Praise for *The Water Boy*

"Every once in awhile I get very, very lucky. I had been looking for over a year-and-a-half for a new President and CEO for the BC Lions and I had interviewed several excellent candidates, but none of them had the proper football background. Bob Ackles was truly a great acquisition for the BC Lions and for the community of Vancouver. With his enormous talent and knowledge he has developed the Lions, once again into a dominant position in both Vancouver and the Canadian Football League."

David Braley, Owner of the BC Lions Football Club

"Everywhere Bob Ackles has gone in football – Vancouver, Dallas, Phoenix, Philadelphia, Miami, Las Vegas and back to Vancouver – he's made things better. We, here in Vancouver, are doubly blessed because what could be better than that?"

Kent (Cookie) Gilchrist, Sports Columnist for the Vancouver Province

"I have known Bobby Ackles for more than 25 years. His football knowledge is unquestioned. It's his ability to relate that knowledge to both the game and the communities in which it is played that makes him unique. Bobby is honest and straightforward. He promises exactly that – qualities that will jump off the pages and make for great reading."

Brian Williams, Commentator, CTV & TSN

THE WATER BOY

THE WATER BOY

From the Sidelines to the Owner's Box:
Inside the CFL, the XFL, and the NFL

BOBBY ACKLES

with Ian Mulgrew

BICENTENNIAL
1807
WILEY
2007
BICENTENNIAL

John Wiley & Sons Canada, Ltd.

Library and Archives Canada Cataloguing in Publication Data

Ackles, Bob
    The water boy : from the sidelines to the owner's box: inside the CFL, the XFL and the NFL / Bob Ackles, Ian Mulgrew.

Includes index.
ISBN 978-0-470-15345-1

    1. Ackles, Bob. 2. B.C. Lions Football Club—History. 3. B.C. Lions Football Club—Biography. 4. National Football League—Biography. 5. Canadian football—Biography. 6. Football—Biography. I. Mulgrew, Ian, 1957- II. Title.

GV939.A25A3 2007   796.335092   C2007-902517-X

Production Credits
Cover design: Ian Koo
Interior text design: Jason Vandenberg
Wiley Bicentennial Logo: Richard J. Pacifico
Front and back cover photos: Lorella Zanetti Photography
Printer: Friesens

John Wiley & Sons Canada, Ltd.
6045 Freemont Blvd.
Mississauga, Ontario
L5R 4J3

Printed in Canada

1 2 3 4 5 FP 11 10 09 08 07

© Recycled · Recyclé
Supporting responsible use of forest resources
Contribue à l'utilisation responsable des ressources forestières
www.fsc.org Cert no. XXX-XXX-000
© 1996 Forest Stewardship Council
FSC

This book is printed with biodegradable vegetable-based inks. Text pages are printed on 100% PCW using Rolland Enviro by Friesens Corp., an FSC certified printer.

To Robert, Ashley, Kyle, Kasey and Robyn
– our grandkids who give me great joy.

Table of Contents

Preface &
Acknowledgements

TO THIS DAY I can still hear the sounds at Vancouver's Heather Park during evening football practice. The Junior Blue Bombers would scrimmage at one end of the small field. From the other end, those of us on the younger, juvenile sister team could hear their Coach Joe Davies. He was always hollering at the young men working out under the pale illumination of a single light:

"Good job McArthur!" he would bark. "Eustis—great throw Ritchie."

John McArthur would become dean of the Harvard Business School for 15 years, one of the longest tenures in the institution's history. Rich Eustis became a major television series executive, handling Dean Martin, Glen Campbell and John Denver.

I still chuckle thinking *The Vancouver Sun* let Rich go because he "couldn't write." He moved to Hollywood to create, write, direct and produce. His prime-time sitcom, *Head of the Class* (co-created with Michael Elias), lasted for five years.

Initially starring Howard Hesseman as idealistic ponytailed teacher, Charlie Moore, some of the characters were based on Rich's high school and community football buddies. In its final year, Hesseman was replaced by Glasgow comic Billy Connolly, whose character Billy MacGregor proved so popular, he was spun into his own series, *Billy*.

There were no slackers on that field—and the sound of Davies' drill sergeant voice made me pick up my step for fear of being labelled a lollygagger. Those were the days.

—⁓—

I have wanted to write a book recording my memories for a long time. I don't recall when it first crossed my mind—my records suggest 1983, but I know it was much earlier. In part, I wanted to tell my story because so many people urge me on after hearing my anecdotes. I also was encouraged by creative writing teachers who said I was a natural storyteller. As well, I wanted to lay it down for the grandkids.

I have a mountain of memorabilia and the biggest problem I faced was what to leave out. This is not a history of the B.C. Lions, although it contains my recollection of the considerable time I spent with the team: from 1953 through 1986 and then again from 2002 until who knows when. It's also about my time with the Dallas Cowboys, my decade-and-a-half in the National Football League, my estimation of coaches, quarterbacks and owners, my time with the short-lived XFL and my abiding relationship with Jimmy Johnson—truly the best coach I have ever had the honour of knowing, and a friend.

This book, as well, is about my experience, my values, my vision of how an organization should operate and my view of how to manage people. Football is a specific sport but the group dynamics are the same in every walk of life.

Winning and losing are everything in sport. The euphoria of success is addictive, the devastation of a Grey Cup loss a black dog of depression. But emotions are only part of the story. Earnestness is not enough for success, though desire and passion are necessary elements. You must also have talent that has been well prepared and is willing to persevere and push through any obstacle to win. There is no easy road, no alchemist's incantation that can replace hard work. You must also be lucky.

I don't think I have anything as grand as a philosophy—I believe you motivate and inspire any team or group by acting with integrity, displaying loyalty and, again, working hard. You lead by example. Transparent, humble, flexible, patient, confident, mature—these are the qualities of leadership. I have come to identify them after a half-century in football—rising from the water boy to the chief executive officer, from washing dirty laundry in the locker room to nibbling canapés in the team suite.

I look back on my life and think of all the people who have helped me have that success. They are legion.

My best friend Kay and the rest of my family—sons Steve and Scott, their wives Sherri and Theresa, grandchildren Robert, Ashley, Kyle, Kasey and Robyn. Kay's sister Carol and husband Jack Kester and her Aunt Thelma—all of them deserve my gratitude for the support they provided and continue to provide. I cannot imagine what my life would have been like without Kay. This is not simply my story, it is very much our story.

My close friends, too, offered encouragement throughout this project and over the years always have been there for me—George and Helen Martin, Tom and Patsy Hinton, David Boyd (who helped create the instant replay technology in football in 1962), Ed and Pat Sharkey, Ron and Alma Jones, and Anne Favell. Jack and Nancy Farley, Norm and Doreen Fieldgate, Vic and Peggy Spencer, Mike and Anne Hurst, Bill and Sandy Lewis, Norm and Mary Bradley, Patricia and Gary Bannerman, Mike and Bev Davies, Moray and Pam Keith, Ted and Marianne Plumb, Doug and Lois Mitchell … I thank them.

Similarly, my professional career would have been less accomplished and I dare say of scant interest without the unstinting assistance of an army of colleagues, board members, assistants, trainers, scouts, doctors, assistant coaches, photographers, media directors and myriad others. They too deserve my gratitude, and these are only a few: "Rocky" Cavallin, Don Cochran, Kevin O'Neal, Otho Davis, Ken "Kato" Kasuya, Tony Eques, Grant Kerr, Al Eaton, Doug Johnston, Al Kipnes, Leo Ornest, Buck Buchanan, Mike Dougherty, John Fowler, Dave Cross, Kim Stahlnecht and Kent Kahlberg, Dave Ritchie, Mike Roach, Dan Dorazio, Bill Reichelt, Mike Benevides, Steff Kruck, Bob O'Billovich, Bob Park, Kevin Witmer, Jamie Barresi, Ken Appleby, Hec Gillespie, Walt Kazun, Bob McCormick, Gerry Altman, Roger Upton, Bill Lowther, Jeff Smith, Josh Keller, Red Robinson, Steve Vrlak, Glen Ringdal, Gail Searson, Lynne Thompson, Tula Janopolis, Connie

Medina, Gail Baldwin, Dana Smith, George Chayka, Lui Passaglia, Carol Longmuir, Karen Hartshorne, Seth Gordon, Birgit Tuckwood, Terri Breker, Neil McEvoy, Jennifer Graham, Debbie Butt, Diana Schultz, Dan Vertlieb, Michele Nuszdorfer, Arlene Stewart-Irvine, Keith Hawkins, Laura Norman, Gavin Bell, Justin McIntyre, Justin Coderre, Alison O'Keefe, Jordan Eshpeter, Chris Kay, Kyle Beattie, Carola Bausch, Phil Adams, Jamie Cartmell, Jacqueline Blackwell, Paul Marr, Chris Pollock, Dave McLean, Brandon Gorin, Natalie Newmann, Cole Renner, John Doukas, Katie Newton, Sherrie Scherger, Alex Janicek, Rosalyn Young, Doug Todd, Greg Aiello, Rich Dalrymple, Paul Jensen, Ronnie Howard, Harvey Greene, Bill Cunningham, Ralph Bower, Ken Oakes, Brian Kent, Bazil King, Bob Olsen, Harry Gilmer, Jerry Hardaway, Leo Knight, Ralph Hawkins, Jim Garrett, Chuck Banker and Andrea Savard, who went above and beyond.

Last but not least there were coaches. I have worked with 23 head coaches in pro football—15 in the CFL, six in the NFL (Jimmy Johnson twice) and one in the XFL. They are all mentioned in the following pages. But there are many others to acknowledge, such as: Vic Lindskog, YA Tittle, Marv Matuszak, Owen Dejanovich, Vince Tobin, Don Lawrence, John Levra, Roy Shivers, O.K Dalton, Joe Pao Pao, Frank Smith, Ted Plumb, Fritz Shurmur, Ray Markham, Bobo Sikorski and Jim (don't call me Jimmy) Johnson.

My old friend Alan Fotheringham and his wife Ann were the catalysts for this book. Alan directed me to Robert Mackwood, of the Seventh Avenue Literary Agency. Robert advised me to sit down with Ian Mulgrew, one of his non-fiction authors and a columnist with *The Vancouver Sun*. We had a chat to see if we could work together. We started creating the manuscript in June 2006 and finished earlier this year. Executive Editor Karen Milner at John Wiley & Sons Canada, Ltd. and the folks at Wiley took it from there. They have been great. Thanks to all.

There are a lot of people who probably should have been mentioned, who are not. People who know me, too, or who have followed my career will probably have an incident, a memory or an interaction that stands out for them that I failed to include here. It was impossible to put more than half a century in professional sports and seven decades of a rich, textured life into a single volume.

These are my professional memoirs for lack of a better way to describe my effort. I hope it gives you some insight into me and my views about football, business and life. I have tried the best I can to be candid and to not mince words. I hope that if you meet me in the stands or in the grocery store lineup, you'll know who I am as a person—my character and my personality. I have also tried to offer a good read. You can judge for yourself whether I succeeded.

I have often thought I would like to do a coffee-table book – *Quarterbacks I Have Known: Lorne Cullen, Jack Patrick, Gordon Carey, Rich Eustis, Troy Aikman, Joe Montana, Broadway Joe Namath* … Maybe next time.

—⁓—

One of my favourite things to do in the world is to walk around a field marked with bright white lines. This is where some of the finest athletes in the world play football. The stark contrast in colour can lead you to believe it is a game of control. But within that grid, anything can happen. It truly is a game that can change from moment to moment, a game that as much as it's played by talented, well-trained men, can come down to a roll-of-the-dice-like chance.

I have walked many football fields during my 50 plus years in professional football—countless on Canadian and U.S. campuses, those in the National Football League and of course those of the Canadian Football League. I am most at ease on the home turf of the BC Lions. The team has been my family for a long, long time.

In 1962, C.B. "Slim" Delbridge became president of the Lions and one day called me and asked me to bring a game jersey to his office at the Burrard building. He was waiting in the driveway in his black Cadillac.

I drove up and jumped out of my pick-up truck. He stared at me.

"Bobby, I thought that you would be driving a Cadillac," he said.

"I will some day Mr. Delbridge," I replied. And I now do.

The Lions and professional football have been very good to me and my family. So has David Braley—current owner of the Lions, who got me back on the treadmill five years ago. An especially deep thank you to David. What a journey!

Telephone Calls & Thursdays

TELEPHONE CALLS have changed my life, and usually on a Thursday for some strange reason. Maybe that's why I don't usually answer the phone at home. At least when my business line rings, I'm prepared. I'm ready, and they want to talk to me. The home phone though, it's rarely for me – why pick it up? Still, once in a while, and I don't know what possesses me, I do answer. I did this morning, a Thursday, wouldn't you know it. Now I'm in the thick of it again. Who'd have thought it? Certainly not me. But I can be slow to appreciate a point.

I wasn't supposed to be at home that morning in the spring of 2002, but it was a professional development day at the University of Nevada Las Vegas. My life in retirement during the week was to get up and drive to the campus, wait for the cafeteria to open at seven, grab a decaffeinated coffee and read the papers. I'm a newspaper junkie. Three or more a day sometimes. I couldn't stay at home, no way. I'd be going through papers, pointing to stuff Kay hadn't read, yakking and generally driving her crazy with talk about things she still didn't know about, asking her opinion while she was trying to just wake up, ranting about something or other on the sports page. Know how annoying that can be? I've figured out a few things after more than five decades with Kay. So I signed up for classes – photography, painting, the novel. Self-preservation. I wasn't interested in a degree; I was just interested – and I had time, lots of time. There was no sense of urgency in my life anymore. I had stepped off the treadmill. No more Dallas Cowboys. No more Miami Dolphins. No more Vince McMahon. No more agents trying to sell me overpriced talent on the downward slope of a career. I was truly at loose ends, wandering around the nicest house we'd ever owned, enjoying the fruits of our labours, as they say, when I reached for the ringing phone.

"Bob, David Braley."

I thought for a second: Braley? Braley? Right. Industrialist from Hamilton, Ontario – Canada. David was the multi-millionaire owner of the British Columbia Lions in the Canadian Football League. We had briefly met a few times in the 1990s when I was with the Dallas Cowboys. While I was in the National Football League, every pre-season I met in Toronto with George Young, general manager of the New York Giants, and Dick Steinberg, general manager of the New York Jets, to grab a couple of CFL games. One occasion, going through the airport, we ran into Braley, then owner of the Hamilton Tiger-Cats. He had been a little gruff as I remembered the short hello. Later, he and his wife Nancy were in Florida and called me while I was with the Miami Dolphins. They came to a Sunday night game, sat in the President's Suite and I introduced them to Coach Jimmy Johnson and his staff over beer and sandwiches. They had a swell time.

"David, good to hear from you. It's been a long time. What's up?"

"I'm sitting here reading about you in the newspaper and your induction into the Canadian Football Hall of Fame."

I laughed.

"I thought," Braley continued, "what's wrong with me? I need someone to run the B.C. Lions – who better than you?"

I was truly speechless. I had pitched Braley for a job a decade before. I was vice president of the Dallas Cowboys when Murray Pezim, the B.C. Lions owner at the time, put me forward as a candidate for CFL commissioner. I was scouting at the Senior Bowl in Mobile, Alabama, and was flattered. I quickly told my boss, Cowboys owner Jerry Jones. He turned and said wistfully, "I wish someone would ask me to be commissioner of a league."

Jones added, "I'd hate to lose you. But why don't you go ahead and talk to them?"

David was on that 1992 selection committee. I told them at the time, though not much had changed, I was a career football man involved in every aspect of the management and leadership of a professional franchise for nearly 40 years. Now, for more than a half-century. As general manager of a Grey Cup winner and as vice president of a franchise that went on to garner three Super Bowls, I had the rare opportunity to be directly involved in the building and the administration of championship organizations in the CFL and NFL.

My entire career rested on a few basic premises. First, I placed loyalty and dedication to the organization above any other professional value. Second, I never concerned myself with the distraction of ego, or who might receive recognition for the job well done. Third, I characterized myself as a team player and a tireless worker. I sincerely believe those with whom I worked closely would eagerly verify those qualities.

The selection committee went with Larry Smith, today president of the Montreal Alouettes. I met Larry a few years later and he told me he cherished a letter I sent him while he was a senior at Bishop's University in Montreal. I was scouting Canadian colleges and universities in those days and I thought he was a top prospect for the Lions. We didn't choose him in the end, but our encouragement was important to him. I always emphasized to my staff: send that letter encouraging prospects. It can loom large to them and have a lasting effect.

I didn't get the commissioner's job back then, but I made an impression on Braley. In hindsight, I'm glad I didn't get the job – what a mess it turned into!

"Anyway," he said, "when I saw that write-up about you in the Canadian Football Hall of Fame, I thought you're the man. So here I am calling. Would you have any interest in moving back to Vancouver to run the Lions?"

"Run the B.C. Lions," I repeated.

Kay, sitting at the table sipping her tea, stared at me quizzically. Who was I talking to?

"I'm sort of enjoying retirement," I said. "But let's say I was interested. In what capacity are you thinking?"

"You'd run the whole operation for me."

I began to pace out the length of the 20-foot phone cord before changing directions. Back and forth in the kitchen as he talked.

He wasn't happy with what was happening in Vancouver. Obviously. They were drawing 18,000 on average in 2001 in spite of winning a Grey Cup the previous year. Not a bad football team. Damon Allen was the quarterback, but he couldn't draw flies. That might have been a league issue. I hadn't followed it closely during my 15-year sojourn in the NFL, but I was certainly aware of the CFL's woes.

In the Eastern Conference, Ottawa had just rejoined the league after a five-year hiatus: they had put together a young, energetic ownership group that seemed to be, sad to say, underfunded. In Toronto, Sherwood Schwartz of New York was pouring millions of dollars into a once proud franchise and seeing it disappear with nary a difference appearing on the field or at the gate. Down the highway in Steel Town, the Hamilton Tiger-Cats, oldest franchise in the country (1869), were struggling too with cash-strapped local ownership. The Montreal Alouettes were owned by Robert and Lisa Wetenhall, another New York–Florida based couple, who managed to operate a solid franchise out of the smallest arena in the league – Percival Molson Memorial Stadium at McGill University, which seats 20,202. It was sold out every game.

In the Western Conference, the overall picture wasn't as dire.

Edmonton remained one of the most solid franchises, with a muscular management team, a committed board of directors and a prescient long-term plan. They hired good people and allowed them to get the job done. Saskatchewan backed the Roughriders through thick and thin, even though they had struggled getting it done on the field since the heyday of the early 1960s and 1970s with Ron Lancaster and George Reed. Winnipeg, also community owned, was limping through financial straits with provincial, city and community support. They appeared to be suffering from constant change in direction. Calgary and the Lions, of course, were privately owned, with solid financial backing.

The league office was a different matter; it seemed to be in constant upheaval. Larry Smith lasted five years as commissioner and since then, a new warm body had sat in the chair every few years.

Even though Braley made the job sound good, I had misgivings. Let's call them trepidations. I wasn't immediately ready to say, "Sure, I'd love the job," even if I was at loose ends.

"I've got to admit I'm definitely interested, David, but I'll have to talk with Kay, we're pretty settled down here, and I'll have to think about getting back in the saddle." Over the years and hundreds of negotiations, I really have learned to play the reluctant bride.

"You don't have to give me an answer now," Braley said. "Just think about it. I'd like you to be president and CEO. You run the whole operation for me. I wouldn't be breathing down your neck. You'd run the operation."

I let the thought settle.

"Let me talk to Kay and I'll get back to you by Monday."

I hung up the phone.

Kay was staring: "Well?"

"That was David Braley," I said. "He wants us to move back to Vancouver and for me to be president and CEO of the B.C. Lions."

She lit up at the thought of spending more time with our family, especially the grandkids.

"Boy, I understand they're really in trouble," she said, not wanting to appear too eager. She's learned a few things over the years, too.

Kay has been my confidante and support structure since I was 19 and she was a 16-year-old driving her mother's car. No matter what I've done over the years, in whatever capacity, I've talked it out with her, we've figured it out together and we've always operated as a real partnership. It wasn't my career; it was our life. Kay's been a big part of any decision whether it's been a job or not. Any decision we've ever made has been a joint decision – even that first big one to join the Dallas Cowboys. It wasn't, "Gee, I've got this offer from the Cowboys and we're going to Dallas."

We talked about it a lot – that was a huge move for us. This would be, too.

"What do you think?" she prodded. "It would certainly be nice for the family."

"Yes, but you know the problems."

Kay had been around football as long as I had and knew the score.

She also had been in Vancouver to a game and saw firsthand the dispirited turnout. We had moved our son Scott, his wife Theresa and new baby Kasey back to Vancouver on January 1, 2002. He had been working with me in Vince McMahon's not-long-dead XFL. But without a job, Scott couldn't stay in the U.S.

"Maybe we could give it a try and keep this place," Kay said.

"You just like the weather."

"It rains in Vancouver," she replied.

We had lived in the Sun Belt for a long time – Las Vegas, South Florida, Phoenix and Dallas. Yet we had family and many friends in Vancouver.

We both looked at each other. We knew exactly what was happening with the Lions; I certainly didn't need David to tell me. The team was a profound part of our lives. Our friend Anne Favell sent us sports and political clippings regularly, too, to keep us up to date.

We looked around the house. It really was the nicest house we had ever lived in – 3,200 square feet on a quarter-acre. Four bedrooms, library-den with a fireplace. We had a huge living-dining area that was great for entertaining. All the windows focused on the big, sun-dappled patio and sprawling back yard. Beautifully treed. Pines – not palms, the Las Vegas special – if you can believe it, tall and even fragrant some days. No pool, you know how it is with pools; you don't use them enough. Gosh, it was a nice house. At the end of a cul-de-sac, quiet, no traffic. It took us about 30 seconds to decide.

I didn't wait for Monday. I called David back the next morning and said, "Let's talk."

The next task was to withdraw from my courses so I would not be assigned an "F" – I didn't know when I might want to go back, I figured. We flew to Vancouver to seal the deal with David. On the way, I couldn't help remembering that I'd left the Lions two decades earlier after a similar fortuitous phone call offering a near identical project – rebuilding a football franchise, in that case the Dallas Cowboys.

It's difficult to believe looking back, but my leaving the Lions after the success of 1985 had its roots in the Grey Cup loss of 1983. We played a great game – up to half-time. Quarterback Roy Dewalt opened the scoring with a 45-yard pass to wide-receiver Mervyn

Fernandez, followed it up with a 20-yard strike to John Henry White and Lui Passaglia added a 31-yard field goal. We rolled down the field like a well-oiled machine. By comparison, nothing went right for starting Toronto quarterback Condredge Halloway. On the final series of the first half he was replaced by Joe Barnes.

We took a 17–7 lead into the locker room and, well, you would have thought we stayed in there. Barnes killed us in the second half. We had a chance late in the game with 1:44 left – Dewalt threw long to wide-receiver Jacques Chapdelaine. The fans hung on the ball as it arced towards him on the Argo 35-yard line. He dropped it.

It would have been a chip shot for Passaglia and an easy win by 2. It didn't happen.

Our coach, Don Matthews, took the brunt of the blame. Every armchair quarterback, Lions fan and sports writer said he blew it starting Chapdelaine.

Matthews' son had been in a car accident during the week, but he got little sympathy. He was pilloried for the late-season decision to cut sure-handed receiver Sammy Greene for disciplinary problems. He should never have gone with rookie Chapdelaine, the critics said. Toronto celebrated an 18–17 triumph.

In spite of the scoreboard, I took heart at the packed stadium, the entertaining football and the buzz in the community about the CFL. We lost, but we won. I considered that 1983 game the culmination of my 10-year struggle as general manager of the Lions to bring the club back from bankruptcy and near-empty houses in the mid-1970s to prosperity and a 42,500-average fan base every game. I was proud of that achievement – and I did not think I would ever leave the Lions for another football team. The board of directors saw it differently.

Roughly two weeks after that Grey Cup, on December 13, I met with the 12 directors of the Lions in the boardroom of Irving Glassner's food-products warehouse in Richmond. It was a new facility and he was extremely proud of it. But I remember it for different reasons.

Each of the directors (with the exception of George Tidball) systematically chastised the way the club was being run: poor marketing, we should be selling more tickets, directors should have input on how the football team was being coached … They went on and on.

You name it, they didn't like it.

We had increased our season-ticket base to 24,517 – 12,000 more than 1982. Our 1984 target was 30,000. Irving Glassner's response was a snippy, "Are we happy with half-empty stadiums?"

John Parks chirped in saying the marketing department hadn't grasped the opportunities available; Harvey Southam said the half-time shows were poor and that alumni membership efforts were half-hearted; Peter Brown complained we didn't have a long-term financing plan, with $1 million coming due in three years (the only suggestion I thought had merit). Pat Claridge, a former player, added smugly, "The promotion of the club is inadequate. And maybe it's time for the board to get involved more. Perhaps there should be discussions about the operation of the club with the general manager and the coach, discussions about the results and the coaching philosophy that's being used."

"Yes," echoed Woody MacLaren, "the board should be expressing their opinions to the general manager regarding game plans, not to criticize but to become more involved as responsible directors as to the on-field performance, not just the general operations of the club."

Maybe at my age today I wouldn't be as pissed off, but at the time, I was steaming. All I could think was these guys had short memories – this club was bankrupt when I became general manager and was now an ascendant franchise. Some of them simply had no idea how to run a football club. It took me by surprise. Not that I expected to be carried around the board room, but two weeks after you contest a Grey Cup – two weeks before Christmas – I expected them to say "let's enjoy the season and the holidays." I figured if they were going to get on my ass, they'd at least wait until January.

When the last of the directors had vented his spleen, I rose from my chair and left. There was nothing to say. I needed time to think. I was tremendously ticked off. It was very, very disheartening.

Kay and I flew to Hawaii and I spent 10 days fuming. The B.C. Lions were my life and I was being chastised for doing the best damn job in the CFL. We were averaging 42,500 a game! We talked about it over and over, Kay and I. I even fired off a letter to club president Ron Jones saying let's meet when I get back.

I eventually called Ron and we had a frank exchange of views. I told him I needed help in a lot of areas but one thing I didn't need was some guy who didn't know his ass from a hole in the ground telling me how to run the football club. I had learned from some good and some bad administrators, and I had been thrown into some bad situations over the years where I'd made decisions that were not only critical to the B.C. Lions' survival but to my survival in the business and my family's survival. And I had made the right choices.

Eventually he came around to realizing the board might have been a little off-base and the conversation became more constructive. We talked about substantive issues – a new contract for me and the makeup of the board.

In those days, the directors were selected by a board of governors led by chairman C.N. "Chunky" Woodward. I went to him for help. He assured me the two directors causing the most trouble would be gone and he'd see what he could do to calm the others. He was as good as his word, but something kept telling me it was over with the Lions. The directors clearly had been stewing about various issues, and items most definitely had been simmering on the back burners. That wasn't a good sign.

Maybe I just couldn't get rid of the sour taste of that bilious board meeting. Whatever it was, it just didn't feel right after that, even when we won the cup two years later. It wasn't as if I was letting things slide. I had already done my planning for the year. In fact, the morning after the Grey Cup I negotiated in the hotel coffee shop with an agent to extend starting-quarterback Roy Dewalt's contract. I was itchy, I guess, the sting of that December 1983 directors' meeting a real burr in my subconscious.

I headed into the 1986 spring training camp in Kelowna, in the interior of the province, still out of sorts. I decided to take a side trip, probably because Chunky was insistent. He and his wife Carol had the coaching staff and their wives aboard his boat, the 75-foot *Peppy San*, for a day of fishing. As we trolled for salmon, he talked me into stopping on my way to camp to visit his 500,000-acre ranch – the Douglas Lake Cattle Company, one of the world's biggest spreads. He wanted me to meet his cow boss of 40 years, Mike Ferguson.

My genial lunch with Mike meant I didn't arrive at the hotel in Kelowna until late into the evening. There was a stack of messages, including one from Tex Schramm – president and general manager of the Dallas Cowboys, arguably the second most influential man in the National Football League given his chairmanship of its powerful Competition Committee. I had met him briefly a few years earlier on the sidelines at a Cowboys practice in Thousands Oaks, California, during their training camp. I was pretty sure he wouldn't know me from Adam. Then, I remembered the 1986 bomb scare in London.

The Cowboys were to play an exhibition game against the Chicago Bears in England. The fear of IRA terrorist activity probably had Schramm looking for an alternate venue and what better spot than the recently opened B.C. Place Stadium, domed home of the Lions, capable of seating nearly 60,000? I got up early the next day and gave him a call.

Tex was a big man with a bigger voice, and it came across even larger on the telephone – a thunderous, booming sound softened only slightly by that unmistakable Texas twang.

"Bobby, I don't think we've met but I've heard a lot about you," he said. "And I'll try to explain why I am calling."

Tex could get flustered sometimes trying to get things out too fast.

"I have a new position I'm starting with the Cowboys," he said.

That took me by surprise.

This conversation wasn't going to be about scheduling dates for a Cowboys game in Vancouver.

"It's kind of a scouting-personnel position only for players already in the NFL or CFL or players who have been through our draft, whether they be on an NFL roster or a free agent."

The Dallas Cowboys. In the spring of 1986, they remained America's Team. Among the most storied sports franchises in North America, if not *the* most successful. The team budget even back then was $30 million. That dwarfed the entire CFL's budget! We were a small business; the Cowboys were a conglomerate complete with its own travel arm and weekly newspaper. Hard to believe there was a time when the CFL paid some players more than the NFL and was a true competitor for talent. But that was before the birth of the American Football

League and the exponential rise in television revenues.

Tex continued to outline the position.

"You'd have authority over everything except college scouting," he continued.

I was flabbergasted. He was offering me a job.

"How much do you want?"

"$120K and bonuses," I replied, without missing a beat and hoping I hadn't undersold myself.

"No problem. Call me on the weekend and we'll sort out any other details."

"When are you thinking about in terms of time frame?"

"Before the season starts."

"But Tex," I ventured, "you're forgetting something – my contract with the Lions."

"See what you can do and call me back," he said.

My first call was to Kay in Vancouver.

"Oh, hon," she said, "isn't that nice. Now maybe they will take you more seriously around here."

There were a few people in the community – directors, fans and the media who still considered me the "water boy." I'm not sure why it struck Kay and me as a slight for so long. It was true. That's how I started. In 1953, before the B.C. Lions even existed as a professional football club, I was their water boy. Their very first water boy. Some people couldn't accept that I'd risen through the ranks to become a successful sports franchise executive. Call it envy, call it whatever, but the name sounded disparaging and it ticked Kay off to hear it.

I remember being at the celebration marking my 25th year with the Lions. I was presented with a plaque commemorating the anniversary. A former player at the back of the room, probably half-drunk, kept yelling: "Water boy! Water boy!"

It really bothered me. I felt like hollering back, "That's right – I started there and here I am running the club. You started at the top and now you're where?"

But I didn't. I swallowed the bile. That was then. I don't give it much thought anymore, but that may be because few people these days say it to my face.

Kay said maybe the message from Tex was a reporter playing a trick, which they sometimes did in the old days. Someone with a pal in Texas roping me in. But that was unlikely. The next morning I called Tex again. After pleasantries, I launched right in. "When I spoke with you yesterday, Tex, there were a lot of questions that I should have asked that I didn't, due to the surprise of the conversation. I wonder if I could ask you those questions now."

"Why sure, Bob," Tex drawled.

"First, I should ask are you offering me this job or are you going to interview a number of candidates?"

"The job's yours if you want it," he said.

"And the job description would be director of football operations with the one exception of college scouting?"

"Yep."

That was a step higher in the chain of command than director of pro personnel.

"Who would I report to?"

"Me."

I wrote "Tex" on my notepad and circled the name.

"Who would report to me?"

"The pro personnel of the operation. You'd be responsible for the budget, preparing and controlling expenditures."

"How involved would I be in the decision about coaching?"

"When [head coach] Tom Landry retires, you'd have a lot of input into the hiring of the new head coach."

He went on to explain that Gil Brandt and Joe Bailey had signed most of the veterans and draftees for the coming season. I would grade the scouts. So it would be important for me to keep up with what was going on in the league. I'd be responsible for suggesting players who might be available on other teams who might help the club, gathering info for the draft, setting up a rapport with other NFL people. ... There would be travel, a chance for advancement, moving expenses, mortgage support. ...

This was my dream job.

"We would give you $25,000 relocation expense money. You would also receive playoff bonuses – four weeks' salary if we make it into the

Divisional Championship or the Wild Card game, six weeks' salary if we're in the NFL Championship and eight weeks' salary if we make the Super Bowl. There's a car. Benefits: pension, medical, insurance."

"Tex," I interrupted, "it looks like I will have to speak to our president, Woody McClaren, today and set up a visit to Dallas as soon as possible."

"That's great," he said. "Call me back."

Tex rang off telling me he would spend the month of June on his 60-foot Hatteras boat, *Key Venture*, in San Salvador in the Bahamas, where he had his own marlin fishing tournament every year.

I hung up feeling excited and almost panicky. The number-one professional sports franchise in the world had called and offered me the vice president's position. My thoughts raced.

I called Woody McLaren and told him about the call from Tex. We talked it through and he said he would speak with the executive committee and for me to make arrangements to travel to Dallas. I called Tex again and he said the Dallas Cowboys Travel Agency would look after everything.

Kay and I flew to Dallas on Thursday of Memorial Day weekend. Woody McLaren flew to Toronto for the CFL meeting I was supposed to attend. He told them I was at training camp. I boarded the plane in Kelowna and met Kay at the Vancouver airport. We were giddy.

It was late, maybe 10:30 p.m., when we landed in Dallas to be met by Tex and his wife Marti. We were no sooner out of the parking lot when Tex turned to me. "Well, are you going to take this job?"

"We've got to talk more in the morning," I told him.

He had already set up a meeting with a real-estate agent who would take Kay out looking for homes. Anne Bixby and her husband Jeff Smith, a scout for the Cowboys, would become two of our closest friends. Kay orchestrated all our moves. She picked out our homes. We would fly her cousin Robert Poburko, an interior designer, and his wife Nicki into town and they would decorate, with Kay managing everything. I would come home to find the furniture in place, pictures on the wall and everything set to go. I never worried about a thing.

Tex ordered a two-level penthouse suite for us at the hotel and once we checked in we ordered a six-pack of Coors Light and made some phone calls. We called our kids: Steve on Vancouver Island and Scott at home in Vancouver. We called Fred and Ann Owens, my high school football coach and his wife in California, and Jack Farley and his wife Nancy. Jack was the former director and president most instrumental in turning the Lions franchise around in the wake of the financial disaster of the mid-1970s. We told them our news was very confidential. It was tough sleeping that night.

The next morning Tex picked me up at the hotel and we drove 10 to 15 minutes to Valley Ranch, home of the Dallas Cowboys – the most opulent and up-to-date training facility in all of pro sports at the time. What an eye-opener. He gave me a quick tour, then we went to his office to talk.

"Tex," I began, "I will require a green card or a permit to work in the U.S."

He looked at me as if I was from another planet: "You need what?"

He had no idea I was not a U.S. citizen. He picked up his phone and dialed: "Larry, come in here."

Seconds later, a tall, handsome black man appeared, Larry Wansley.

"Larry, this is Bob Ackles. He's coming to work with us. Bob, tell Larry what you need."

I did.

"Larry, would you look after that?"

Larry, a famous, veteran ex-FBI agent, rolled his eyes. "Yes, sir."

Tex and I continued talking about what it might take to turn the Cowboys around.

The franchise was on a slide and Tex needed answers – just as the Lions did when I took the helm in 1975 (and then again later when Braley called in 2002). Tex recently had forced legendary head coach Tom Landry into changing his offensive coordinator. Now he was adding a new department to the football operation – pro personnel. I would lead it.

One of the biggest problems facing the Cowboys was their success. Every other team hated them. Viscerally. Their reputation as the nation's team, as the team that got the best of every deal – all of it worked against them. Other teams not only easily motivated their players for a game against the Cowboys, but also it was nearly impossible for the team to make a trade. The Cowboys needed someone to turn it around. I was to play a big part in it, although at the time I didn't even suspect the pitfalls.

Tex dropped me off so I could lunch with the Cowboys' head of college scouting, Dick Mansperger. I went way back with Dick, to the first year of the Seattle Seahawks, 1976, when he was director of player personnel. We were good friends and he gave me the rundown on the organization. He even tried to tell me things I would eventually learn on my own, but I wasn't listening.

Dick told me there were some subjects, such as the March owners' meeting, that I must discuss with Tex. Make sure you attend, he said. He insisted I should sit in on all player personnel meetings and be involved in all trade discussions. Make sure, he said, to discuss secretarial staff, an assistant and part-time pro scouts.

Dick drove me back to Valley Ranch where I had another meeting with Tex. Larry Wansley arrived and said he could probably get an H-1 permit that would allow me to work for up to five years. In the meantime, he said, I could apply for my green card. In Tex's mind, everything now was taken care of – no more hurdles. He clapped a hand on my shoulder and said, "See?"

Tex drove me back to the hotel and we shook hands. He was that kind of guy; he didn't need a piece of paper to seal a contract.

Kay had had a great day with Anne Bixby, and we both thought this move felt very comfortable. We boarded the plane back to Vancouver, very excited about our prospects.

Next morning, I was up early flying back to training camp in Kelowna. The first person I had to speak with was our head coach, Don Matthews. I found him at the local racquetball club. He was playing handball with Larry Donovan, one of his assistants. I broke the news. Don looked stunned.

"I'm pleased for you and Kay of course, Bob," he stammered.

I shook his hand and told him we'd have more time to talk later. Back at the hotel, I found a stack of messages from reporters and our media relations director, Josh Keller. I called him.

"Bob," he said, "has something happened to you with the Dallas Cowboys?"

"You'd better come over to my room," I replied.

He was there in a blink. I told him what was going down and he suggested I move to another hotel under an assumed name. I called Woody McLaren and told him the story had been leaked. I suspected Tex had done it in Dallas. Woody said he was catching the next flight.

I picked him up at the airport. A dozen reporters and cameramen scrummed us. We begged for time and headed to the team's hotel.

Woody said the board was unanimous and would release me from the final two years of my contract. They would give me a rousing send-off on the floor of the B.C. Place Stadium: "Bob & Kay's 'Bye Bye' BBQ." There would be a going-away dinner with Bob Hope. They would even create a scholarship to fund studies in Sports Management at Simon Fraser University and the University of British Columbia. I was very touched.

Regardless, I was off on a great adventure.

Little did I realize it would end six years later as suddenly as it began, when Cowboys owner Jerry Jones fired me – on a Thursday, coincidentally. Little did I anticipate how much water would flow under the bridge after that. Or that in 2002, at 63 years old, I would be offered the job I at one time had coveted more than any other.

Of course, I told David Braley I would take the job. But I would need to spend the first year evaluating the organization, figuring out what needed to be done. I said I would need his support carrying out that plan.

"Done," he said over the phone.

In Vancouver, we met at Davis and Co., in his lawyer Doug Buchanan's office. I had Jim Carphin, a friend and former player, and attorney at Fasken Martineau DuMoulin, handle my side of it. We basically ironed out the legalese. There are always little things with contracts. But David and I pretty well had a handshake deal over the phone. We didn't discuss much in the way of money.

"If I'm going to do this," I told him, "I should be paid equal to the highest-paid president in the league."

He replied, "No problem."

"I run it."

"You operate it," David said. "I'll talk to you once a week."

I told him, "I think we can be in the Grey Cup within three to five years."

It would be quite a challenge. But do-able. When I left in 1986, the Lions were defending Grey Cup champions, we had a season-ticket base of 30,000 and a new training facility in Surrey. In the 1985 season, the Lions drew 452,275 fans for 10 home games, including pre-season, an average of 45,000-plus per game. They won the Grey Cup and carried away two Schenley awards – Mervyn Fernandez as outstanding player and Michael Grey for best rookie. By comparison, in 2001 the Lions attracted just 178,709 fans to nine regular-season home games, an average gate of 19,856. The team lost close to $1 million that year, and David had lost some $14 million since he bought the Lions, although Vancouver was the league's second-biggest English language market. I had my work cut out for me.

This, however, was a chance to put my experience and knowledge to work for another organization in search of direction and quality leadership. I saw it as both a challenge and another opportunity for exciting change. I'm someone who still has a very strong desire to accomplish more and help develop another champion. And I had time on my hands.

What I had learned over a half-century in the game was worth a dozen MBAs and then some: rebranding a business, motivating a demoralized organization, building a winner. I know how to do that, I thought. That's why Tex Schramm and the Cowboys came calling. I had learned so much in the CFL with the Lions, so much more in the NFL with Dallas, Arizona, Philadelphia, Miami, and even more with Vince McMahon and the XFL ... That's why David Braley had called. Now I had another opportunity.

And Bring Your Playbook!

Vancouver, British Columbia
April 15, 2002

I DIDN'T know how bad things really were in Vancouver when I arrived. I'm not talking about the finances; I'm talking about acceptance in the community. There's no rocket science to the football end of this business. There really isn't. Anyone can win at any time; anyone can lose at any time. Having the right head coach, having the right quarterback, avoiding injuries – that's all it takes. That's the easier part of it.

The tougher thing is getting people in the seats. That's incredibly important when you are a gate-driven business like the CFL and can't rely on the kind of television revenues that support the NFL. In Vancouver, when I arrived back, nobody cared. A sea of change had happened since I'd left in 1986. We had 30,000 season-ticket holders back then. We were averaging 45,000-plus fans a game. We were winning. It was really a high. Sitting in the stadium the first game back in 2002, attendance was 12,000, although we would average out at about 18,500. It was a nightmare. I knew turning around an apathetic city and community would be tough. When I asked about the business operation, what I heard wasn't good either. The rumour mill suggested there was a difficult working relationship with David Braley. With 3,000 miles between him and the operation, even with modern communication, I knew there were undoubtedly some problems. But I quickly suspected there might actually be a systemic problem.

Football teams, or any sports franchise, are not like manufacturing companies feeding a specific need or a business with a clearly defined market. They require the alignment of a greater number of elements to produce success. You have to understand the pulse of the community, the pulse of fans, the pulse of the team and understand what will make the mix come together and gel. No matter how conscientious, no matter how dedicated, that's difficult if you're sitting in Hamilton with 15 other businesses to run. Especially when someone needs an immediate answer, which is often. It's difficult to say, "Yeah, do that. Go ahead and do that." Because later you're wondering, "Oh god, did I just give away the farm?"

I arrived in the office to find there wasn't a budget. I asked our financial administrator, "Do we have job descriptions? Do we have a policy manual?" Carol Longmuir shook her head. There wasn't anything in writing. No business plan. No budget. No job descriptions. No policy manual.

I'm not big on everything's gotta be in writing. You can't run it like that – not a small business. Still, you want to have an idea of what you're doing, where you're heading and why. Something that says where you want to be in two years or five years and how you expect to get there – your goals and targets. In my mind, every department had to know what they were doing. We didn't seem to have that. I learned it was in David's head. He has an incredible mind for numbers and details. Ask him and he could tell you: you're going to spend X number of dollars on football operations, and you're going to spend this on promotion, and that's the cost. He had it all up there. I was truly amazed. He checked all the financials and all the business documentation himself.

"Don't you have auditors?" I asked.

"Nope," he said. "This way if I'm signing a cheque for an invoice, I know all the paperwork is there. I know we've received the services and the goods."

"Like a restaurant," I added, "that way you know the stuff isn't going out the back door."

"Exactly," he replied.

Still, that's fine if everyone else has a photographic memory, too, but I've found that until you put it down on a piece of paper, the employees tend to be in the dark. The people who have to operate the business don't actually know what's going on, and they're the people who must agree this is what it will take to get from here to there. Just as the team needed a playbook, the organization needed a business plan.

In this case, the lack of a plan was aggravated because they had to pick up the phone and call David every time they wanted to order something or run a promotion. It's almost impossible to be successful in this business operating that way. The time it takes going back and forth is inefficient. Yet even with those drawbacks, the club had some success.

It seemed to me, in spite of the challenges the Lions faced, the core staff in marketing, promotion and ticket sales were competent and solid. They needed a plan. Once I finished evaluating the staff, that would be my second order of business.

That first week, David and I went to see the Canucks. When I left in 1986 they were not a force on the sports scene and were still playing at the Coliseum on the eastern boundary of the city. Now they were downtown in GM Place and a hot ticket. It was a great game and with the enthusiasm I saw the Canucks generate, I began to think everything was going to be great. Until the next morning when I got to the Surrey offices, the centre of the football operation.

I was just sick. There was no indication anyone had any pride whatsoever in the operation. The building was decrepit. The carpet was awful. It was embarrassing. It was the original carpet installed 20 years earlier! Threadbare. On top of that, I thought, someone is going to be coming down those stairs, trip on that carpet and kill themselves, or sue the hell out of us. It was unbelievable.

We needed to replace the carpet, just for a start. I called a staff meeting for everyone in the organization.

It had taken only my first visit to realize the split offices the Lions operated weren't working in tandem as well as they could. The football, finance and some of the ticket operation were in Surrey with the practice facility. Most of the marketing, sales, promotion and some ticketing were in offices at B.C. Place Stadium. I needed to get a handle on people in both areas and what they did.

Everyone came together at Surrey to meet with me. A lot of them I didn't know. We sat in the boardroom, even the coaches (who were getting ready for training camp, which was a few weeks away) – football people, business people and sales people. I said we were going to go around the room and introduce ourselves and give a brief job description.

Adam Rita, the general manager, whom I've known for a hundred years, went first. As we went around the room, I got a good sense of who everyone was, what they did in the organization and to whom they reported. It was the beginning of what would become our policy manual and our job descriptions.

Later, I followed up by sending everyone a form asking him or her to write out the information and return it to me. We now do it annually to adjust the descriptions to reflect changes in responsibilities or in the organization. Little things like the Internet, for instance, changed everybody's business drastically.

We started working on our business plan, too. It began at about 30 pages, grew to 50 and now nudges 100. It's kept in a binder so everyone in the organization can open it up and see how we're doing and how we're supposed to be doing.

I thought it was a good start. Yet, with my first impressions being so bad, I soon thought I was out of my mind for taking the job. I had no idea the fan base was in such bad shape. The club had squandered the good will established in the 1980s and allowed the fan base to dwindle and community interest to evaporate. I attended functions and people would look at me and ask, "Why are you here?"

The Lions had had no presence for years. Worse, I discovered that, after 16 years away from Vancouver, the whole business landscape had changed. None of the people I knew, none of those I had previously done business with, were here. It was a whole new younger group. I would really struggle.

About two weeks after I arrived, I sat down with the coaches and reviewed the personnel and listened to them tell me about the players. I felt relatively good about what I heard. A fortnight later, I went to training camp and got another rude awakening.

I didn't like the way the camp was being run from the moment I arrived. I've never been to a training camp where you were supposed to have two practices a day, but everyone agreed to meld them into one. The players were taking a 30-minute break between drills before going back at it. They didn't change or shower.

Most recently, I had been through the XFL and NFL systems, where you had the morning practice from nine to 11. You showered and changed, had lunch and enjoyed a two- to three-hour respite during which you could relax. You then got taped up and went back on the field from three to five or three-thirty or four to six. You had dinner and the coaches had their meetings. Then the players and the coaches met. We also used this system in the CFL, last time I had looked.

This was one screwed-up training camp, I thought. My god! It didn't seem right to me.

"This is the new way of doing it," said head trainer Bill Riechelt.

"Gee, Bill," I replied, "I haven't been out of football more than six months and I've never seen this done."

I discovered that if Damon Allen was having an off day and not completing his passes, we weren't completing anything. The other quarterbacks in camp couldn't make a throw – David Rivers from Western Carolina University, Ortege Jenkins from University of Arizona and Scott McEwan from UCLA, who would be released at the end of camp. I thought, where the hell did these guys come from?

The whole training regime was odd. I was really flabbergasted. Still, though we didn't look sharp in pre-season, we didn't look awful either.

David stuck to his word even when we got off to a bad start. He talked to our financial officer if he had any questions about monetary issues. He got a daily copy of our ticket-sales report. Quite often he'd pick up the phone and call Adam. How are the injuries? How's the team? He liked that. He was involved in the game. He understands the game a lot better than many owners.

Wayne Huizenga, the owner of the Miami Dolphins (who hired Jimmy Johnson, who hired me), is very seldom around. He lets the guys he hires do their job. Tex Schramm, in Dallas, wasn't the owner; he ran the club. I saw the owner, Bum Bright, twice at Christmas parties. He let Tex run the show, and believe me he ran it.

Now, the second owner in Dallas when I was there, Jerry Jones, he came in not knowing anything about the NFL, with a coach who didn't know anything either. Jimmy Johnson was a great college coach but no one knew how he would fare in the big show. It took both of them a little bit of time to adjust. But they're very bright guys, so it didn't take them long to figure things out and go on to win two Super Bowls together. I think they could have won five if their egos had been kept in check – and Jones had stayed away from the football operation.

In Arizona, Cardinals owner Bill Bidwill was hands-on, too, with similarly bad results. He was there every day – and they've never won anything. I'm not sure they ever will. His problem is he hires somebody, they get to a certain level and then, for some reason – again, ego is my bet – he's turned off and he makes a change again. The team is in constant flux.

Jeffrey Lurie, in Philadelphia, bought the team in 1994 for $195 million US (a record at the time for a sports franchise), after a failed bid to buy the New England Patriots. A college professor-turned-Hollywood television and movie producer – best known probably for the 1991 Kathleen Turner crime comedy, *V.I. Warshawsky* – Lurie was still unsure and feeling his way when I worked for him. His critics called him the egghead in the boardroom and snidely suggested his mother had bought the team for him. I found him a bright, engaging man who was a quick study.

His family had amassed enormous wealth from their base in Boston. Lurie's grandfather was Philip Smith, who owned General Cinema, a movie theatre operator. The family invested in Neiman Marcus and Harcourt General, a publishing firm that sold for $4.5 billion in 2001.

Lurie cherished vivid childhood memories of attending sports games with his dad, Morris, who died of renal failure when Jeff was only nine. He and his friend Joe Banner (now also the president) were fantasy football players. They were draftniks. They would sit for hours in Jeffrey's garage as teenagers in the 1960s and put together a football draft board. They'd do their own draft, they were such NFL fans.

For Lurie's first few years in the mid-1990s, the Eagles struggled financially. Lurie spent most of his time talking to people with other clubs trying to get his mind square, rather than listening to his own people. But he is smart – a professor of social policy at Boston University before he went into business, so he figured it out.

He hired good people, listened to them and let them do their jobs. In early 2001, the Eagles also moved into the $37-million NovaCare Complex and began construction of their new stadium in partnership with local government. That's why they developed into Super Bowl contenders – good people, smart investment with strong community backing.

The football business may not be rocket science, but it is not a widget factory either. I don't think you can run it like a normal business, as I said, but there are certain principles you must adhere to. I've found in football that if you don't know something, all you have to do is pick up the phone. Someone in the league will tell you. Now they're not going to tell you their game secrets – like how that end-around works. But you can ask a question like what do you guys do about this or how do you do that? Guys are great at sharing business advice and saying, "Call me again."

I didn't need to call anyone about the situation in Vancouver. I had been in this mire twice before. I needed to finish assessing the rot and figure out how to fix it. Unfortunately, before I got a chance to analyze much we were 1–3 Right off the bat, I had to do something. One win and three losses. That's unacceptable.

I had to make a change or we were going to chase away the 12,000 people we still had in the park. It's never easy but you get to a point where you know it's not working – losing is a sure sign. But why is it not working? Is it because the plan isn't in place or because the people aren't in place? Do you have the right people to make it work? Or is the plan not workable? Well, for one thing, we really didn't have a plan yet. I hadn't had a chance to formulate one.

David and I discussed the situation over the phone and I told him I was going to fire the coach. He flew to Vancouver and we discussed it further. We agreed it was probably the best thing to do.

I called Adam Rita, the general manager, into my office and we kicked around a bit of everything just to make sure there wasn't some option I had missed. Finally, I said that I wanted him to take over as coach for the rest of the year and to tell his best friend, head coach Steve Buratto, he was through.

Adam didn't argue.

Firing people is never easy. I had been fortunate over the years. I've been fired twice: once by the Cowboys and once by the Cardinals. The second time was one breath before I quit, so it doesn't really count. But the first time, when Cowboys owner Jerry Jones punted me – that's a different story.

Just shy of a month following the 1992 draft, on Thursday, May 21, Jerry's secretary called me about 10:30 a.m. and said Jerry wanted to see me. She didn't say "and bring your playbook," the classic line a coach uses when cutting a player.

I walked over to Jerry's office, about as far as you could go from one side of the building to the other in our complex, and Marilyn ushered me in. I took my usual seat in one of the padded leather chairs beside the massive, square, marble coffee table that dominated Jerry's office.

Jerry sat on the sofa and we chatted idly for a few minutes. Soon he was talking about scouting. Were we paying our scouts too much? Our assistant coaches were doing most of the scouting and other teams were starting to cut back, he said.

"I don't think that's a great place to cut," I told him.

He disagreed, and I tried to steer him onto another subject. But Jerry didn't want to let go of the scouting costs and he worried the issue like a terrier would a bone. I should have picked up on that.

Jerry had been questioning the worth of the scouts ever since he learned they were peeved at being denied a share of the previous playoff's bonus money. I had advocated on their behalf shortly after the season ended, and here I was again telling the owner of the club he didn't see things properly.

Jerry always claimed that he lived by the "do-right rule." Earlier in the year, I had told him not giving the scouts their bonus money was not fair. This time, I told him it wasn't right and he should do the right thing. He took that as a personal insult.

He exploded. Jerry jumped up from his seat, stabbing a finger at me, "You're outta here!"

He shook with rage.

"I want you out of the building at 5 p.m. today," he said. "You'll get two weeks' severance."

My first thought was to give him a shot to the side of the head. I had the perfect angle. Instead, I got up from my chair and walked out the door, down the long corridor, past Jimmy Johnson's lair and into my office. Jack Mills, an agent from Boulder, Colorado, was waiting.

He stared.

"Bobby, what's wrong with you? Are you feeling okay? You look a little pale."

We went way back; we were friends as well as business associates.

"Jack," I said, "I've got something important to do. I'll call Jerry and tell him you're here."

I called Jerry and explained why Jack was coming to see him.

"You understood what I said, didn't you?" Jerry growled. "You're still outta here!"

"Yes, Jerry, I understood," I replied.

I hung up, Jack left and I called Kay.

"How are you feeling?" she said.

"Better," I lied. "I'm going to tell Connie [my secretary] to pack up and I'll see you soon." It was the first time in my life I had been fired or told to leave. It wasn't a good feeling. Hollow and empty, actually. I had fired people before but I had never lost a job. From my first job at eight or 10 years old picking fruit and vegetables on the neighbour's farm, to becoming general manager of the B.C. Lions, I had never been fired. I had always done the firing or, as equipment manager, I had told players the coach wanted to see them and, by the way, "Bring your playbook."

I arrived home about 7:30 with a van full of stuff. Kay was upset but not too concerned about us landing on our feet. Within a half-hour, running-back coach Joe Brodsky and his wife Joyce showed up with a bottle of wine. Scout Jeff Smith and his wife Anne arrived soon afterwards. Within days we received more than 200 telephone calls and notes from concerned friends.

We had 24 hours to come up with a plan because our daughter-in-law Sherri and three grandchildren – Robert, 10, and twins Ashley and Kyle, seven – were arriving in Orlando for a week with us at Disney World, Epcot, swimming, MGM, collecting bugs and geckos, the Kennedy Space Center, Gator Land and more swimming. Afterwards, we would travel across Texas. During our impromptu six-week vacation, we would visit such exotic locales as Galveston Island (Gary Cartwright has a very interesting book on this area), Texas City, Huntsville, Nacogdoches (a John Levra favourite), Kilgore, Austin, Fredericksburg (Admiral Nimitz Museum), Kerville (don't miss the Cowboy Artists of America Museum) and one of our favourites, San Antonio.

We landed with the Phoenix Cardinals, who hired me almost immediately afterwards as director of college scouting. I didn't miss a season. The experience of being fired taught me a lot and probably improved my sense of compassion.

I've never had to fire a player – coaches see that as their responsibility. They should look the player in the eye and say, "It's not working out. We're going to have to let you go."

Or, "We're going in a different direction." Whatever. Most coaches I've been associated with usually did that – though admittedly there's always the equipment guy or some in-between messenger who tells the player, "Hey kid, Coach Johnson wants to see you – and bring your playbook!" So he's really the first guy that says, "You're gone." And very seldom do you see a guy take his playbook and come back to the locker room.

I make the decision, though, when it's time to let the coach go. I always know what I want to say. But it depends on the coach. Two out of three I had to fire were very volatile and each reacted differently. But they handled it very emotionally. Mind you, that comes with the turf. If they weren't emotional, they wouldn't be in the game.

Although Vic Rapp with the B.C. Lions handled it well when I talked with him, "Yeah, I understand … no hard feelings," and so forth, afterwards he got hot under the collar. It was understandable. Once he left my office, he had to go tell a whole other group of people – his assistants – their lives were changing too. His coaches would also lose their jobs in all likelihood. Their families would be upset. In the end, they were all going to be mad at me because I was the man who did the dirty deed.

But coaches calm down.

Coaches, when they get to this level, understand that being fired is just part of the process. Before I fired Vic, I had fired Cal Murphy – less than two years after I offered him the job in my first decision as general manager with the B.C. Lions in 1975. In my view, under Cal we had hit a plateau as a football club by 1977 and we needed somebody to take us to the next level.

That firing was difficult because Cal was a local hero (a well-loved, hometown product) and he's no wallflower. He told me what he thought. That's why you must be so careful what you say and how you handle it. The media want juicy quotes. They want you to say, "That guy's a son-of-a-bitch; I never liked him and he's a bum." They try to coax it out: "Hey, you can tell me, I'm your friend – we had beers after that bad loss."

In this case, they were ugly. It almost cost me my job; some of the directors were pretty upset over the move. I'm sure they and Cal discussed it within minutes of it happening. The first piece of mail I received the following morning was a card that read: "I want to be the first to tell you, you are a fucking asshole!"

It came from one of Murphy's close Catholic friends.

I thought Cal was a good football coach, but he was not ready to take us to where we needed to be. We needed someone with experience who could kick some ass and put a team together. We were drifting. We were also two rookies and that wasn't a good combination.

At the time, I tried to hire Leo Cahill who had been fired by the Argos. I even flew to Toronto and spent four days in a hotel talking with Leo about the job. We hammered out a deal, I hand wrote a 15-page contract and Leo signed it. His lawyer made a couple of changes and witnessed it.

Leo drove me to the airport in Toronto and said, "Okay, buddy, I'll see you Tuesday for the press conference."

It was a Friday afternoon. I flew back to Vancouver and fired Cal Murphy. I was celebrating the Christmas season with friends that Sunday night when I was paged at Puccini's Restaurant.

I knew what it was. I knew the only thing it could be. Kay says my face went ashen.

I picked up the phone. It was Herb Soloway, the big-time Eastern Canadian lawyer who had approved the contract. He was obviously at a party in Toronto. It was 11 o'clock there and I could hear the background revelry.

"Leo doesn't want to come," he said.

I knew immediately Bill Hodgson, owner of the Toronto Argonauts, had got wind of my deal with Leo and offered him more money.

"I don't believe it," I replied. "I just don't believe it. Leo took me to the airport, we shook hands, he said, 'I'll see you on Tuesday, buddy.'"

I paused.

"So if Leo tells me he's not coming – I'll believe it. But not till I hear it from him."

Two hours later at home, I got a call from a sheepish Leo who blamed the breakup with his wife for everything.

"You understand how she is – my kids are here …"

He went through the whole sob story.

"Leo," I said, "I just can't believe it. You're under contract as far as I'm concerned and we'll discuss this Tuesday when you show up for work."

There was no way he'd be coaching the Lions, but I wanted Leo to twist in the wind for a while. Immediately, I went out and interviewed 35 coaches. I ended up hiring Vic Rapp, who was an assistant with the Edmonton Eskimos. He turned the franchise around on the field.

Rapp was the guy we needed to take us to the next level. He did a helluva job. But again, there was another level above that we could not reach under Vic. We'd get to the playoffs and lose. We could not win a Grey Cup. After a few years I fired Vic for the same reason I fired Cal: we needed to move up another notch. We couldn't beat Edmonton, and that's what we needed to do to win the cup.

He sat there and said: "Okay, I understand."

Later, he didn't. But he told me he did – and I know he did.

Coaches understand, even if they don't like it. Professional football is a small world and no one can afford to burn too many bridges. That's why, as I said, you've got to watch what you say – especially when it's during a firing. It's the comments that come out after, when you face the media and are asked why this? Why that? Those cause the most harm. Sometimes you say things that are taken the wrong way by the person who reads them. Some people get bitter. But I have found it is the wives who display the most emotion because it disrupts their whole family life and because, by implication, you've said their husband isn't worth a damn. He's usually feeling back on his heels, and he knows why it's happening, but his wife usually doesn't see it in football terms; she sees it as disrupting her home and an attack on her family.

Kay and Joyce, Cal Murphy's wife, for instance, had been fairly close. Kay wallpapered their house in New Westminster with three kids hanging off her. Yet, Cal's wife was very, very upset. It took a long time for her to be able to talk to Kay or me. I don't matter. But Kay? It was very difficult for her. Those are the kinds of repercussions in your personal life that happen, given how close everyone comes to feel, how much everyone shares on any kind of true team.

In Vic's case, he became very bitter about it for quite a while. I think it was his wife Carol's doing, or maybe all the assistant coaches, most of whom lost their jobs too. It all wound him up. I don't know what, if anything specific, did it. Nevertheless, I hired Vic in Philadelphia years after this firing, and Kay and Carol are good friends again.

In terms of wives, I also know that when I got fired in Dallas, Kay was very upset at Jerry Jones because he had told her not six months earlier, "Kay, Bobby and you will be with me forever."

He'd said the same thing to me. I just never put any store in it. Kay did. I hate to think what she might have said to him had she had the chance.

I was hoping a coaching change would have the desired effect with the Lions on my return in 2002 after the bad start. Adam Rita took over and just-fired head coach Steve Buratto became our offensive line coach. They were true friends. We ended up having a decent season – a 10–8 record, which was respectable enough for third place in the West. Still, even before the playoff game with Winnipeg, I had decided to replace Adam.

We got our asses kicked – 30–3 – which made my job easier. But I had already made up my mind. I needed to make a complete change, I decided. I couldn't help but think of a comment one of the women assistants on the football side made shortly after my arrival, "I hope he doesn't think he is going to interfere with the football operation."

"Give your head a shake," my informant replied, "That's what he has done all his life."

She would go with the others.

I thought part of our problem throughout the season was our lack of work ethic, especially compared with my experience in the NFL. I worked for a year with John Gruden, when he was the offensive co-ordinator for the Philadelphia Eagles. During the season, he worked from four o'clock in the morning till midnight. I could argue with him that was excessive, but he felt he needed that time.

Now, he's extreme, but most NFL coaches work from 6 a.m. to 10 p.m. early on in the week during the season. As they get closer to the game, say on Thursday, and begin to feel more comfortable with their preparation, it will be 6 a.m. to 6 p.m. On Friday 6 a.m. to mid-afternoon, Saturday is pre-game stuff – a light workout and then most of the afternoon off – or it's a travel day. Sunday, of course, is game day. That's their routine. If it's Christmas day, it doesn't matter. That's their routine during the season.

That's where I come from, so when we were struggling and Adam was wandering into the office well past nine and was gone by five, I thought, oh my god! I don't like working with guys who are nine-to-fivers in this business, and he was a bit of a nine-to-fiver. I have a problem dealing with that, and that's my fault and my problem, not his. I've known Adam since he was an assistant coach at Boise State, Idaho. I just thought, Jesus, this isn't it. This isn't going to get it done. It didn't.

I began to organize my thoughts about what I needed to do to resuscitate the franchise. I don't think I knew what goal-setting was until I read a book on it. Now I sit down every year and list my goals – personal and business. As water boy, I wanted to be the assistant equipment manager. As the assistant equipment manager, I wanted to be the equipment manager. And so on. It was time for me to sit down and establish my goals for the Lions.

I had scrutinized the organization and evaluated the staff. I realized how fortunate I had been that Lui Passaglia was hired six months before I arrived to coordinate the club's community relations. He was a natural for the job.

George Chayka, the vice president, also had been with the organization for over a decade in various capacities. I was exceedingly lucky he was around to lean on. George was an institutional memory, loyal, hard-working and completely capable. He could easily run a CFL franchise on his own and do a great job. George had played football at Simon Fraser University and become a player agent in the 1980s. I had a number of disagreements with him over the value of his clients. He usually thought his guys were worth more than I did. He held two of them out of training camp one year and went to Hawaii on vacation. We eventually worked it out with the clients but I was not too happy, and we still joke about it today.

I didn't have a lot of problems with the business staff. I had determined what happened, why it happened and I was intimate with the issues regarding the season ticket base, the sponsorship base and the team image. It wasn't a personnel issue. I mainly needed to repair bridges into the community.

My business goal-setting list had "season ticket base" at the top. I wanted to move it up from 11,029 in 2002 to 20,500 by 2006.

With the season over, I got on a plane and flew to Toronto. I knew what I wanted to do.

I got a room in the airport hotel and David drove up from Hamilton the next day. We met for about three hours. I laid out what I thought I should do, and he said okay – even on the biggest move. I wanted to fire the head coach and general manager, David's close friend, Adam Rita.

I've always maintained the most important person you hire in a professional football organization is the head coach. You've got to have leadership. You've got to have loyalty. You've got to have an eye for talent and be able to put talent in the right place. You must have that one guy, the head coach, who is a good football guy, who knows talent, who can organize and who is not afraid to hire good people. Some guys won't hire good people because they don't want them taking over their jobs.

The head coach doesn't have to be a great X's and O's guy because he can hire them. It's like me being president: I can hire a financial person so I don't have to be a mathematician. A head coach manages the team, he manages his staff, and he has to spend time and express the right attitude dealing with the media. That takes a lot of time for a head coach.

When I look at the bottom line at the end of the season, it always comes down to how many games you won and how many you lost. That determines everything else – whether you break even, make money or lose money. It determines whether you've got support in the community. Too many losses over too many years will get you fired, erode the team's market value and cause people to say, "Oh, I'm not going to see them." There are very few places like Regina or Green Bay where a team can lose for a long period of time and still get support.

Hiring the right coach is the most important thing I can do, I explained to Braley. The right person can put the right people on the field, can win games, can sell tickets and put money in the till. But timing and the team dynamic are everything.

"It's not that Adam is not a good head coach. He's not the best head coach for us right now," I said.

"Are you sure?" David asked.

"Yep," I replied.

He still said okay.

David thought maybe it was time to revisit Wally Buono. We had talked about Buono in the past, when David first heard he might be available. The head coach of the Stampeders was out of favour. The owner, Michael Feterik, was miffed Buono wouldn't play his son, a third-string quarterback, if you were generous. A couple of months before, Feterik called David offering to pay some of Buono's contract if the Lions or another team would take him. I told David at that point to wait until after the season – I was still focusing on Adam and wasn't ready to make a decision. David said Feterik called another couple of times after that and even asked David to shop Buono around the league.

I couldn't believe that. Wally was the second most-winning coach in the CFL. He'd done it. He'd been there. He knew. He would be perfect, I thought. I wouldn't have to go out and start scrambling for a guy I didn't know. Not that I knew Wally. We had met at a few social functions but I knew his career. I actually recommended him for a head coaching job in the World League of American Football for the Montreal franchise. He played football there. He coached football there. He is bilingual – English and Italian. And he's good-looking.

But he had already moved to Calgary back then and was on the verge of getting the head coaching job. He wasn't prepared to move at that time. He'd be a great solution, I said.

"Why don't you call Feterik and get permission for me to talk with Wally?" I told David.

I flew back to Vancouver and the following morning went looking for Adam. He wasn't in his office so I waited for him. I wasn't going to send for him. I'd look him in the eye. He arrived about 11:00.

I told him, "Adam, I think I've just got to make this move." I didn't ask for his playbook.

"Okay," he said, and we talked about how to handle the media. It was very low key.

Three of his assistant coaches approached me later and told me they had an interest in the job. But I felt I had to make a change and couldn't elevate an assistant; I had to make a clean break and hire my own guy.

David called and said Feterik had given us permission to approach Wally but he wanted me to speak with his chief lieutenant, Fred Fateri, first. I called the Stampeders' vice chairman and asked him if it was okay to talk to Wally. He said sure.

I made plans to fly to Edmonton for the Grey Cup and hopefully have a talk with Wally. I wasn't in the best of moods, given the disappointing season. The vibes I was getting from the Stampeders organization didn't help. They put me a little on edge. Maybe it was something simple. They were new kids on the block and no one I knew had really dealt with them and neither had I. I dunno. But something made my Spidey-senses twitch – maybe it was just the way they had been treating Wally, the things they said about him. From a distance, he looked like a great coach – but they acted as if they couldn't get rid of him fast enough.

Starting Over

Grey Cup, Edmonton
November 22, 2002

MY WIFE and I arrived in Edmonton late in the day and went down to the bar. It was packed but we found a spot at a table with a couple dressed in Calgary Stampeder colours. Kay and I introduced ourselves and we'd no sooner ordered drinks when this ostentatious, swarthy thirty-something with a much younger woman on his arm arrived. He was very full of himself – all flash and bling. They squeezed in beside our table.

"I'm Fred Fateri," he said, extending a hand.

I thought, Oh my god!

He went around the table telling the Calgary couple, "I'm going to turn the Stampeders around, don't you worry."

What a coincidence!

"I'm Bob Ackles," I said, as he turned back to me.

"Oh, yeah, oh yeah, Bobby Ackles," he said, at a volume as if talking to the entire room. "We're supposed to talk about Wally Buono's contract."

Everyone within a half-mile was listening. I've got to get out of here, I thought. He's loud and obnoxious. "Oh, there are some friends of ours," I said pointing across the crowd to no one in particular. "We'll talk tomorrow." His girlfriend was pulling at an arm and he wasn't that interested in me anyway. Kay and I slipped away. That was the start of it. My dealings with him got more outrageous from there.

I think he was like a lot of people who watch football, hockey or any professional sport on television. They sit there and think they could coach better than the professional. Some people really think that. They watch a lot of games, they read a lot about it in the newspaper, and in their own mind they think they can do a better job than those who are doing the job. It doesn't matter who the person is. It's just that they know if they had that opportunity they would be winning Grey Cups, Stanley Cups, Super Bowls, World Cups …

You'd be surprised how many people out there think that. Fateri was like that. It's the same as someone who goes to a restaurant a lot and thinks: "I could own one of these and make a go of it."

Toughest business in the world. Look at the bankruptcies. Football and professional sports are a business, too. People can forget that. They get lost in a fantasy and forget that what they see on television or on the field is like an iceberg and represents perhaps only 10 per cent of the whole. People forget there is another 90 per cent below the surface, a support infrastructure that requires enormous care and attention and is equally important to fielding a competitive team as playing talent.

—ᴡ—

The following afternoon, we stood in the middle of the meeting room after the board of governors adjourned at the Macdonald Hotel. Everything with Wally Buono had gone sideways. First of all, Wally wanted a letter saying he had permission to talk to me. Fateri said a letter wasn't necessary. But Wally was skittish. So there we were – Fateri, Wally, Stampeders owner Michael Feterik, David and me, other owners milling around behind us, and I'm saying, "So, it's okay if Wally talks with me?"

"Now what's this about no permission to talk?" Fateri said to Wally.

"You've given permission?" Wally replied.

"Yes, I've given permission."

"It's okay then, we can…"

"Yes," Fateri said. "Go ahead."

With that, they left and Wally and I agreed to meet over breakfast the following morning before the Grey Cup game.

Wally and I met for two hours, mainly getting to know one another and seeing if we could get along. We finished pretty sure it would work out, agreeing we'd talk later in the week. During the game, David and Feterik met and clarified the terms of Wally's contract. The Stampeders' owner also said he'd cover part of the cost.

I didn't pay a lot of attention to the game that cold Sunday afternoon due to the various discussions that took place in the stadium suite. David Braley was acting CFL commissioner and there was just much too much going on. The best I can say is I loved the half-time show – Shania Twain. Montreal beat the hometown Eskimos 25–16.

Kay and I flew home to Vancouver the following day. As we walked through the airport, my cell phone rang. Fateri. He was steaming.

"We're getting blasted in the media and our phone lines are lit up with fans angry that Buono's leaving," he said. "We're going to need compensation for this deal."

"What?" I was dumbfounded. "Compensation? No one mentioned compensation. You were going to cover part of his salary."

"We want compensation."

"Both David and I talked with you and Michael over the last month and no one ever mentioned compensation. Ever."

"We want compensation," he insisted.

"You're full of shit!" I replied. "We all stood there together and you know there was never any compensation mentioned."

"I'm mentioning it now."

"We're not giving you anything," I snapped.

With that, we hung up, agreeing to differ.

—⁂—

A week later, a Calgary newspaper named five B.C. Lions players the Stampeders wanted in compensation for Buono. I hit the roof. It was blatant tampering.

I called the league office and complained loudly to Commissioner Tom Wright. I couldn't believe what was happening. I was even thinking of drawing up a short list of other coaches who might be available.

Fateri called me on December 6 and told me I had a week, until December 13, to sign Buono.

"You let me know what Lions players you want to give us."

I slammed down the phone.

Four days later, on December 10, he called back and said I had to make my decision by the end of the business day. It was completely out of control. The following day, on December 11, he sent me a form letter, copied to the commissioner:

With respect to discussions held between yourself and Mr. Wally Buono, please be advised that the Calgary Stampeder Football Club Corp. hereby withdraws permission for any further negotiations to take place in this regard, effective immediately.

I couldn't believe it. It got ugly, too. Fateri called me a liar. I'll never forget. Acerbic, opinionated radio sports commentator Neil McRae came to my defence saying I was a lot of things, and I could be a son of a bitch, but he'd never known me to be a liar. I called a press conference and reiterated my position. I had four key points:

· Wally has behaved in the utmost professional manner throughout this whole process. This man has a lot of integrity. I have nothing but good things to say about Wally Buono.
· Plan B can now move ahead. We have not been forced into a situation; there was always a possibility that this could not be finalized. I have full confidence we will find a great head coach for the Lions.
· We were willing to participate and work with Calgary. They did not accept our offer.
· I thank the fans of our organization for their patience in this process. As in all businesses it takes time to find the best person for the job.

I laid it out for the media and gave each reporter a copy of a chronology of what had taken place. "Make your own decision about what happened," I told them.

Afterwards, I picked up the phone and called a friend of mine who was head of security for an NFL team and said, "Would you check on a guy for me? Frederick Fateri – F-A-T-E-R-I. From California." About 10 days later, he sent me reams of stuff. I put it in my file and said, "Hmmm. Asshole, say one more thing ever again and it's going to someone in the media. They can check it out."

I mean, these guys in Calgary were really weird. They said at one point, "Wally's on the downside." You've got a head coach under contract for three years and you come out publicly and say he's on the downside? That's crazy. This Fateri was one strange dude.

The commissioner was fuming over what I'd done.

"Tom, I'm tired of the guy," I told him. "He's an idiot."

"I understand, but you've got to keep it out of the media. It makes everyone look bad."

A week after my press conference, cooler heads prevailed. Stan Schwartz, the president of the Stampeders, managed to get Fateri and Feterik, who usually ignored him, to realize they were making the team a laughing stock. He stepped in and calmed things. He called me on the phone and said, "Bob, let's sort this thing out."

It didn't take us long. He said it was fine for me to give Wally a call and the Stampeders recognized he'd probably be signing with the Lions. Stan said the only issue with the team was they wanted Wally back in town in January to resign in person and do a little PR to mend some of the fences with the fans. It was a good conversation and it helped erase some of the tensions.

Wally and I had the deal done early in the new year. I called Stan and told him Wally was joining the Lions as coach and general manager.

After this episode, no matter what they did, the reaction in Calgary against Fateri and Feterik was so bitter the dynamic duo returned to California a year later. The only reason Feterik ever came to Canada in the first place, Wally told me, was to find a place for his son to play quarterback. He didn't have the skills – not for the NFL, not for the CFL. He was a small-college quarterback.

The day after we reached a deal, Wally and I sat down to plan the future.

In terms of the coaching staff, Wally kept three of the assistants who worked for Adam – offensive coordinator and former head coach Steve Buratto, defensive coordinator Paul Arslanian, and the defensive-line coach Richard Harris. He brought in from Calgary his own offensive-line coach, Dan Dorazio, his special teams-linebacker coach, Mike Benevides, and his offensive coordinator, Jacques Chapdelaine, who became our quarterback-receiver coach.

Adam's son had been our videographer and he went with his dad to Toronto. Wally brought in Justin Coderre from Calgary to be our video coordinator. We kept our training and equipment people. But we made a couple of changes in the football office support staff.

In terms of the team, as soon as Wally got his staff put together, after he had a chance to look at the video and assimilate all the information on our players, we sat down. We systematically went through the team. He gave me a report on each and every athlete. Player personnel decisions are coaching decisions and I was primarily interested in where he thought we had to make changes. But that would take him much of the season – this was his preliminary assessment.

In terms of a key player, I had started negotiations with quarterback Dave Dickenson. I had seen tape on him while he was at Calgary in 1998 and 1999. He got a Grey Cup ring in '98 as backup and later was named the CFL's most outstanding player. But he had then gone to the NFL. I went to see him play in San Diego because I knew he would be available from what I was hearing on the grapevine. I went down for a pre-season game and he was the best quarterback on the field that day – of the four of them!

Nevertheless, Dickenson was number-three pivot on the depth chart, possibly number four, and the Chargers had drafted a quarterback fairly high – Drew Brees. I figured Dave's days were definitely numbered so I kept an eye on him. Sure enough, San Diego released him. Miami picked him up on waivers, then they let him go. Detroit took him, they dropped him, and then Seattle picked him up. He drifted through 2002 on practice rosters not playing much. I told Wally I thought he was the guy we needed.

Wally was Dickenson's coach in Calgary, I figured this was a no-brainer. So did he. He asked what I thought about Damon Allen because he was our starting quarterback. He had played well for us. But Damon wasn't selling tickets; he didn't excite anybody. Wally and I agreed we needed to make the change.

We got Dickenson under contract without incident and told Damon not to report to training camp because we were trying to trade him. That was difficult. Damon is a football player, that's what he does, that's his job, and every spring he needs to be in camp. That's his life. It was very tough to tell him to sit out.

Toronto, where Adam had gone, was keenly interested in Damon, not surprisingly, but we couldn't get a deal done. They figured we would eventually let him go and they'd pick him up for nothing. Fortunately, there were a couple of other teams interested. Still, no one wanted to surrender a lot. We played it out and finally, during training camp, we made a deal with the Argos.

Going into the season I felt good about the team and the football operation. I also had to continue addressing the business challenges. George Chayka, the vice president, and I met daily to discuss the uphill battle we were facing in the community. One morning, we met over at Moray Keith's office at Dueck on Marine Drive. There were three acres of cars stacked up on three levels. A mammoth modern showroom of more than 30,000 square feet. Chevies, Cadillacs, Corvettes, Hummers and Novuranias. Moray is a big sports fan, a big football fan and he had been a major backer of the club for years.

When I left Vancouver to go to Dallas in 1986, the Lions had an awful lot of good corporate support programs in place. We had a season-ticket program, for instance, with many large companies participating through payroll deduction plans. That made it easy, easy, easy for an employee to become a season ticket owner for only $3.75 per paycheque. Or they could just buy a pair of season tickets. That's how we got our season-ticket base from 24,000 to 30,000, programs like that. I don't know why or how those programs withered. I guess the management decided while I was gone they weren't going to put any money or effort into the community.

"Moray," I said, "We need help."

I knew Moray had been on committees in the past and could be counted on to pitch in. The three of us tossed around a few ideas and decided we needed to bring in a few other people. We decided to approach Tom Malone, a Scotiabank vice president (they were a big sponsor) and Dennis Skulsky, then publisher of *The Vancouver Sun* and

The Province for Canwest Mediaworks, and his lieutenant, Jamie Pitblado, vice president of marketing for the Pacific Newspaper Group. The big dailies were the dominant local media players and long-time Lions' partners. The six of us met again at Moray's office.

We needed to get people involved, particularly from the business community. We decided to hold breakfasts to which we would each invite people we thought might have an interest, who would maybe get on board or who would give us some sort of help.

We decided to hold the first meeting at the Vancouver Aquarium where they have a boardroom in which one wall is glass and you can see the dolphins swim past. Moray got up and said, "I love sports. I love what the football team and the hockey team can do in this town."

He looked around the room.

"I guess our motivation for getting involved was we just didn't want this football team to die," Moray said. "Let's face it, it is in bad shape and something needs to be done to repay an owner who has stuck by this team and suffered his share of losses without asking for much help."

I gave a little talk. It was all very positive. Then, everyone was handed a little piece of paper for suggestions or questions, and we asked them to fill it out and give it back or take it with them and send it along later. If they wanted to get involved, we said they should invite two people to the next breakfast. It was a bit like the shampoo commercial – you tell two friends, and they tell two friends and they tell two friends …

I was out of town when the group decided they needed a name. I heard about it afterwards: The Water Boys. I don't know whether they were being ironic or just goofing around. Few of them knew the emotional resonance of that title for me. Starting as the water boy for the Lions before they were a professional team had played a huge part in shaping me as a person. The team was my family. At the same time, "water boy" was an epithet flung at me at times like an insult – it cut both ways. Kay knew that. Still, self-conscious about it or not, I couldn't help agreeing with them; it was a good name – I liked the idea of the business community helping to sustain the team, keeping it refreshed. And I was proud to have been the water boy.

After the Aquarium breakfast, then mayor, Larry Campbell (he's now a senator) came on board. We met at City Hall, the first time they've ever allowed coffee and breakfast wraps into the council chambers. Vancouver fire and rescue services chief Ray Holdgate became a Water Boy. We went to Firehall No. 1 for our next breakfast, and when Vancouver police chief Jamie Graham joined, we celebrated in the police museum, a former morgue. Everyone stood around the autopsy tables eating their breakfast while a morbidly obscene picture of a dead Errol Flynn stared down at us. We decided to hold the breakfasts every six to eight weeks in interesting locales, and they did wonders for building my rapport with the business community and fanning interest in the Lions.

Some of the Water Boys – both men and women – began promoting corporate suites in the stadium, some got involved in sponsorships and some just promoted the team. We gave them small football-shaped cards that entitled the bearer to two free tickets. The Water Boys gave those to people they thought might enjoy a game and become supporters. It was a huge success.

I could see throughout the season how much it helped us rebuild bridges in the business community. We began emphasizing other programs too – in elementary schools we had Read, Write and Roar!; in secondary schools, it was Lion in the House (our players gave talks about the importance of education, or discussed bullying) and Punt, Pass, Kick, a skills competition that drew 12,000 to 15,000 kids. The players were out all the time helping coach community kids.

It didn't ultimately matter why things had deteriorated. They had. And once that happens, it takes a long time to build it back. And a tremendous amount of sweat and effort has to go into it. But that's what we did.

To create some football consciousness in the spring, I started the Orange Helmet Dinner, an awards night for those who work in football at a neighbourhood and school level. We got about 400 people out. To see how touched the coaches were was amazing.

All of these efforts would have their effect over time in nurturing our fan base. There was nothing like a kid going home and saying, "Mom, do you know who Dave Dickenson is? Oh, he's a nice guy. I met him today at school and we threw the ball around. We played basketball." Or whatever, because you know the next line: "I'd like to see him play sometime."

I know that if I get that response, that if someone goes to one game, gets their parents to go to one game, then maybe they'll go to more. Those kids grow up to become your season-ticket holders.

We lost a generation of fans in Vancouver between 1986 and 2002. For a whole cohort of young people it was basketball, and then hockey. Football fell off their radar. The Canucks are so popular, I believe, because they pay attention to the kids who are their future fans. I've never put my finger on any one thing that the Lions did that sank them in the community. Certainly during the 1990s, before David took over in 1997, I think laziness may have played a role. Some people seemed to have the attitude: I'm being paid, I think I'll go on an extended scouting trip. Or whatever.

Still, more than that contributed to the team's alienation. When I left here in 1986 there was a solid group of local business people on the board of directors, the team was community owned and we were active throughout our market. A year later, the team lost the TV contract, started scrambling and seemed to drift onto the financial shoals.

During my era, before I left in 1986, we had it so our season-ticket renewals were in the mail at the end of October. We deposited roughly $2 million in the bank by the middle of December, thanks to our Early Bird Special sales of season tickets. They stopped doing that after I left in the mid-1980s. Why? That was $2 million you had in the bank to tide you over! Why would you stop? I have no idea. Someone decided, "Oh, that's a lot of work. Let's not bother."

Of course, I restarted the program in 2002.

The biggest challenge by far for the Lions on my return was the business side. In the NFL, you didn't face those problems. The NFL is corporate America. It's big dollars. No, it's humongous dollars. It's about turning people away. After I came back to the Lions, many people said, "You must have learned a lot of marketing stuff down in the NFL."

"No. Not at all. They don't market. They don't have to."

The brand name, "NFL," is a platinum mine. A little patch emblazoned with those initials, flash that anywhere, and watch the reaction in America – Wow! Where can I buy it?

The difference is population: 300 and some million versus 35 million. The money difference is a quantum leap. If you're dealing with a player in Dallas, you might give him $2 million or $3 million as a signing bonus on a three- to five-year contract. In the CFL, he might – maybe – get between $25,000 and $50,000 to ink a three-year deal.

No, in America, put up a sign saying "NFL" and you sell out. The biggest challenge truly is to field the best team to win. In Canada, you not only need to win on the field, you also need to survive financially. That is the challenge.

We were doing a lot of things after the first year I returned, but people didn't realize how much we were doing yet. The Canucks did one little thing somewhere, not that they don't do a lot of things, but they got front page all the time. We did a hundred things and rarely got a mention. And we were being criticized by the media for our marketing.

I asked some of them one day: "Tell me what marketing is."

They hemmed and hawed.

Nobody but marketers know what marketing is. People don't really know what it is. Is it buying ads in the newspaper or on radio or on TV? Yes and no. It's a whole host of ineffable things. But to get our message out, I started inviting the media to what we called round-table discussions. We took them down to Vera's – the burger shack at Kitsilano Beach owned by a former Lions defensive lineman, Noah Cantor – and gave them lunch. We didn't talk football, we told them about our latest community outreach programs. I gave them a complete run-down on the non-football activities we were up to and it began to have an effect. The carping about our marketing died off anyway.

I think the biggest change with Wally's arrival was in attitude. Attitude and professionalism. You could feel the organization start to take a little more pride. We'd done some things to physically clean up the place – replaced that disgusting carpet for a start. But more important, I think our staff began to realize this was serious business and it was not a nine-to-five operation. If you want to work here, you've got to have that attitude – do whatever it takes to get the job done, but get it done.

My first year back in Vancouver, I wasn't involved at all in the draft. We got one significant player – Jason Clermont, a slotback from the University of Regina who was our fourth pick in the first round. There was no one else really. We drafted Brett Romberg 17th overall in round two, but we never seriously expected to see him. He was a University of Miami offensive lineman and ended up in the NFL. You take a chance on those guys. If they get drafted by the NFL and make it, you've wasted a draft choice. But, if they don't make it in the NFL, you can be a big winner because they will then come to Canada to play.

For Wally's first year, I sat in on the coaches' meetings in preparation for the draft so I could understand their thinking: why we were drafting this guy instead of that guy. Mike Benevides, our special teams coordinator and linebacker coach, handled the Canadian college draft for us. He put together a package with Neil McEvoy, player personnel coordinator. They got everything ready and all the tapes prepared. There is a camp every year put on by the league for all the teams that features 30 or 40 of the top draft prospects who are run through a battery of tests. Wally and four of our people had attended that and met the players.

We used our first pick to draft Paris Jackson, sixth overall in the first round, a wide receiver from the University of Utah. We chose Javier Glatt, 15th overall in the second round, a University of British Columbia linebacker. We also got Carl Gourges, 24th overall in the third round, an offensive lineman from Laval University. They would all prove their worth. Not a bad draft for us, not bad at all.

In the end, we had a decent year on the field, finished 11–7 but lost to Adam, Damon and the Argos in a cross-division playoff semifinal 28–7. They must have whooped it up.

I don't like any loss. Ever. This was no different. In spite of the personal overtones, it was only another defeat. Honest. I didn't like it. For sure. Never do. Especially when you have to wait until next year to get over it. That it was Adam and Damon didn't matter much to me. We had to let Damon go or we would have stagnated. We would have had a lackadaisical fan base and drawn maybe 5,000, even 7,000 fewer fans a game. There was no excitement under Damon. Right off the bat, Dickenson arrived and the Lions became an exciting product. Yes, we had lost – but we were rebuilding and I felt good about that. Optimistic.

Over the next few weeks Wally and the coaches reviewed the game tapes from the season and re-evaluated the players. Every tape of every game. Coaches look for things they didn't see in the rush of the season. Looking at the games consecutively you see things – whether a player improved over the season, stayed the same or tapered off in the final games.

Older players can often tire and tail off late in the season because of their age or because of the compound effect of injuries over their career. As a coach and as a general manager, you've got to keep that in mind. With young players, there's a different problem.

Coming out of college, most rookies run out of steam halfway through the season. I think it's mainly psychological, but it may also be conditioning. They're used to playing between 10 and 11 games a season; they join us and now they're playing 20 to 22 games. It's considerably more demanding. To be able to go 22 weeks at a high level and compete is difficult. But rookies should improve as they get into the league and generally you see that in their second and third years. If they don't, it's time to cut or trade them.

One of the other big things to keep in mind is that coming into a pro camp, rookies don't know what to expect. They watch it on television; they hear their buddies talk about it. But until they are there, they don't know. If they're going to make the adjustment in their sophomore year, in the off-season they must prepare themselves mentally and physically knowing what is expected. That's what coaches have to figure out: do they lack the skills or do they need experience and maturity?

The system that individual coaches use to evaluate each player is exceedingly complicated. They evaluate a player on every single play during the season, assigning a point value for each aspect of playing a position. They do that after each game, but then, at the end of the season, they go back and re-evaluate – looking at the tapes to ensure they made the right call. It's all logged in a computer database. In modern football, coaches in some ways have become geeks.

The first technocrat coach I ever saw was John Gruden, now head coach at Tampa Bay. He was a really macho man but also a computer nerd when we worked together at Philadelphia. Computers began arriving in a serious way in the 1990s as the younger coaches came into the business from the college teams; the old-time guys really struggled to switch over. It was a major technological revolution. John was on its leading edge.

I remember an incident in the old days before video, in 1959, the Lions' head coach at the time, Wayne Robinson, a really hard-nosed guy, was screening game film. The old 16mm stock was dark, so you couldn't always see very clearly. It wasn't crisp like digital images are today. And you only saw one angle. On this occasion, Robinson saw an offensive lineman go offside but couldn't tell exactly who it was. He played it back and forth, back and forth, back and forth, while all of the players sitting in the room squirmed. You could have heard a pin drop.

You know that player and probably both guys on either side of him knew who it was – but no one said boo. Robinson was doing a slow burn – back and forth, back and forth, and back and forth. Finally, he managed to make out the three stripes of an Adidas-brand shoe. Bob Brady, the offensive guard and a local guy, was the only player wearing Adidas. Well, Robinson mercilessly embarrassed the kid in front of everyone.

Now, there would be no question of who that was. There is no place to hide on the field today. No place at all to hide. If I want to see play 37 of game such-and-such, boom! There it is immediately on the computer screen. With a click, you can generate an instant graph of anyone's performance. Technology has made the video guy important. He doesn't only take film and develop it. He creates a fundamental coaching and management resource. Now, when coaches watch the play, it's broken down – they get a sideline view and an end-zone view of the same play. You see both angles back to back. Immediately. It's amazing how much scrutiny players are under.

For coaches and managers such as Wally Buono, this information is invaluable for evaluating performance, documenting the decline of a player and making personnel decisions. The first big call you make about a player is whether he should be on your team. The second big call is when he should be let go. You don't want to hold on to any player too long. Today, the computer has put an enormous set of diagnostic and comparative tools at a coach's disposal. Wally and every top coach relies on them, although not to the exclusion of their own gut instinct and hard-polished experience.

When the dust had settled that year, Wally and I got together and went over his report – a distillation of the coaching analysis of each player. But simplified. A line or two and a few icons – arrows pointing up, down or sideways to indicate the trend lines. Nothing nearly as elaborate as the coaching reports.

Wally and I knew for sure that we'd made the right choice in Dickenson. But I thought we needed overall improvement in the number and quality of Canadians on our roster. Wally was a little more specific about the adjustments. He thought we needed to replace a couple of offensive linemen. We had to find another deep-threat receiver. Neither of us was happy with our kicking game. We had a young kicker who did a decent job but he had decided to retire and coach. We had to find a replacement. Wally had kept three coaches from the previous staff, and he decided he wanted to make a couple of changes there, too.

The player changes would look after themselves. We had talked about the following season's contract issues: whose deal we needed to extend, that type of thing. Wally and Bob O'Billovich, our personnel guy, would work together on player acquisitions. A former head coach, Bob had been in personnel for a long time. He understood the type of player you need to win in this league.

As I headed to Mexico for that winter's vacation, I didn't think everything was fine, but finally I felt we were rolling in the right direction. Wally had a season under his belt and knew what he needed to do to make the team work. I was beginning to think I had not been crazy to return and take the helm.

Water Boy

THEY CALLED me Robin. It was a girl's name, much to my disgust, and they chose it because my mouth was always gaping to be fed. Hungry, that was me, and that hunger drove me. I was born in Sarnia, Ontario, on September 16, 1938, a little more than a year after my brother Ken. My mother, Molly, was a petite woman, four-foot-nine inches tall, 100 pounds. I weighed 11 pounds.

Molly was from Toronto, and we soon moved back there when World War Two broke out a year after my birth. My parents had met there, probably in 1935 or 1936 but no one made a note. My father, William Allan Ackles, arrived from Amherst, Nova Scotia, moved into the neighbourhood and they married not long afterwards. My brother Ken was first born. Dad took him and Mum to Sarnia afterwards because he found work with Imperial Oil crewing on the tankers that plied the Great Lakes. That's why I was born in that corner of south-western Ontario across from Port Huron, Michigan.

I don't know much about either side of my family, but I researched my dad's clan a bit during a trip to the East Coast. He was born on April 6, 1911, and came from a fairly large brood that lived in a rambling Victorian house that's still standing. There were two boys and four girls, I think. A baby, I heard, died at birth, and my grandfather married twice. But my grandfather was apparently a son of a bitch, and it sounds like my father ran away from home.

On September 14, 1939, my father was one of the first Canadians to enlist and head overseas. I wouldn't see him for another six years. He would earn a France and Germany Star, a Defence medal, a Canadian Volunteer Service Medal with Clasp and a War Medal 1939–1945. But that's why I never got to know him very well – the war and its aftershocks.

Living in Canada during the war, your whole existence revolved around news from Europe. We occasionally received a letter and sporadically a package bearing exotic stamps affixed to brown paper wrapping arrived. Once, a parcel came from Holland containing a pair of wooden shoes for each of us.

My mother and my grandmother, who lived with us, both worked in the war effort. As my father was one of the first to enlist, the radio station CFRB chose us to attend the studio one night to speak with him on air. I was four, perhaps five, at the time and it was my first recollection of hearing my father's voice.

You can imagine the excitement around our house when my mother received a telegraph from the government saying he was coming home. He was discharged April 22, 1946, and did not waste any time deciding the place to raise a young family was in the nearby farming community of Locust Hill, about 26 miles northeast of downtown Toronto as the crow flies, population 56.

He didn't have enough cash to buy a farm, so he purchased a quarter acre for $1,500 – our address was 7926 Highway #7, a garage about 20 feet square with a very thin, pebbly concrete floor. A hand pump was affixed to a wooden bench at the back door. There was no other indoor plumbing.

I recall confiding in my dog Chippy, a black cocker spaniel cross, that it didn't look too good. Still, there were plenty of nearby farms, a creek, which I considered a veritable St. Lawrence River, a train station, a cemetery and a general store.

My mother operated a truck-stop featuring coffee and sandwiches from the house while Dad was off trying to earn money in construction or any other job he could land. When Mum got pregnant with my sister, we closed the truck stop. While we were closed, Dad made a deal with Reliance Petroleum Ltd. to install gasoline pumps. We reopened as a truck-stop and filling station.

The elementary school for the surrounding district was a one-room, red-brick building two miles away. It had a large furnace in one corner at the back of the room, kept stoked in winter by the senior boys in grades 7 and 8 (if there were any kids that old that year). I yearned for the job.

The school was surrounded by maple and fir trees. There was a softball diamond and we built a great bicycle jump. It was idyllic. We spent summers at the creek, about a half-mile from our garage, which we called the Dew Drop Inn. My brother Ken, good friend Wayne Thurston and I prided ourselves in being the first kids in the creek each spring – usually during Easter break. The ice had not totally disappeared yet, but the three of us would skinny dip under the highway bridge. Wayne lived just down the highway from us and had come from Toronto, too. There were many days later in the summer we would sit in the same spot, satiated from a mess of fried chub. My best friend in elementary school was Ken Burrows, and we're still connected. Ken was always working on the family farm near the school. As I grew older, I got part-time jobs picking fruit or vegetables. Beefsteak tomatoes for five cents a hamper. My favourite farm was our neighbours', the Armstrongs. Their spread was one of the larger family properties in Markham Township – covering between 400 and 500 acres. They had owned it for generations. It usually didn't take me long to earn enough folding money to enjoy a good time at the Markham Fall Fair.

One night my mother woke me up and said, "I want you to go to Napanee with your father."

As I rubbed sleep from my eyes, she said he wanted to visit his brother Norman, but he had been drinking. "I want you to keep him awake."

I was nine or 10. Can you imagine? It was an old panel truck and off we sped down the two-lane highway. Of course, I fell asleep – and so did he. I awoke to grit sandpapering my face and a god almighty screeching. We had missed hitting a tractor-trailer head-on and were scraping down its flank. It took out one whole side of our van.

No wonder I grew up with such an independent streak.

I remember the summer my pal Wayne Thurston and his family rented a cottage at Wasaga Beach on Georgian Bay for a week. I went with them to visit my Aunt Barbara Bilton and cousins, John and Dave, who lived there. A week later, when the Thurstons had to return to Locust Hill, I begged my mother to let me stay another week. She acquiesced. When it came time to leave, I said my goodbyes, walked out to the highway and stuck out a thumb – a 10-year-old hitching a ride for 100 miles. I can't imagine that happening today. Different times.

In spite of the sub-zero temperatures, the scouring wind and thigh-deep snow, I enjoyed the winters, even if it seemed we were always shoveling the driveway at home or the sidewalk at school.

Ice hockey was my first love. There was plenty of natural ice during most of the winter. At 11, I decided to try out for the local peewee team.

The Unionville Arena was the only artificial ice surface in the township. I hitchhiked the five miles to practice and the games, packing my goal-tending equipment. I was extremely proud to be a starting goalie in the competitive North Toronto League named after Maple Leaf great King Clancy. I idolized Leaf goalie Turk Broda. Years later, when I was the general manager of the B.C. Lions and Clancy a vice-president of the Leafs and the Hamilton Tiger-Cats, I told him about it with enthusiasm. He loved the story.

Near the end of my senior elementary school year, I learned we were moving. My father had itchy feet. He pulled out the atlas one day and said it was time to pull up stakes. He considered Acapulco, Mexico, but settled on Vancouver. I'm not sure why. I think he was having trouble doing what he wanted to do. He wasn't getting anywhere and he had three kids. In the summer, the truck stop did okay, but they were building the new 401 highway. Soon we wouldn't have the traffic.

One of our neighbours had lived in B.C. and he and my dad were drinking buddies. I think he kept saying, "Oh, Vancouver is the place. Lots of work there."

I don't think my father ever stopped to check that out. Someone told him Vancouver was a great place to live, and in B.C. there was always lots of work. He just announced one day, "We're going to Vancouver."

We sold our place March 10, 1952, for $3,100 and moved into a little apartment above a restaurant in Unionville until we finished school. Then we got in the car and drove to Vancouver.

I was sad to leave Locust Hill. It was a perfect place to grow up. I have many fond memories of the area and the people. I always had something to do – playing touch football on the station lawn, lazing about the Armstrong farm, especially at maple syrup time, skating, playing hockey on open fields and ponds, fishing in the creek, erecting tree forts, re-enacting the famous battles of World War Two or mimicking a dust-up after a western at the Markham Theatre. I've often thought about my father's decision. Life seems to me about being in the right place at the right time. Had we stayed in Locust Hill, or moved to the next town, to Markham, say, or someplace like that, who knows? I might have been a farmer.

With most of our belongings sold, some shipped to the west coast, we loaded the balance into the only new car my parents ever owned, a 1952 Chevy coupe. My younger sister Nancy had chicken pox and my mother was pregnant again as we headed west. I thought of it only as a new adventure.

We spent the rest of the summer living in the car and eating meals cooked on a small green Coleman stove. I have pictures of us in odd places like North Dakota clustered around a picnic table eating supper. We stayed twice in rented cabins only because of the inclement weather – in Minnesota or Wisconsin we ran into bad thunderstorms, and coming out of the mountains in Montana we hit a snowstorm and had to pull in and find a place to stay. Other than that we slept in the car.

It took us the better part of two weeks to drive across the country. That trip shaped me forever, as surely as if we'd emigrated across an ocean. Of course, there was no work for my dad when we got here. Yet I never thought of us as poor.

One of my high school coaches, Fred Owens, years later called it "a great Horatio Alger story." It certainly has all the elements of those hoary rags-to-riches tales, which is funny, because I don't think of it that way. Looking back, it's hard not to recognize my dad's hardscrabble for what it was.

When we first arrived, we stayed in Richmond with a young couple who had lived near us in Ontario. But they had three kids and we had three kids, and they had this little matchbox house out by the old airport. Within a week, it was clear we had to find a place of our own. We couldn't.

My father drove into Stanley Park and we set up camp. We would spend the better part of July and August squatting. Every so often, the police would arrive – usually at two or three in the morning – rouse us and say, "You can't stay here."

We'd get up, strike camp, drive to another spot and set up again.

My mother was pregnant so it was pretty tough on her. My brother Ken and I spent the day running wild, returning at meal times. We had no supervision. My father spent his day searching for work, returning at night to cook dinner. He always cooked, a habit he'd apparently picked up in the army. We'd sit there at the picnic table at Lumberman's Arch and he'd simmer and sauté on our little Coleman stove. There was a bucolic quality to it.

Still, for a long time I wouldn't tell anybody about this period in my life. I was embarrassed. For a kid, it was terrific. The park was a big back yard with a great swimming pool. My brother did his thing, I did my thing, and my little sister was with my mother all the time. It was Eden. But as I grew into adolescence, I realized other people didn't view it as I did – a camping adventure. Like being called "water boy" for a time after I became general manager, remembering the experience worried at my self-image.

My dad finally got work in construction doing floors and, when September rolled around, he found a little house at 7th and Laurel. But we couldn't move in until October so he moved us into an apartment above a storefront in Marpole in the meantime.

What was funny, however, was he took Ken and me to Fairview High School and tried to have us enrolled. He didn't know it was primarily a business school for girls. The woman fortunately explained it and directed him to King Edward High School.

I was staggered by the school. Just its sheer size. There were hundreds of kids – I was used to a score. Ken at least had gone to a much larger school in Markham. But it turned out I was better off than my brother. I was 14 and in the same boat as everyone else. I had arrived from an elementary school, and my classes were filled with kids who had similarly arrived from different feeder schools. Most didn't know each other. Ken went into Grade 10 and there were already established cliques.

I quickly got into athletics, too, which helped immensely; Ken was never into them. To this day, I think that's a key to fitting in. I played sports from the time I was old enough to run until I was 37 years old, huffing and puffing at Sunday morning hockey. I played football, soccer, hockey, rugby, lacrosse … I was always on the go, going somewhere to play something. And in all that time, my mother and father never saw me practice or play a game. Not once did they ever see me practice or play. Not once.

Thinking back now, with our two boys, we were always going some place, Kay or I. One of us always saw them play the game. One or both of us.

—⚹—

I went into King Edward looking for hockey jackets and asking every guy I met "Where do you play football? Where do you play hockey?" In those days, they played rugby in the fall, football after Christmas, and hockey ran from late September until spring. So I started playing rugby even though I initially had no idea what it was. In Ontario, the "rugby football union" was what they called the football league. I really had not seen true rugby played. I learned.

There were only three sheets of ice in the Lower Mainland and the guys I hung around with played at the Forum. I went for tryouts but it didn't look good. I wasn't used at all in the exhibition games and figured I had better find another team. The coach, John Gorman, called a few days later and asked why I had dropped out.

"It just looks to me," I said, "that Abby Branca is your number-one guy, and Ray Creed looks a shoe-in for backup."

"Abby quit," he replied, "and Ray Creed played the first game and was a sieve. Will you come back?"

"Hell, yes."

At the Forum, manager Peter Kerr said I had to sign a card to play because in those days the rights to minor hockey players were owned by a parent major-league team. To play in the Ontario Hockey Association, I had signed a card that made me the property of the Toronto Maple Leafs. Now, Pete told me, the team would have to seek a release from Toronto so I could become the property of the New York Rangers. At 14. It was ridiculous, and no wonder the system was eliminated.

The guys I played with were a great group that included John Ferguson, legendary tough guy with the Montreal Canadiens, who sipped from the Stanley Cup and later toiled in professional hockey's executive offices; Joe Jeroski, who became a golf pro; and Ken Bailey, the number-one thoroughbred trainer at Hastings Park. Terry Mc-Kibben was probably our best athlete. But he wouldn't leave Vancouver to go anywhere. He could have gone with Ferguson to Saskatchewan to play junior hockey, and probably could have gone to the NHL as well. McKibben was just as great a soccer player and could have gone to England to play Premier League. He became a fireman. We're still in touch. Same with Kelly Hood. Dan Kolesnik, who played hockey and high school and junior football with me, is a good friend today as well. That's one of the great things about sports; you never lose touch with people. We all became lifelong friends. They can disappear for a while, but they come back and we pick up where we left off, on common ground.

The first pair of real goalie skates I owned I bought off Gump Worsley, the great netminder who at the time was with the Canucks in the Western Hockey League. Ferguson and McKibben were stick boys for the team and Fergie arranged it – $10 for the pair.

We were real Forum rink rats. In the age before Zambonis, on Saturday, Sunday and evenings, we cleaned the ice. The rule was you had to be going over the boards before you got to yell what job you were going to do. The lazy guy always wanted to handle the hot mop, next easiest job was the squeegee and so on and so forth. The guys who wanted to push themselves used the scrapers. Fergie, I remember, would never open his mouth. He would grab a scraper and start from the boards, which was always the toughest place, cause you always get those little chips and things. And he would push that scraper around and around the rink, just to build up his legs. Even at that time he was thinking: I've got to get myself stronger and bigger if I want to make the National Hockey League.

We got paid 25 cents a clean one year and 35 cents the next year. On a Saturday and Sunday, I could maybe make between $5 and $6. I supplemented that with stooping at the racetrack on Saturday – picking up untorn tickets, because you'd be surprised at the number of people who go, "Oh, shit," and throw away a winning ticket. I always came out with two, four, five bucks. I was always an entrepreneur.

I remember the 1953 newspaper story that led me to become the Lions' water boy. My friends and I had just finished a touch-football game in Heather Park and we were talking about this new team they were starting. We had a newspaper and I'm sure the headline was, "Dr. Stukus hangs out shingle."

Annis Stukus was one of three famous brothers from Toronto. He, Bill and Frank were known as "The Stukii" and led the Argos to Grey Cups in 1937 and 1938. Annis, who was nicknamed "the Big Stukus" and "the Loquacious Lithuanian," had helped found the Edmonton Eskimos in 1949 and was a natural choice to come to Vancouver and do the same.

The professional league in those days was known as the Western Interprovincial Football Union. Its eastern rival was the Ontario Rugby Football Union in central Canada. Together, they formed the Canadian Rugby Football Union, precursor of the Canadian Football League, and every year the champion of each met and did battle for the Grey Cup. I thought it would be great to be the water boy if Vancouver got a team. The next morning I skipped school and headed down to the office at 411 West Hastings.

It was a walk-up, and Stukus wasn't there. Vida Scott, his secretary and assistant, was in the office and so was Eric Cameron, one of the team's directors. I told Vida I wanted to become the team's water boy.

"Mr. Stukus will be back at noon or maybe closer to one o'clock," she said.

I came back and he was there. I introduced myself and he had Vida take down my address and phone number.

I didn't hear back.

Still, I kept following the team – initially called the B.C. Cubs – in the newspaper until I saw the first team practice announced. I made a point of being there and I vividly remember walking onto the field at Heather Park even though it's more than half a century ago. I waited till practice finished and followed Stukus as he headed for the clubhouse trailing a gaggle of reporters. I grabbed him by the shirtsleeve.

"Coach, can I have a minute?" I said.

"Yeah sure, kid," he said, turning to face me.

"I applied for the water boy's job, remember?"

"Right. I remember you. Come on. I'll put you to work."

He turned and strode to the clubhouse.

"Tiger," he called out. "What's your name, kid?"

"Bob Ackles."

"Tiger," he said to a short burly man who emerged from somewhere in the back of the locker room, "Tiger, this is Bob Ackles; he's the water boy. Put him to work."

Tiger, I would soon learn, was from someplace in Ontario but you'd swear he was a wise guy from the streets of New York, given his chutzpah. We would become great friends. He talked through his nose, which was more a broken beak. He was solidly built. He had wanted to be a football player but was just too small.

Tiger had worked with Stuke for years. He took me into the locker room where the players were stripping down and told me to start picking up the soiled towels and jockstraps. That first season, the team played exhibition games against semiprofessional and pick-up teams from Kamloops, Victoria, the Navy and UBC. We even played the Fort Lewis Four by Fours, a U.S. Army team that featured Les Richter, who became a great linebacker with the L.A. Rams. We opened as the Lions the following year – 1954. I still remember my first road trip.

We stayed at the old Macdonald, a classic Canadian railway hotel where years later I'd meet Fateri. I bunked in with Tiger, who told me, "Kid, you know Stuke and I were here for a couple of years. So if I come home with a couple of broads tonight, you sleep in the bathtub."

He did. I didn't tell my mother.

The trip was memorable, too, because the locker rooms in old Clarke Stadium were so bad the team always dressed in the hotel. It was chaos after the pre-game meal. Guys were coming into our room for extra socks and all kinds of odds and ends when the phone rang. It was Bill Hortie, one of the linebackers.

"Tell Tiger I got no pants."

Tiger took the phone.

"What do you mean? Your pants were in your bag. I put your bag in front of your locker. You must have taken them out and left them in Vancouver."

Any equipment manager with common sense takes extra stuff. Not Tiger. Now we had a team that wore white jerseys and bright orange pants. It's 4:30 in the afternoon. Imagine trying to find a pair of pumpkin-coloured football pants in Edmonton.

We borrowed a pair from the Eskimos; they were, of course, canary yellow. Hortie was a starting linebacker; he couldn't wear those pants, so he took the third quarterback's pants. Quarterback Gene Robillard, who I saw occasionally in Ottawa up until his death in 2006, wore the yellow.

Tiger looked after me. He never had any money but he always had one of the directors' cars – a Buick, a Cadillac, something grand. Quite often he'd run me home after practice. But Tiger lasted only the year. His whole life revolved around football, women and horseracing – and not necessarily in that order. That became a problem.

It was a gruelling time for me. When school finished for the summer, Tiger got me a job at Wilson's Stationery, which sold furniture and business supplies. They had a warehouse downtown across from the old Sun Tower. I lived at 7th and Laurel and I started at 7:30 in the morning. I worked full-time at Wilson's and part-time with the Lions.

Sometimes I walked; if I had money, I took the bus and a bag lunch. When I finished there at four o'clock, I got on the bus and went out to UBC for the Lions practice, which began about 6 p.m. Most of the players worked, so they couldn't start much earlier.

After practice, the team gathered for dinner in one of the fraternity houses. The trainer and equipment manager were allowed to eat, but

I couldn't. Eric Beardmore, the director in charge, said I wasn't a full-time employee and didn't contribute enough to the team.

"You're not doing enough for us to feed you," he told me.

I'll never forget it.

I sat in the lobby, night after night, hungry and embarrassed, hoping one of the players would give me something to eat. I left the house every morning at seven with only a sandwich for lunch, I remember telling Beardmore.

"That's not my problem," he said.

No, I thought, that's not your problem, but maybe it will be some day.

Now I'm not a guy who holds a grudge, but years later when I became the general manager, Beardmore's son wanted to assume his father's community membership when his dad died. That was something we didn't usually do. We could, you know, nudge nudge, wink wink, for friends, well, we could find a way. When I got this request, without hesitation I scrawled "no."

He could have let me eat.

After the team dinner, Tiger or his assistant, Danny Rose, would give me a ride home.

I didn't realize it at the time, maybe not for a long time afterwards, but I was trading my biological family for a football family. We weren't close, my family and I, and really, we just didn't gel after my father came home to Ontario from the war or when we came west.

My father got a job on the ships eventually and was always gone. On weekends, he'd come home and go to the liquor store at 8th and Main and grab a bottle of what he called "bingo" – cheap red wine – and a dozen beers. That was his weekend. Two beers would put him under the table and then he would want to sing "Danny Boy."

The biggest thing that ever happened in his life was the Second World War. The biggest day of the year in our house wasn't Christmas, it was November 11 – Remembrance Day – because he could go and get together with all the boys and tell war stories. That was the biggest day each year. He struggled to make ends meet. He always worked, but he just never seemed to get ahead. He was always very critical. He would say to me, "Why are you going out and working with that football team – they aren't paying you."

He didn't get it.

My older brother, Ken, was his favourite. He had curly red hair and a fiery temper to match. Ken was Dad's kind of guy. And like Dad, he was never successful. Ken was always going to do this or do that – he had a lot of ideas, he wanted to do things, but he would never follow through with anything. He was very intelligent, very smart but didn't have a lot of common sense. He wanted to be more than he was, but he never put the time or the energy into one thing. He was always shifting from one thing to another and another and another. He never zeroed in and said, "This is what I'm going to do."

Ken joined the army young. Got married young. Had kids young. He was always trying to make ends meet. If he had stayed in the army for 25 years, he probably would have been successful. Later, he had medical problems. He had a bad car crash, back trouble, one thing or another, and diabetes. He came to see me when I was general manager out at the Surrey Office, and he really looked bad. He had been divorced twice by then and his life had taken on a tragic hue. I don't know how long after that I got the phone call saying they had found his body. They figure he jumped off the Patullo Bridge. I knew he was distraught. I knew he was in pain. I guess he decided it was too much.

My sister Nancy got married, had kids and moved to Saskatchewan. Dad followed her there. My other sister Jeanne married and moved to Nanaimo. Her glass is always half full. It doesn't matter what life throws at her, she finds the silver lining. At least every time I see her, that's the impression I get. She's got a couple of kids, too. And my younger brother, Doug, who was very much an afterthought, lives in Langley. We were never a close family.

I was shocked when I was named executor of my father's will. He died in Saskatchewan at 65. Not that there was anything there. The house, but I think once the bills were paid and everything, each of the five kids got $5,000. Still, that's $5,000 more than I ever expected.

My mother died earlier – of a massive stroke at 53. She'd had an earlier stroke, before she hit 50, and it left her debilitated. She couldn't talk, though she tried to. She had a bad limp and one arm hung listlessly. She sat around and watched TV. In 1957, we got her this little black-and-white television set. She drank coffee and stared at that little screen.

In those years after we arrived in Vancouver, I guess subconsciously I knew the family wasn't cohesive and I had to make my own way. I wanted to work full time for the Lions so bad, it became my central goal. My first year I didn't get paid, but the second year I started charging players $1 a week to look after their lockers. I'd clean their shoes after practice, brush all the mud and dirt off, put them up to dry, hang up all their stuff, get the laundry done.

It was the time in my life, between 13 and 17, when I could have ended up heading in the wrong direction. The Lions and sports – football and hockey – saved me. I got a sense of the other directions I could go in during the summers. There was a hiatus in sports, and I hung out with the rough-and-tumble neighbourhood crowd down at Kitsilano Beach during those formative teenage years.

We headed to the beach at 10 o'clock in the morning – three, four, five of us – singing and just having a hell of a time. We'd spend the whole day swimming and harassing anybody – girls, whoever. We'd end up leaving at dark, nine or 10 o'clock, at night. We were a bunch of teenagers with nothing to do.

At Cornwall and Yew Streets – there's a pub there now, where there used to be a service station and a little corner store – we'd go in to get our odds and ends. Many evenings we bought a little jar of mustard, half a pound of baloney and a loaf of bread. For the group of us, that was dinner.

One evening as it was starting to get dark, there was a hell of a ruckus and I came out of the store to find 50 to 75 kids in the service station parking lot watching a brawl. The guys were between 19 and 21 years old and they'd obviously been drinking. Two of them put the boots to another – stomped him to death right there. It was unbelievable. They would be sentenced to hang.

That was the kind of group that congregated around there. We were always three, five, seven guys, so we always felt protected. My life could easily have gone sideways when I think about it. We regularly got a dozen beers or a bottle of wine, and would sit and have a bonfire. All under age. The police very seldom were around, it seemed.

Or on Saturdays, one guy had a car and we'd head out to Vancouver's now-renowned nudist Wreck Beach. Back then, Wreck Beach wasn't yet a nudist hangout and was about as big as a small office. Mickey, an attractive, tall blonde in her 20s who lived in our neighbourhood, would join us. Four or five of us would pile into this 1947 Chevy convertible at 10 o'clock in the morning, head over to the 8th and Main liquor store and she'd go in and buy us "minors" a couple dozen Labatt Blue, a bottle of wine or two and we'd head to Wreck Beach.

It's not that what I was doing was wrong or all that risky, but nothing good happens at four o'clock in the morning and eventually something bad occurs. I remember walking home one night with a buddy of mine, just a block from my house, when a car stopped. A '32 Ford Coupe convertible. It was a car young guys drooled over. A local boy named Frank was behind the wheel. He gave us a wave and shouted, "You guys want a ride?"

I went over and I leaned in the car, my hands on the door. I could see the kid in the passenger seat had his hand on the foil-wrapped hotwires to keep the car running.

"No," I said with a friendly grin, "not tonight. I'm going home. I live just down the block." I had nightmares for years that police would lift my fingerprints off the door and come knocking.

Lorne Cullen was one reason that didn't happen. Lorne became my high school football coach in 1953, weeks after I started school in Vancouver. He's been in my life ever since. He became my coach with the junior Vancouver Blue Bombers. He kept me in sports and that made a difference for me.

Lorne let me arrive late for practice because of my work with the Lions; he says he wouldn't allow that now. I played primarily offensive guard and offensive centre (doing all the deep snapping) and nose tackle. I liked all of it. It was enjoyable to me – you were getting smacked all the time or you were smacking someone. I enjoyed the camaraderie, even the practices.

I played football until I was 21. At King Edward High School we won one championship and tied with Kitsilano another year. The year I went to Vancouver College, for the 1956 football season, we lost our opening game and then won every game, and that was against U.S.

opposition, the junior varsity team at the University of B.C. (a high school team beating a university squad!) and one other high school that we trounced. We had a very strong team; from that team there was a handful of players who went on to the CFL.

With the Bombers we won a B.C. championship. We went to Alberta and lost in the B.C.-Alberta final. In juvenile we won one B.C. championship too. I had some success in high school, in both juvenile and junior. So those guys and I became a very close-knit group. We still get together and talk about when we played this game or that game fifty years ago. It's a startling bond.

—⁂—

I still see Lorne. He's 78 and plays hockey a couple of times a week. He's amazing. He's been a very close friend and had everything to do with keeping me headed in the right direction.

Up until they moved to White Rock in 1956, I lived at my parents' home on 7th Avenue in a basement room with the furnace and mice for company. After they moved, I was peripatetic. Sometimes I'd stay at the stadium in the equipment room; sometimes I'd stay with my brother; at training camp, I stayed with the team, and when the team came back from training camp, I got a place at the Admiral Hotel with the rest of the players for about a month.

I attended Vancouver College that year on a football scholarship and the coach was Fred Owens. He said I could stay at the school, which was boarding students in those days. But you had to be in by 6 p.m. and I couldn't get back from the Lions practice to meet that curfew. Fred took me home to his wife Ann in Richmond and said I was moving in with them. They had two daughters at the time and Ann was pregnant with their third – they would have six girls in all. I became Fred's son. They became my surrogate parents. Fred went back to school at 50 and got his doctorate in education. Kay, Stephen, Scott and I continued to visit them for years after they moved to California.

That year I also grew close to Ed Sharkey, a big lineman, who at the end of the 1957 season said to me, "Do you want to go to Miami Beach?"

I was 19, had finished school that spring, and Sharkey was a character, a complete rounder. He had gone to Duke and enlisted in the Marine Corps. When he was cashiered, he moved to Reno. Harold Smith, who owned Harold's Club casino, was spending a lot of money recruiting players for the University of Nevada, which was a bit of a renegade school. Ed went there for his last two years of eligibility before playing professionally. He came to the Lions to finish his career.

I had nothing to do and an adventure sounded like a great idea. So Sharkey, his wife Pat, two little kids and me piled into their '53 Chevy coupe and headed to Miami Beach via Reno. We planned to spend a few days in Reno, pick up their belongings in Tahoe and continue to Florida.

We got a little motel in Needles, a suburb, and at that point Ed announced we were not going to Florida after all. We were going to stay there for a while. So we fell into a routine. He and I went out every evening. I hit the movies and he looked for a job as a card dealer. It didn't seem that far-fetched. He had learned the trade while he was going to school and he knew a lot of people in town.

He and Pat put a $5,000 deposit on an upscale home. About the same time, Sharkey got a call from Lions general manager Herb Capozzi telling him that he had made the all-star team.

Sharkey told him he didn't think he'd make the game in Montreal, but he'd let him know.

And every night off we went – he'd scour the hotels for work, I'd go to the movies and then the clubs – watch Louis Prima, Keeley Smith, Sam Butera and the Witnesses, great shows like that, or play the nickel slot machines. As long as you gave the girls a quarter, they'd be by like clockwork with a drink or a beer. I'd go home at 2 a.m., up five or six bucks. Pat woke me one morning, though, worried.

"Bobby, Ed's not home."

I rubbed the sleep from my eyes.

"I know what's happened."

I wasn't sure what she meant at first and it must have registered on my face.

"He's lost all his money and he's trying to win some money back and he's at one of the casinos. Go bring him home."

I pulled on my clothes and headed down to cruise the casinos. I finally spotted him. He didn't look too happy, and I didn't think he saw me. Damn, I thought, what are you going to do? Go up to him and say, "Hey Ed, your wife wants you to come home?"

I went across the street to Woolworth's and ate breakfast at the counter. I returned 30 minutes later.

Sharkey saw me across the room and got up.

"I wish you had come and got me when I saw you walk through the casino a half-hour ago. I was up $5,000; now I'm down $5,000."

"How was I to know?"

We walked over to Harold's Club. Sharkey got another $500.

He lost that too.

Sharkey managed to get most of his deposit back on the house. He called Capozzi and said he'd play in the all-star game. We packed up the car and drove to San Francisco. He, Pat and the two kids flew to New York where she stayed with his family and he continued to Montreal to play in the game.

They left me for almost two weeks in San Francisco.

I didn't have a driver's license and I was staying at the Cable Car Motel down by the San Francisco Airport on El Camino Real. I eventually ran out of money even though the hotel room was paid for. Every day I drove into San Francisco along El Camino Real, which was the long, winding route, to avoid the highway patrol. In town, I phoned one of our former quarterbacks, Maury Duncan, who lived in the area, and he and his wife took me out for dinner. He loaned me $20. I hit the burlesque joints and had a hell of a time.

I finally ran out of money and went to this little restaurant where I convinced the owner to let me wash dishes for food until Ed phoned and said to come pick him up at the airport. We drove back to Vancouver. Ed ended up becoming vice president and GM of the General Brewing Corporation of America.

It was late when we got back into town and I ended up sleeping on the porch. A few nights later, I joined a group of friends who worked for *The Sun* at their Christmas party at the Commodore. It was quite a night. I thought I might have lost my job and any chance at a future career after I broke the leg of the assistant sports editor in a wild west-like bar fight that featured bodies flying down the legendary club's entrance staircase.

I moved into a basement suite over by King Edward High School with another couple of friends after I came back. It was a party palace for a group of 19-year-olds in 1957.

The following summer, 1958, I moved in with Tommy Hinton, a big guard, and Urban Henry, an even bigger defensive tackle, when they arrived from Louisiana to play for the Lions. They didn't know each other initially. One was from northern Louisiana, one from southern. They went to different schools. But they both signed with us and Capozzi said to them, "Why don't you guys drive up together?"

They did – and they became great, great buddies. Both were great players, too.

The three of us, in fact, became very fast and strong friends. They were only about a year or so older than me, in their early 20s, so the three of us got a triplex over on 11th Avenue, just off Fraser. Our apartment was at the top of the three-level building. Urban had the back bedroom, Tom had the front bedroom and I had the couch in the living room. It was the funniest half a year in my life.

Urban was an incredibly talented artist and he had a great career going from the Lions to the NFL. I have a pencil sketch he did of the great Packers' receiver corps from the Super Bowl teams – Boyd Dowler, Ron Kramer and Max McGee. Urban wasn't on either of the Super Bowl squads, but he played with the Packers in 1963. The sketch is photographic. Oil paint, porcelain – he was a wizard in any medium and a giant on the field.

Tom was married and his wife Patsy and child were in Louisiana. Urban, who never did marry, was reared in the bayous of Morgan City, Louisiana. Depending on his mood he claimed to be part Cajun, all Cajun, or just a coonass. He brawled, boozed and womanized as much as he could. He'd fight at the drop of a hat. He was a hell-raiser.

At the same time, hard as it is to believe, I was still playing junior football for the Vancouver Blue Bombers. We practised at Braemar Park, just off Oak Street, behind the Children's Hospital. Danny Young, one of my best buddies, was dating a girl named Sally who had a cousin named Kay. One day, Kay drove Sally to watch the practice in her mother's new Buick. They were parked just off the side of the practice field when I spotted them.

"Hey, isn't that Sally?" I said to Danny. "How about getting me a date with the blonde with the Buick?"

He tried. But Kay at that point didn't like me.

"I'm not going out with that guy," she told her cousin. "I hear he's fast."

Apparently, a girl in her class whom I'd dated told her she dumped me because I was "too fast."

"I'm not going to get stuck in the backseat of a car with him," she told Sally.

But I pestered Sally and eventually I got a date with Kay at Theatre Under the Stars, which was a huge deal in those days. We've probably spoken on the phone or been together every day since. I think she was 16 at the time; I was 19, working for the Lions and bartending.

If I wasn't working, I'd meet Kay after school and walk her home. I didn't have a car until we were married. I used her mum's car, the Buick, because it was an automatic. Her older brother would usually have the family Ford station wagon because he could drive a stick-shift. If her mum and dad wanted to go out the same night, they went out in one of the trucks from their bakery.

Kay's mum, Molly was a very strong, strong individual. I think she might have been the first woman to have a driver's license in Vancouver. Molly drove that bakery truck back in those initial years from 1934 through 1938 without thinking twice.

Kay's dad, Stan Francis, was the size of a jockey, a really good guy who loved to fish. He had a boat, and he and his buddies would go off on Saturdays over to the Gulf Islands. They owned a slice of land up on Gambier Island where we have a place now. It was a huge piece of property with a large, old lodge that used to belong to a long-defunct hardware company. Kay's aunt and uncle bought it, and when they couldn't afford it, Kay's mother purchased a portion. She was very astute.

Still, Kay's mother wasn't very happy about me dating her daughter for a long time, not very happy at all. She thought my friends and I were thugs. Who could blame her?

My best friend at the time was Danny Young, who was gruff. The first Christmas he and I were invited to Kay's Auntie Thelma's, we went over and they had a buffet laid out on a ping-pong table down in the basement. You can't imagine the food. Thelma's husband was Polish so there were cabbage rolls, latkes, sauerkraut, perogies – all kinds of central European fare. Danny surveyed the spread and snickered, "What's this DP food doing here?"

Within minutes he was throwing fists with someone's favourite son. Boy, Kay's mother really did not like me for a while.

I came from a working-class neighbourhood and I hung around with a rough-and-tumble gang. We weren't from wealthy families. Some were from single-parent families. Weekends with this group consisted of a few beers and … what can I say, we had some tough, tough cookies. Some would fight at the drop of a hat. That was their weekend entertainment – have a few beers and a brawl. One became the chairman of a large, international industrial firm, another a police officer, two became fire fighters, one a celebrated junior high school principal, another a prison guard … Many of us became very successful, but we were orangutans as kids.

I landed my first full-time job in 1959 when Lorne Cullen talked Bill Adshead, the majority owner of Sparling's, into hiring me. Adshead had been a great local athlete in baseball and handball. He became a scratch golfer and was instrumental in starting Little League baseball in the province. I was 20 and Sparling's was the only real sporting goods store in the lower mainland at the time. It probably supplied 85 per cent of the sports equipment, from club to team to school. They probably had five guys on the road most of the time and they had a huge fishing and hunting section run by Don Traeger. It consisted of a main floor and an upstairs where there was an office and huge storage space. They eventually got a basement from the furniture store next door and the ski harnessing shop was set up down there.

I thought it would be right up my alley, and I did spend seven years there. But it really wasn't for me. Sparling's was good because I handled the Lions' account. I was selling to myself, for instance, when

I became the equipment manager. They also let me take time to be involved with the team. If game travel conflicted with my hours at work, I got to go to the game. They were a great bunch of people, but that was not what I wanted to do for the rest of my life.

—∞—

Molly and Stan played cards every night. They'd sit in the kitchen and argue. Kay's aunt and uncle or another friend would inevitably be involved, the four of them in the kitchen playing cards and bickering. I'd show up when I got off work, have a shower and usually have dinner with them. When we decided to get married, I wanted to ask Stan's permission. We sat tentatively in the living room on the appointed night, hoping to catch his attention. Finally, Kay got too antsy and went into the kitchen and prodded him. "Bob wants to talk to you about something," she said. "Will you make sure you're available?"

"Sure, kid," he said.

But he just sat playing cards, drinking his rye and milk.

It was getting to be about 10 o'clock and he was still in the kitchen drinking and playing cards. We were watching TV but we could hear them arguing. Finally, Kay said she was going to bed. She went upstairs just as Stan came out.

"I'd like to marry your daughter," I said to him.

He looked at me, clearly surprised by this particular interruption on his way to relieve himself.

"Okay, kid," he said, "but maybe in another year or two."

I nodded.

"So it's okay?"

"Sure," he said, "in a year or two."

"Great."

He headed into the loo and I went to tell Kay.

I guess Stan forgot to tell Molly afterwards because all hell broke loose the next morning. They were in bed when she started calling.

"You come in here, young lady," she said sternly. "What do you think you're doing?"

Kay told her and Molly was certainly not amused. Molly was so set on sending Kay to university and keeping her from the altar she offered to buy her a cute little Thunderbird convertible from the neighbourhood dealership.

"Why don't you get the car," I told Kay later. "We can elope."

"Yeah, right!" she said.

What can I tell you, as Bogie said, from the moment I met her in the fall of 1958, it was a beautiful friendship. And eventually Molly and I became good friends too.

Stan, sadly, got cancer, which is why we got married a year or so sooner than expected. We tied the knot on June 4, 1960, so Stan could give Kay away. It was the best day of my life. How could I be so lucky to marry a girl like Kay? What a wonderful person.

Yet in many ways, it was an awful time. Really, really painful for Kay and everyone to watch what Stan went through. In those days there wasn't much treatment for the cancer that ate away at Stan. He probably shrank to 80 pounds towards the end. It was dreadful.

Kay went to business college and had a job for about two months after she graduated. Then she was home with kids and the manager of our family. I was able to devote myself to football because I knew she had everything else under control. We were rolling down twin tracks. At the same time as we were struggling to create our own family, we were becoming part of a larger football fraternity – the Lions.

What It Takes

WALLY BUONO was the rock on which I decided to stake the Lions' franchise. There's no question you have to have great players to win. You've got to have good players, too. You've got to have competent backups, even, to support those great players – no one disputes that. But if you don't have that one guy – that head coach – it will all come crashing down like a house of cards. It is the head coach who makes it all work. He puts togeter all the components. He's the person who must hire a staff that can construct an offence, organize a defence and select special team members who are exceptional role players. He and his staff know what kind of players are needed to get the job done. The head coach ensures that happens. For me, that is the key to success in football. I suspect it's true in all team sports. To get the job done, you need an ideal head coach.

Sure you need a good quarterback. You need a good centre, too, and a great left tackle, but it's for naught if you don't have that one guy, the head coach who can bring it all together. He has to select the best players from camp, the 46 guys who can win. If those 46 can't, if there are some on that roster who don't have what it takes, he's also the guy who must find the players who can. His job is tough – to lead a group of men on a physical and emotional journey that's different every year, but produce the same result – a championship. And then it starts over again. He gets up and goes to camp the following year only to find four or five guys who were on that roster missing because of retirements. Then there are the guys who now are on the verge of losing their edge.

That's a problem for a lot of coaches – they fall in love with their players. And rightly so that they would feel that way about those guys who have played hard for them, played their hearts and their bodies out for them. Unfortunately, from a business and competitive stand-point, the key is to catch those players just as they are about to decline – and deal them. The worst thing a coach can do – and this happened with Dallas icon Tom Landry – is wait until players are past their prime before replacing them. The Cowboys suffered and declined as a team because of that. And, in all fairness to Tom, some of the Cowboys' draft picks couldn't play.

For me, when I think of football teams, I visualize the coaches. They are the defining personality that matters. I don't remember the on-field plays over the years as the way someone managed the team, the decisions they made and the way in which their personality came to permeate the organization – as it should, if it's the right energy. In many ways, I've become as fascinated by organizational psychology and the business parameters that shape sports franchise decisions as I am by the game of football.

A team should be the embodiment of the coach, an avatar of his personality and strengths. That's how I look at the teams I've been associated with, that's how I evaluate them. Not that this individual player or that offence was better than any other, but how did this coach motivate and teach his team, how did that coach inspire and lead, why did that coach fail in spite of the talent and desire at his disposal? Ultimately, that's what dictates whether a sports franchise succeeds or fails. Performance. With the B.C. Lions, I saw the orga-nization struggle to find a head coach for its first decade, and then after our Grey Cup win in 1964, stumble through to 1983 without the right leadership – a long fallow and lean stretch for the franchise. Each coach did certain things excellently, but there was only one, surpris-ingly, who put it all together – Don Matthews.

Watching the birth of the Vancouver franchise from about 1954 through to 1961 was the beginning of my true education in football from the field and locker room up. I started as the water boy and that gave me a unique perspective on the team, the organization and the dynamics that make it work. I saw how certain elements changed over the years and witnessing that process was essential to developing my understanding of the game and the business. Of course, it also drilled into me the importance of the head coach.

Some things, like rank and sweaty jockstraps, haven't changed. Others, like the sports business environment and the game itself, have been utterly transformed. The difference between then and now is night and day. Most professional sports leagues today, for example, provide some kind of equalization draft to provide a new entry with some talent to ensure a competitive team. Not in 1954. It was Alice in Wonderland a half-century ago. Think of a world where flying over the Rockies was such an exotic expense that football-franchise owners balked. They were used to bus and train travel and couldn't imagine making such an onerous and expensive journey. They insisted Vancouver pay for airline tickets to fly in visiting teams.

The wackiness continued with the other owners demanding we have a 15,000-seat stadium. They said we had to have 6,500 season tickets sold. And forget about an equalization draft to ensure we had a competitive team – the other owners said find your own players. It was a hardship, no question, and the Lions had to scramble.

The people who owned the club, the fans who bought $20 memberships and the community volunteer directors who put up their own money hired Annis Stukus because he was a big name in Canadian football. But they made a mistake when they said Stuke would be GM *and* head coach. They should have hired him as the GM and had him hire a head coach. Stuke, god bless his soul, was a great promoter. He could sell football. He'd meet three people and sell two of them season tickets. "We're going to win 15 games," he told people that first year we were in the league. "We might lose one."

Well, we were one and 15 that year – one win that is! He was a born salesman – people believed him.

Stuke was not a very good coach. He wasn't an X's and O's guy and he didn't know where to recruit. He knew how to recruit if you put someone in front of him, but he didn't know where to find talent.

There is a magazine called *Street and Smith*, a fabulous publication on college football. Every year they bring out a scouting report – two, three, five paragraphs on each of the major college football teams. Back then, that's how a lot of CFL teams did their recruiting, as those in the know sniggered, nudge nudge, "scout by *Street and Smith*."

Occasionally, Stuke or one of the directors might know somebody at Notre Dame who would send us a film. You'd look at this grainy black-and-white film and go, "Oh, look at him. Did he catch that?"

Stuke was fortunate to stumble across a great Canadian, Norm Fieldgate, and to luck into some pretty good athletes who had played out an option in the NFL. Arnie Weinmeister, one of the all-time great defensive linemen, lived in Seattle, and classified as a Canadian because his mother and father were from Saskatchewan. He signed with us because we gave him $15,000 and he was making only $12,000 in the NFL. By Bailey was another player from Washington State who had kicked around in the NFL and even won championships at Green Bay and Detroit. But he wasn't a starter down there. We gave him a little more money, plus he was closer to home, so he came to Vancouver. Bailey played 11 seasons for us as a fullback and defensive back who also ran back kickoffs.

That parity seems odd now, but up until the 1970s, the American and Canadian professional football teams paid about the same. For instance, even in 1972, we signed three players from the South East Conference who were All-Americans, the cream of that year's crop. They were drafted in the NFL but came to us because we gave them more money – Johnny Musso, a fullback from Alabama, Ray Nettles, a linebacker from Tennessee, and Ron Estay, a defensive end from LSU. They had all played in one of the last All-America Bowls, were top-notch players and we signed them. Back in 1954, we had a handful from the NFL for that one reason: money. Stuke benefited from that.

He also picked up a quarterback from Notre Dame who was a classic, drop-back, hand-off-or-throw-from-the-pocket pivot. But Stuke's playbook was based on a single-wing formation, the kind of offence he was familiar with as a player in the 30s and 40s. It forced quarterback John Mazur to do all this spin-a-rama stuff instead of doing what he did best – drop back into a pocket. Stuke's playbook was out of date

Gilbert Avenue, Toronto, Ontario. With my mother Molly and brother Ken (left) in 1944 or 1945. My mother wrote on the back of this picture, "How do you like us? Love from all, Muriel," and sent it to my father who was overseas during World War Two.

This used to be a nice little red-brick, one-room school house in Locust Hill, Ontario, until someone bought it and painted it green. I attended grades two through eight in this school.

My father, Bill, cooking dinner on our Coleman stove in Roosevelt National Park, North Dakota, in July 1952. We were moving to Vancouver and driving across the continent to get there. My mother Molly stands watching and looking very tired.

My first team photo with the BC Lions – the first of 54 in pro football. There are some good friends in this picture, "Tiger" Kozak, Danny Rose, Norm Fieldgate, Brian Mullhern, Annis Stukus, By Bailey, Doug Reid, Bobo Sikorski and Don McKenzie, to name a few. I am sitting in front, holding the football.

The 1959 Junior Blue Bombers, BC Champions. My coach and good friend to this day, Lorne Cullen, is in the hat, along with Assistant Coach Ray Markham (seated on the left side of #61), and all of my buddies who played for the Bombers and King Edward High. We are still a very close-knit group. I am the short guy wearing #41, in the middle of the top row.

With one of my best buddies,
Dan Kolesnik (left), at King Edward
High School in Vancouver in 1955.

The best day of my life, June 4,
1960. Kay and I were married
at St. John's United Church,
and approximately 150 friends
and family attended a sit-down
reception at Oscar's Restaurant
in downtown Vancouver.

With his Excellency Earl Grey's Cup at Ruby Foo's Restaurant in Montréal following our 32-17 win over the Hamilton Tiger Cats in 1985 – our second Cup win. Left to right: Jack Farley dressed in his Captain Vancouver outfit; Ron Jones, President of the Club; Nancy Farley; Alma Jones; Kay and me. We always enjoyed ourselves.

SEC ROW SEAT

INVITATION
FIELD LEVEL
ENTER GATE A

BOB & KAY'S 'BYE BYE' BBQ
B.C. PLACE STADIUM
FRI. JUNE 27th, 7:00 P.M.

BOB & KAY'S "BYE BYE" BBQ
A Fun Farewell to Bob & Kay Ackles.
Fri., June 27th 1986
B.C. Place Stadium
7:00 p.m.
$25.00 PER PERSON

SEC ROW SEAT

INVITATION
FIELD LEVEL

JUNE 27th '86. $25.00

Bob and Kay's Bye Bye BBQ on the floor of BC Place Stadium before we left to go to Dallas and the NFL. Left to right: Molly Francis (Kay's mother), Steve and Sherri Ackles, Robert Ackles (Steve's first son and our first grandson), Kay Ackles, Bob Ackles, Scott Ackles.

Two old war horses, great Canadian and broadcaster "Big" Bill Good (left) honouring Annis Stukus after his induction into the Canadian Football Hall of Fame in 1974. "Stuke" hired me as the first water boy for the BC Lions in 1953.

A return to Vancouver during my first season with the Dallas Cowboys for a very special evening put on by the BC Lions, with special guest Bob Hope, October 1986.

With the legendary Dallas Cowboys Head Coach Tom Landry, always a gentleman, shortly before he was fired from the Cowboys in February 1989.

Pre-game at Texas stadium in 1991 with Head Coach Jimmy Johnson. Pre-game is a great time of the week, time to visit with coaches of visiting teams as well as the media and your own staff.

Starting to turn it around in Dallas. In Jerry's suite after a win at Texas Stadium in 1991 with (back row, left to right) owner Jerry Jones, me, Jimmy Johnson, Jimmy's youngest son Chad Johnson, (front row, left to right) Jerry Jones Jr., and Stephen Jones.

With two of the many guys in the broadcast media: former quarterback and Hall of Famer, Pittsburgh Steeler Terry Bradshaw (left) and Verne Lundquist (right).

even in the 1950s and defences shut us down quickly. We got into the season and Mazur got hurt, so our backup, Gerry Tuttle, came in and that forced Stuke to change things around.

The bottom line was we couldn't compete. We didn't have enough real players and our whole philosophy wasn't very good. Still, we had a lot of people in the park and they were easily excited. You got a first down and you'd get a standing ovation. Even I will never forget that first ever touchdown, which By Bailey scored.

After that one game we won, 9–4 against Calgary on September 18, 1954, Lions fans tore down the goal posts and marched downtown with the pieces. They were overjoyed at winning their first ever game. They were incredibly supportive all season long in spite of our usually poor performance on the field – we were habitual losers.

They fired Stuke after the next season. Even though we had managed to win five games, things really weren't getting any better. They elevated Clem Crowe, a nice old guy who won a Grey Cup in Ottawa and later became Stuke's assistant coach. Unfortunately, like Stuke, he was long past his prime. The game had passed him by. I remember that 1956 season, however, not because of the coaching change, but because of a true tragedy.

The first East-West All-Star game was played that year at Empire Stadium. It should have been a celebratory time, and it was – until after the game. On December 9, Trans-Canada Air Lines Flight 810 flying from Vancouver to Calgary (continuing to Regina, Winnipeg and Toronto) crashed, killing all 62 aboard. All-Star game official Ed Pettit and five players – Winnipeg Blue Bomber Cal Jones, Saskatchewan Roughriders Mel Beckett, Mario DeMarco, Gordon Sturtridge and Ray Syrnyk – died. The plane hit Mount Sless near Hope in an area so rugged and remote, searchers didn't find the wreckage until the following May. The next season for Saskatchewan would be a write-off; you couldn't replace four players of that calibre. Jones, too, was a great player who probably wouldn't have stayed in the CFL for very long. That was his rookie year, and you could see he was something special. The trauma shook everyone in the league.

I was still in school and had played hooky to be the equipment manager for the Eastern team. I stayed with them at a Kingsway motel.

The game was Saturday, and Sunday morning I was going room to room packing the players' bags. One of the hotel staff heard the news on the radio. It was still early in the morning and it was a terrible shock for the players as they stumbled out of their rooms to learn what had happened. Devastating. We initially didn't know who had died. We knew players were on the flight, but we didn't know who. It was a fluke it was all western players.

I wasn't close to those who died, but it was fascinating to see the lore that came to surround the flight – much like the aura that glows around the plane crash that killed rock and roll idol Buddy Holly. Over the years, it seemed to me that plane was awfully over-booked given the number of guys who claimed to have had a ticket for the doomed flight.

But the two I knew were Hamilton fullback Cookie Gilchrist and coach Jim Trimble. Both should have been on it. Cookie had slept in and Trimble told me he actually had got on the bus to the airport. He had forgotten his overcoat, however, and asked the bus driver to let him out to retrieve it. In the hotel, he ran into Saskatchewan Roughrider DeMarco, who had missed an earlier flight. DeMarco was eager to get back and Trimble handed him his ticket. "Take my seat. I'm going to go get my overcoat and I'll catch another flight."

It was like an episode from *The Twilight Zone*. Trimble and I became close friends. Twenty years later, he was a pro-personnel specialist for the New York Giants. He introduced me to Wellington Mara, the Giants owner, at their training camp. Wellington had been the owner back in 1954 when I was with the Lions and the team persuaded Arnie Weinmeister to leave the Giants and come play for us. He said he was upset at the time because Arnie played so well for the Giants, but he got over it.

Wellington, who died in 2005, was a gracious giant in the executive suites of the NFL. He was highly respected and I came to admire his acumen and sense of fair play. During my years with the NFL in the 1990s, I learned a lot watching him at meetings and how he handled controversial issues by avoiding conflict.

He was a visionary and league builder. He was a key architect of the revenue-sharing formula for NFL television rights that gave each team an equal share regardless of its market size. That avoided the problems troubling other professional sports leagues with their television deals that enrich big-market teams at the expense of smaller franchises. Wellington always saw the big picture.

—⚏—

Stukus and Clem Crowe were nice guys but anachronisms. That happens with coaches. They can get stale. Outlive their own eras. The Lions finally fired Clem mid-season 1958 after five straight losses. We were making no progress. It was inevitable.

Danny Edwards was appointed interim head coach. He was a first-class receiver we'd picked up from the NFL. Injured, he joined the coaching staff rather than return home to recuperate. He salvaged the 1958 season for us with three wins. But Herb Capozzi, general manager at the time, and Ralph Henderson, the club president, decided not to give him the job. They hired Wayne Robinson, an assistant from the staff of Winnipeg Blue Bombers coach Bud Grant.

Robinson had been another very good player in the NFL forced to retire early because of injury. He arrived in 1959, bringing along assistant coach Dave Skrien. That was the first year we made the playoffs. Mind you, we went to Edmonton and got thrashed. It was a two-game, total point series. They crushed us 20–8 in the first game in Vancouver and 41–7 in the second game in Alberta.

I won't forget that one. It must have been 25 below. The field was ice. The aptly named Eskimos used broomball shoes, and Robinson came up with this idea for us to use cleats fitted with hollow, aluminum spikes. They used them in Winnipeg, he claimed. But the holes filled with ice. The players said it was like being on roller skates. We got killed.

Still, there was great hope for the 1960 season, especially when we added Neal "Crusher" Beaumont (who won Rookie of the Year honours), Lonnie Dennis (a short but incredibly powerful all-star tackle dubbed "Charlie Tuna") and Steve Cotter. We also had Sonny Homer – boy could he fly, an incredible receiver who also played defence for a few seasons – and Jim Carphin, an outstanding local receiver who had played at the University of Washington. Robinson knew what we needed to win.

That was the season I became equipment manager – 1960.

Robinson never did get along with the guy I replaced, Danny Rose, best man at my wedding. Danny was among the last of those guys from another era: real characters. We roomed together in training camp at Kelowna. He was charming but also a sad alcoholic. The first sound you heard in the morning was the telephone wake-up call at six, the screw top coming off a bottle of rye whiskey and a long slurp.

"Up and at 'em," he'd say.

Danny kept a bottle underneath the seat of his car, a little Plymouth coupe. Driving to training camp, every so often he would reach down between his legs and pull up the bottle and take a long drink. He drank all the way up the serpentine Hope–Princeton Highway. He always carried a flask and constantly had to have a drink.

Yet the players loved him. He brought them little extras all the time. But the equipment, which was his real job, took a backseat. Like Tiger, who came from Edmonton with Stuke, Danny's job didn't always rank top priority. Both of them wanted to be one of the boys. Danny learned from Tiger, or more to the point, *didn't* learn from Tiger. He didn't realize professional players must look sharp for practice and the game. Worse, he was very slow when he did anything.

Players were often impatient: "Shit! I've got to play this game – where's the stuff?"

Danny existed on island time.

Robinson was the opposite. He was a guy out of the Big Ten, a guy out of the NFL. He understood pride. He understood discipline. He had a sense of professionalism. It was his way or the highway. Whether you were an assistant coach, a trainer or an equipment manager – it didn't matter, if you worked for him, it was Robinson's way only. For me, seeing that focus on winning for the first time was impressive. Robinson assumed command – there was no mistaking that. I came to realize that projecting authority and how you exercised it were the essence of leadership. But Danny was Danny and he did things his way.

"Yeah, yeah, I'll get it done," was his refrain.

It was only a matter of time before Robinson fired him.

We were at training camp in Courtenay. Robinson snapped when he saw Norm Fieldgate on the field in a torn jersey. He came steaming over.

"Danny! I thought I told you I didn't want to see players out here wearing that crap," he hollered. "I've had enough!" He stormed away.

General Manager Capozzi had left training camp to return to Vancouver. But that night Robinson called the motel where Kay and I were staying.

"Come on over," he growled. "I've just fired Danny. I want you and Dave Skrien to come down to the equipment room and go through it with me."

We got there and he was still mad as hell.

"This is horseshit," he said, tossing worn-out and dirty pads aside. "We can't put up with equipment looking like this and in such disrepair. I want this mess fixed."

"You got it, coach," I said. I was ready, willing and able to make the transformation.

The next morning, as the players came in to get their towels and T-shirts, they were shocked that Danny had been fired. They really liked him. They didn't take it out on me, but I'd replaced their guy and it took a few days for everyone to make peace with that.

Dealing with Robinson, I had to change the way things were done. So it also took a little while for the guys to come around to the new way of doing things. But it didn't take long since I'd always been friendly with them.

Capozzi returned from Vancouver livid that Robinson had fired Danny without his approval. He only reluctantly gave me a letter confirming my appointment as equipment manager. Capozzi and I were never close, but he could see that now we had an inventory, now we knew where we were, what our costs were going to be – how many socks we'd used so far in training camp, how many more we'd need, how many towels …

There, again, when I took over as equipment manager there was no budget. If Danny needed something, you know, he just went and got it. I organized the operation. Capozzi liked my budget and inventory system; he liked that I was organized.

And I had my own way of economizing – I issued numbered jerseys at training camp, white for offence, black for defence. I gave defensive rookies with no chance the number of an offensive veteran and vice versa. When the rookie got cut, I didn't need to juggle the numbers. If a rookie asked for new boots and I didn't think he had a chance, I said wait a few days. I hired a couple of kids later – George Oswald and Ken Howell – who ended up working for me forever. Under Capozzi, while I was equipment manager, I also travelled down the coast once a year to scout college and pro teams. It was our family vacation. The Lions gave me $500 to cover expenses. Kay and I supplemented it with a couple hundred from our savings and the money I earned from the stadium pop machine, usually another $200. We'd take two weeks to drive down the coast visiting the University of Washington, Washington State, University of Idaho, Idaho State, Oregon, Oregon State, the 49ers, the Rams ...

It was half a day here, half a day there. We'd spend two or three days in L.A., maybe flip over to Las Vegas for a night and then go right home. It was a working vacation, but a lot of fun and we met a lot of people, many who became invaluable professional friends later. We also saw a lot of talent. That was something Robinson knew about as head coach – talent. He imparted that to me and he, more than anyone else, laid the foundation for the team that would go to the Grey Cup – and win. But he would not be with them.

In 1961, Robinson traded for all-star quarterback Joe Kapp – who became the nucleus of that Grey Cup–winning squad. It was a blockbuster trade in its day. Kapp was the Calgary Stampeders' quarterback, a leader of men for sure. He had been an All-American at the University of California, Berkeley, and had won a Rose Bowl. We gave Calgary four players and a prospect – a Canadian playing for the New York Giants. That was a lot, unless you realized Kapp was indispensable to winning the Grey Cup. Robinson was investing in the future of the team but not everyone could see that. Robinson was someone who saw the big picture. He was thinking not only about the next game and this season, he was mulling a season or two in the future.

Kapp wouldn't help immediately, but he would be pivotal, pardon the pun. Ironically, he wouldn't help Robinson, the man responsible for putting him in a position to excel.

A week after the mid-season Kapp trade, Capozzi fired Robinson and his assistant, Dave Skrien, took over. We finished out of the playoffs again with a dismal 1–13–2 record – as sports wag Denny Boyd put it, "Football's answer to post-nasal drip." But that was because of the instability. That season was a write-off because of the mid-season change in coaches and the disruption to the team's chemistry that followed. Confusion reigned in that locker room in part because it was a young team. They were much better than that record, which in my mind underscored the head coach's importance in bringing focus and direction to the group. In 1962, we had a decent year – Skrien steered the club Robinson had built to a 7–9 record. That was the start of the momentum that propelled the team to two Grey Cup games and to win one; you could feel that energy. We had some pretty good talent and they were coalescing as a group. It was palpable.

We went 12–4 in 1963 and you could tell the team was solid. But it remained for the most part inexperienced and immature; you could also feel that. Going into the Grey Cup at the end of the 1963 season, I never thought we were going to win. Forget about the hit on Willie Fleming during that championship game that still riles many fans half a century later. I'm not even sure it was all that bad a play. Certainly standing on the sidelines, I didn't erupt with, "That dirty Angelo Mosca!" I didn't like it, but didn't think it was illegal.

By the time we got to the 1963 playoffs we were already pretty beaten up. Conditions weren't with us either. It was a decent Sunday afternoon for the Grey Cup, but the field was chewed up. The pitch at Empire Stadium was never worth a damn. That day it was especially dreadful. A bog. They tried to repair it, even bringing in helicopters to dry it out. But it was a mess – abysmal drainage coupled with the abuse of too many recent playoff games on top of the damage caused to the turf by the Pacific National Exhibition's musical horse performances.

As for the famous hit, Willie already had been partially tackled and was stumbling out of bounds, as I saw it. Hamilton's Mosca hit him right on the touch line. Sure, it was a savage hit, but I thought it was legal. The way the media wrote it up, and columnist Jim Taylor was the instigator, Fleming was way out of bounds when he was crushed by a foul rat named, as headlines across the country proclaimed: Mosca!

Whenever Fleming saw Mosca after that, he shouted, "Mosca, I made you!"

Mosca loved it. He lived off the notoriety for years and even used it when he went into the wrestling game.

There is no question, though, after the final whistle, with the Tiger-Cats 21-10 victors in that 1963 Grey Cup, we put the champagne back in the case, and the Fleming hit became a motivator for the next season. It was a hell of a motivator. We went to Toronto for the 1964 Grey Cup, bent on beating Hamilton handily for revenge. But the year before I didn't ever think we were going to win that game. And we didn't.

I think the Tiger-Cats were a better football team than the B.C. Lions in 1963. They were already veterans of many playoff games. That was our first Grey Cup game in franchise history. That was the best season for us – ever. I don't recall us ever being in the 1963 game. Maybe early. But I did not ever think we were going to win that game.

The next year I knew we were going to win the game from the moment we triumphed in the Western Final. Our players exuded confidence. We had gone 11–2–3 to win the West. We arrived in Toronto to play Hamilton knowing what it would take to win; we were prepared to pay the price. And we did. We won 34–24.

We had a very good football team. We had a good offensive line and a really strong defence. Kapp was a good quarterback who provided solid leadership on the field. We had a good kicking game, good special teams. But I think Skrien was successful because he inherited and fine-tuned the football team Robinson imagined.

Robinson as a head coach was such a hard-nosed guy, a tough, mean son of a bitch who gave no quarter, and the players eventually turned him off. He would not give an inch to anyone and that kind of constant antagonism wears on staff and on an organization. That's why Capozzi canned him, which was a good lesson for me. Because I respected him. Robinson put together good personnel, he ran a tight ship, he knew what it took to get the job done. But he couldn't win in the end because he couldn't motivate the players to make that extra effort to get to the ultimate level. They wouldn't pay the price for him. They were not in emotional synch.

Skrien, by comparison, was laid back. He was an easygoing guy. That was a huge change that paid off in the locker room because strong bonds developed among the players and a handful of natural on-field leaders emerged. The players reacted positively to being un-bridled because the nucleus of the team by that time was very good. We had very good leadership at all levels on the field.

Linebacker Norm Fieldgate, the captain, for instance, was a stalwart in the locker room. He knew the rule book inside out. He understood the game, the import-non-import mix – he understood the commu-nity. He was from Saskatchewan originally but got released by the Roughriders, and Stuke brought him to Vancouver. He was the thread running through the team from 1954 until he retired in 1967. After he stopped playing, Norm was very involved on the board of directors and as president. He and his wife Doreen became active with the alumni and remain involved with the team today. He was a model player.

Off the field with that 1964 squad was an entirely different matter. The players were more than I suspect anyone could have handled. Certainly Skrien couldn't handle them. He proved to be too soft a guy. Strong personalities such as Kapp, Dick Fouts, Tom Brown, Beau-mont and Pat Claridge really clashed with him – and they won.

They were party animals. Fouts drained a 40–pounder of gin a day. He was known to drop a post-dated cheque into the hands of an assis-tant coach to cover his curfew violation fines on the way out of the hotel with a cheery, "I shall see you on the bus in the morning, my man."

Those guys loved to party with each other. They were always get-ting into scrapes. Nothing huge: bar fights with each other, with civil-ians. Some of them were unquestionably malevolent. They loved to raise hell. The problem was they decided that they alone had won the Grey Cup and it had nothing to do with those guys over there – the coaching staff. Skrien lost them; their respect for the coaches vanished with that 1964 victory and it was obvious.

There were subtle indicators and blatant flags.

Bill Munsey, to take one case, had been a great force in the 1964 Grey Cup win. He played both ways and scored a TD on offence and on defence. The headline in *The Vancouver Sun* read, "Munsey for Mayor." The next year he came to camp 30 pounds overweight.

There was that mental thing with these guys. Everyone told them, "You're so great; you're so great." Those guys believed it. We had 15 to 20 guys who didn't just go out celebrating Friday or Saturday night, they were out every night. They didn't prepare themselves the following year. Which was also a symptom of the times – athletes today are much different. In those days, in the off-season the players went home and went to work at a job. The coach sent them a letter to the effect, "Training camp is four weeks away, guys, so here's what you need to do." Some did almost nothing to stay in shape between their last game and the first day of training camp. The loss of mental and physical edge was phenomenal.

This was also a tremendous lesson for me. We won a Grey Cup in 1964 and went into the '65 season expecting to repeat or at least compete. Instead, we went into the toilet, 6–9–1, and finished out of the playoffs. The next year was even worse. There were a lot of dark days, in fact, after we won the Grey Cup. The team disintegrated. Skrien couldn't control the players and the tail started to wag the dog. Rancour and a kind of malignant mood began to grow. Skrien, it turned out, was not so much a coach who had moulded and shaped a team into a champion, he had been at the right place at the right time. He was carried along for the ride.

We were in Toronto, for example, and Kapp was out on the town two nights before the game. He and a handful of other players had been off boozing it up. They had gone to see Ronnie Hawkins at his club, Le Coq d'Or, on Yonge Street. The Hawk, whose backup musicians gained fame as The Band, had lived with Ronnie Morris, one of our running backs. Morris had come to the CFL from Tulsa University and Hawkins had come to Toronto as a musician. We closed Le Coq d'Or and went up to a little coffee shop and sat around until the wee hours of the morning before returning to the Westbury.

I made it a practice to never arrive back at the hotel with the players. Call it an instinct for self-preservation. This night, as it turned out, offensive coach Frank "Blackie" Johnson was sitting in the lobby at 2:30 a.m. or so when Kapp staggered in. The next morning, Blackie demanded Skrien suspend him.

"Forget it," Skrien said, "Guys stay out all the time; we've got to win a couple of games."

Johnson wouldn't stop complaining about the Kapp incident. But let's face it, you're not going to suspend your quarterback on the eve of a must-win game. And the heat was really on Skrien, so much so that Johnson's wife Boots had invited the team wives over to rally around Skrien's wife Dee.

Kay told me it was a great idea.

But the next day, when the team arrived back in Vancouver, Skrien fired Johnson.

It was another of a growing list of distractions. Among the silliest, lineman Rudy Reschke bit a waitress on the butt in the Admiral Hotel. It was Labour Day and he was a rookie, the others egged on. We settled out of court with the waitress for $125.

Things really deteriorated after Kapp signed a contract with Houston in the American Football League. It was a major eruption. Lions president and acting CFL commissioner Allan McEachern, later chief justice of the province, suspended Kapp.

It would take an extraordinary round of negotiations between the leagues, which respected each other's contracts, to sort out the mess. Kapp wasn't allowed to play in Houston, but it was also obvious he wasn't going to be much of an asset for us. We made a deal that allowed him to play in the NFL with Minnesota, and we got the rights to Jimmy Young, a Canadian playing for them. But the team was coming apart at the seams. I think the players liked Skrien, but they lost respect for him.

We were 1–14–1 in 1966, if you can believe it. Two years after we had won the Grey Cup, we won only one game. I mean, you can see not repeating, maybe even losing in the Western Final or in the semifinal. But within two years of winning the Grey Cup – of being a team that went to two Grey Cups – we became a team capable of winning only one game. That's unheard of. When the team went 0–3 at the start of the 1967 season, Skrien was gone.

Capozzi was elected to the legislature in 1966 and the board of directors replaced him as general manager with his assistant Denny Veitch. He and I had our differences. While he was Capozzi's assistant, for some reason, Veitch thought he could come into my equipment room and take stuff. I finally talked to Capozzi about it and said: "Hey, this is coming out of my budget!"

He agreed and I put another lock on the door.

Veitch was ticked off, and I think he carried a chip when it came time to fill the vacancy for his job. I put together a proposal but he said he wanted someone with a little more education. A couple of the directors went to bat for me and said give the guy a chance, he's been with the organization for years and loyalty should be rewarded.

He gave in and I got the job – minor football coordinator, which meant I had enlarged scouting responsibilities and nurtured our relationship with the amateur football associations. For the first year, I also worked as equipment manager as well.

Denny and I sat down to negotiate my salary, and I kept the paperwork. He wrote out what the job pays and everything else – roughly $12,000 with car allowance and other benefits. I left elated and headed down to Sparling's to resign.

"I'm going to go full time with the B.C. Lions," I told everyone.

Lorne Cullen, my old high school coach, who got me the job, pulled me aside.

"Bob, are you sure about this? You go full time with a football club, you're putting yourself in a position where you could be gone at any time. There's security here."

He was right. But it wasn't what I wanted to do.

I went home to tell Kay. We thought we were the luckiest couple in the world. The next day, that world caved in.

Veitch greeted me and added as an afterthought, "Oh, by the way, I couldn't get you what I told you I could get you."

"Pardon?" I replied.

"I couldn't get you the money I said I could. It will be more like $6,000."

I was devastated.

"You're kidding, right?"

"No, sorry, Bob. But $12,000? Come on – I can get a high school teacher for half that. I've even got a half-dozen who've left me messages. How can I justify giving it to you?"

There was nothing I could do or say. I had to go home and tell Kay. She was devastated.

I tried calling one of the directors, but he couldn't help.

Kay and I talked long into the night. We couldn't continue to live like we were on a $6,000 salary. What could we do? We had to sell everything. We sold our nice split-level home in Richmond and moved into a Cracker Jack box–sized house in Vancouver on 22nd Avenue. We began working ourselves out of the hole. We sold our car, a brand new 1967 Malibu Sport convertible; we were determined to make it work. And I was determined not to display even a hint of bitterness.

I spent two to four nights a week at minor football events; during the season, I'd work from 7:30 a.m. at the downtown office and finish up between 9 and 10 p.m. at Empire Stadium doing laundry. There was little time for Kay, Steve and Scott. But Kay never lost faith or groused. Whenever we talked about me finding another job, she told me, "Forget it – you love what you're doing."

I am a lucky guy.

I'm not a vindictive person, but looking back, there are only a handful of people in the business I look at and say, "What you did wasn't right." Eric Beardmore was one – the director who wouldn't let me have supper. Veitch was another – he didn't have to lie to me. I lost all my respect for him. It was a devastating time, but Kay and I struggled through it.

Jim Champion, the next coach I encountered with the B.C. Lions, had been our defensive coordinator when we won the 1964 Grey Cup but he had moved on to the St. Louis Cardinals. The Lions got him out of his contract and made him head coach when Skrien was fired. The trouble was, Champion was a very good defensive coordinator and not a very good head coach.

Champion didn't have a philosophy or a larger vision of how the game should be played. I had come to realize this was essential from watching Robinson. If you ask what resources and support staff they need, most good head coaches will respond with a list – I need this guy; I need that guy. Good assistants are essential. Champion was the opposite. He figured he was going to do everything himself and it didn't matter who else you hired.

The media loved him. He had great one-liners. He was always accessible. He'd sit down for an interview, he'd play golf with reporters – but as a head coach, he wasn't very solid.

Champion couldn't handle the task facing a head coach – giving careful attention to the many different facets of the game and the organization. As an assistant coach or a coordinator, you worry about one aspect of the game. In terms of motivation, it's easier because you are working with a much smaller group. You also have a squad's camaraderie that you can rally around. That 1964 Grey Cup–winning team had a great defence, "The Headhunters." It was great, to a large extent, because of Champion's coaching and his ability to motivate a small group. But he never managed to make the transition to head coach where the task is to motivate a much larger, more diverse group. It was just one horrible thing or another under him and we finished 3–12–1 in 1967 and 4–11–1 in 1968. We couldn't get on track.

The highlight of the 1968 season, though, was the arrival of Jackie Parker. He was without a doubt the greatest CFL player of all time. No question. He was unbelievable. A five-time all-star as quarterback and a three-time all-star as running back. They nicknamed the big blond, the "Fast Freight from Mississippi State." Born in Tennessee, he played both ways, helping Edmonton win the Grey Cup in 1954 as a defensive back returning a fumble 84 yards. That was the first of three straight cups with Edmonton.

Parker came to B.C. as an assistant coach in 1968 and even suited up for eight games that season. When those games ended and Jackie got out of the locker room, he'd go to a little room we had under the stands at Empire Stadium where the players and coaches could have a few beers and sandwiches. Afterwards, Kay and I helped Jackie's wife Peggy practically carry him to his car – he could hardly walk after those games, the pain was so bad. It was sad. Here was the greatest player that's ever played in the CFL moving like an old man.

We went 1–10 in 1969. Champion was let go and Jackie took the helm.

After two lacklustre years, Jackie talked the club into hiring his pal, Saskatchewan Roughriders coach Eagle Keys, as general manager. The trouble was, Eagle didn't want the job. He didn't want to be an administrator: he wanted to be head coach. So Jackie went back to the club and said he'd become general manager and Eagle would become coach. As it turned out, Jackie wasn't an administrator either. That gave me my real opportunity. Eagle and Jackie were happy to let me do the paperwork, even negotiate contracts, while they talked football. They loved to talk football. Boy, could they spin a yarn.

During those years, I met more people in football in North America than I met in my entire life. Jackie knew everybody in football; Eagle knew anybody else. Together, there was nobody they didn't know.

At the coaches' convention every January, our suite was open practically 24 hours a day and always filled. It was a Who's Who of professional and big-time college football, all drinking and telling stories. Bear Bryant would be over here, Johnny Majors there, Jackie's brother Fred, who worked for the Associated Press, 30 to 50 guys, the biggest bullshit poker game in the world on the go, arm-wrestling … I got a chance to meet everyone and soak up pure professional football culture.

That was a huge advantage for me. I could pick up the phone after that – anytime. Even later, when Jackie was gone, those relationships endured. I could always pick up a phone and call someone at an NFL team, a U.S. college, a Canadian college or wherever, and they knew who I was. I had met them. I had met them through Eagle and Jackie. It was always: "Hey Bobby, what can I do for you?"

Jackie taught me the importance of connections. A head coach has to have an extensive network, a trap-line of information to keep himself abreast of up-and-coming players and gossip you won't find in scouting reports.

One year, Eagle told me an old pal was joining us at the coaches' convention – Danny Edwards. I went to the files and dug out Danny's folder looking for anything he might find funny after all those years. I copied his contract and scooped a couple of old publicity photographs to take along to the convention. As I flipped through the file, a page torn from a notepad fluttered to the floor.

I recognized Herb Capozzi's handwriting.

The note indicated Capozzi was meeting, probably in November 1958, with Ralph Henderson, club president, and Edwards about the coming year. He had scribbled down figures for Edwards as coach and two assistants: Eagle Keys and Don Shula, who achieved greatness with the Miami Dolphins.

Edwards laughed with glee when he saw it.

"Yes, yes," he nodded. "Wouldn't that have been a different world? I was sure I was going to get the job. Eagle was scouting in Edmonton at the time and he was all set to come; Don was coaching a university team and he was eager too. Then I didn't get the job and they hired Wayne Robinson."

A few years later, I had a chance to bump into Shula at the Senior Bowl and we shared a chuckle over how close he came to coaching in Canada.

"My wife was pregnant at the time and I remember it well," he said. "We were all packed and ready to go. When Danny called and said he didn't get the job, we were so disappointed. Danny was one of my best friends."

And talk about stories that go around! A decade later, when I was with the Dallas Cowboys, Jimmy Johnson arrived as head coach with Don's son, David Shula, as his offensive coordinator. When I got to know David, I said to him: "When were you born?"

"1959," he said.

"Do you know that you were almost a Canadian?"

His dad had never told him and he thought it very funny. So did his dad later, he said, when he reminded him of it.

It's such a small world.

Still, those were very dark days for the Lions. Even under Eagle and Jackie, the team couldn't put it together. It would seem to be headed in the right direction, you'd have a spurt every year, you'd have weeks of enthusiasm and excitement, but we always stuttered and stalled. I've often wondered why.

Jackie was a great football guy. As great a player as ever there was in any league. He was a good addition to our team. He had good personnel skills. He knew players. Boy, did he know talent. He could deal with people. But he wasn't a very good paper guy, and perhaps most importantly he drank too much.

Jackie's routine was to come into the office in the morning around nine. At lunchtime (he was smart), he'd slip out the back door and head over to the Mark, the nearby athletic club. He'd play raquetball; sometimes there'd be a round of golf but always drinks – as much as a bottle of Beefeaters a day. Then he'd head to his apartment down-town around 4:30 p.m., call his secretary Gail Searson, pick up his messages and return his calls. You couldn't sit Jackie down in those days for a day, a week, a month and say, "Jackie, you have to put to-gether a business plan," or, "Let's make sure we have job descriptions for everybody."

He only did things by the seat of his pants. That gave me an op-portunity to do all the things he didn't want to do or didn't like to do. Jackie was very much a mentor to me. We worked closely together for a long time. I respected him enormously as a coach – I thought he should have stayed a coach. We hit it off. He was just such a good guy. His flaw as a coach, though, was he didn't like to get into conflicts with players. He was a players' guy. He loved the players so much he didn't ever like to say "no." That became my job.

He turned a lot of the administration over to me. I dealt with the agents and the players, and I learned on the fly. You must have a plan going in – what was that player's value to your team? You negotiated in the range. At first, for me it was a trial-and-error thing. Or I'd phone people and talk to them, get an idea without getting into collusion by asking outright, so, how much are you paying a guy like that?

You have to be careful with salaries. You can't give a backup line-backer more than your starting cornerback, even though he's great on special teams as well. There must be a certain uniformity. Of course, as your team gets more veterans and improves, you start hav-ing problems.

Today, the contracts are filed with the league. So, let's face it, as soon as you sign a player for a dollar more than the guy next to him, the first thing he does is go in the locker room, sit down and drawl, "Hey, guess who got a new contract?"

Still, there's a sense of the market value of most players, and there is the grading system used by coaches that tells you exactly where that player is in his career. Every player is evaluated up the ying and yang at this level. So you always look at the grades at the end of the year. When I was doing contracts I always had a spreadsheet showing age, injuries and grades – everything we could possibly know about a guy and where he fit in with our football team.

Age and injury are critical factors. If you have a player who is a running back, for example, and he's 30 years old with a past knee injury and a recent shoulder injury, you're not going to give him a bunch of money. But you have to be cautious. There is always an exception. Look at Warren Moon or Damon Allen. And agents always say, "My guy is different."

At the end of the day, when I was negotiating contracts, I tried to be fair. I felt that if the player, the agent and I left the room, could shake hands and be relatively happy about getting the deal done, then I could feel good about it. Sometimes I gave a little more than I wanted, but I was satisfied if we all felt good when we left the room. I absolutely hated that in the NFL, every six months guys were coming back to renegotiate. By contrast, 25 years ago, you would shake hands, "Great to have you back, looking forward to a good year," and you wouldn't hear from the guy until his contract was up. Still, it's delicate. You have to understand the players. The last thing you want is a guy who is totally ticked off, and I never believed in trying to screw players.

Jackie Parker was a good coach. Probably could have been a great coach. He was very bright, knew the game inside out, knew talent very well, knew everybody in the business. There isn't anyone in the business who wouldn't do anything for him. But he wouldn't spend the time it took to be a great coach. Jackie hired good assistant coaches, but I don't think he wanted the pressure of being the head coach. That's why he schemed to have Eagle hired. They were going to be the greatest head coach-GM combination in the history of the Canadian Football League. It never happened.

In taking over the team in 1969, Jackie encouraged them to rally and win four of the last five games. Jackie could really help on the sidelines. He knew what was happening in a game. He knew what the opposition was doing to us and what we could do to them. He was a great tactician. Jackie knew what could be done and how to do it. Move this guy here, block him there. But we didn't have the talent to execute. We had some. They were good enough to get us into the playoffs but we were trounced by Calgary 35–21.

In 1970, Tartan Turf, the first artificial turf in Canada, was installed at Empire Stadium and our luck was as hard as the phony field. What a tough year that was. We finished 6–10 and out of the playoffs. More than that, the atmosphere was rancid and Ernie Pitts, one of our well-liked receivers, was shot dead in Denver while visiting his estranged wife and daughter. I got the phone call about four in the morning. Like I said, nothing good ever happens at four in the morning.

Ernie was a veteran who had a great career with Winnipeg. More importantly, he was a leader on our team especially among the young black players. It was 1970 and the locker room was rife, like the rest of society, with Black Power, afros and attitude aplenty. Ernie had kept things calm and his loss was a big problem for our football team in terms of chemistry.

We went a less-than-mediocre 6–10 that season, and Jackie started lobbying for Eagle. They had played together in Edmonton – Eagle was Parker's centre. Again, even with such an amazing duo, the team responded with a sub-mediocre performance – 6–9–1. As the team foundered, the fans abandoned ship. I think Eagle was a pretty good coach and he was successful in Saskatchewan. But there he had quarterback Ron Lancaster and a pivot with that ability makes a huge difference.

We had some great players at different moments during those doldrums years – Rocky Long, Johnny Musso, Al Wilson, Jim Young (who captured the Schenley Award for outstanding Canadian twice), and linebacker Ray Nettles (who won a Schenley as the league's most outstanding defensive player).

Don Moorhead from Michigan was our quarterback, a classic six-foot-three, 210-pounder who threw decently. He wasn't a great thrower, but a smart enough athlete. He had played major college football and won. But we wouldn't make the playoffs again until 1974 and we got stomped in the semifinals by Saskatchewan 24–14.

The nightmare only continued the following season.

In the off-season, two of our big linemen – Garrett Hunsperger and Bud Magrum – went to Prince George to go hunting. They stayed at the Inn of the North where they got into a fight and beat the crap out of a waiter. Now here were two big guys. Magrum was a

Vietnam demolitions expert, a Marine Corps guy. Both were hulking guys. They beat this little waiter to a pulp.

I went to see Jackie.

"Better go see Eagle," he said.

We did. Neither of them wanted to do anything, so I talked to a lawyer who said, "I don't want the Lions to do it. They both have to send me a personal cheque for $100 as a retainer saying that they want me to represent them and I'll represent them."

I went to lasso the two clowns and bring them into Eagle's office. We laid out the story. I said, "If you each give me a cheque for $100 that will retain this attorney and he'll do what he has to do."

They said, almost in unison, "Yeah, yeah, yeah."

They might as well have said, blah, blah, blah. A couple of dumb adults who'd never grown up, the Dumbo-sized duo planned to ignore it. Eagle should have taken them by the scruff of the neck and said, "Write that cheque now! We're going to get this thing straightened out." They would have still been in trouble but at least they would have been in good hands. Instead, they threw the summons in the waste basket, and you know what the judge thought of that. They didn't have a lawyer and they both got nailed. The publicity was horrendous. I don't know how many seats were cancelled.

Worse, before we knew it, the team lost five of its first six games. I was summoned to a special meeting of the board on August 29, 1975, in downtown Vancouver. They told me to wait around and "be available."

I sat in my office while they conferred in the boardroom for most of the morning. Eventually, they made their decision. The resolution, moved by W. Munsie, past president at the time, and seconded by T.E. Blossom, read: "That the services of J. Parker be terminated and that the position be offered to R. Ackles for the balance of the year, 1975."

They brought me in the room and offered me the job.

What was I going to say? "No?" I took it.

They asked me to step outside again.

The next resolution, moved by T.B. Prentice and seconded by W. Munsie, decreed "the resignation of head coach Keys be requested and if not then his services be terminated."

They ushered me back into the meeting and told me to go tell Parker and Keys they were through. "Which of the three assistants do you think can take over as interim head coach?"

"Cal Murphy," I said.

"Fine. Hire him."

All this took less than half an hour.

Director and pal Tom Hinton and I drove to Empire Stadium to break the news. After we told the three assistants that their boss had been fired, I offered Murphy the job.

Of course, he played hardball because he had me over a barrel. What was I going to do if he said "no"? It was mid-season. We had a game in a week. I knew he was not going to say "no," still it was a really tough spot. I was fortunate in that Murphy didn't exploit the situation. I had helped him coach at Notre Dame High School in the mid-1950s and we had a good relationship.

It was a difficult day for everyone. Jackie was so well liked. But always the bottom line wins. If the team wins and performs well, the finances usually look after themselves. If they don't, you can usually survive because owners are often happy to say it's more important to win than make money. I'm not sure there is any other business like it. In football, people with a lot of money really believe it's more important that you win than if you make them a lot of money. Usually those people are making money from the other things they do. They don't like to lose money in any business, but winning in football is more important and they'll subsidize it. That's the nature of the business. Look at the NFL. You'd have to be a bumbling fool not to make money owning a team, but the most important thing to those guys is winning. They go to their clubs, they play golf and if they've won on the weekend, it's a whole different feeling. If you're in last place versus first place, it's a big difference. The league is probably the most exclusive men's club in the world – only one woman owner – and there are enormous testosterone-charged, chauvinist egos at every level. That's why Jerry Jones and Jimmy Johnson finally split – they both wanted all the credit for putting together a Super Bowl winner like a couple of major Alpha males beating their chests.

Testosterone can often get in the way in football. The next morning I had barely settled into my office as general manager when the phone rang.

"Pat Peppler," this deep, deep, voice of doom said, "general manager of the Atlanta Falcons. Now you listen to me, you rotten little son of a bitch!"

"What?" I had no idea what I could have done.

"If you don't get Monroe Eley out of that contract," he continued angrily, "your name will be mud in the NFL. Forget about buying a ticket; you'll never be able to visit."

He hung up.

—⁂—

Monroe Eley was a hell of a running back for us – a big strong, quiet kid with good speed. He had dropped out of school, which is why we got him early. When he was eligible for the NFL draft, Atlanta took him and he wanted to go there to play. At that point, Jackie Parker made a deal with Peppler so that Eley would go to Atlanta and we would get a Canadian kid from the University of Hawaii, Henry Sovio, a huge tight end. We were also going to get $20,000 US. But things went sideways.

Eley was required to clear waivers in Canada if we wanted to send him to Atlanta. Jackie had called around and learned a couple of the general managers might not pass on Eley.

Sure enough, when Eley was placed on waivers, he was claimed by Toronto and we had to pull him back. You could only do that once. So we were reluctant to put Eley back on waivers because we might lose him entirely. It was one of those tasks that had languished on Jackie's desk since. Now Jackie and Eagle were gone and Peppler figured he was getting screwed since Sovio had signed with us and there was no Eley in Atlanta. I had to rectify the situation.

It took a bit of doing, there was still a wrinkle at the last minute with Toronto, but we negotiated waivers and the kid was soon on his way to Atlanta. We received a cheque for $20,000 US. The funny thing is, I was watching the opening pre-season game of the Atlanta Falcons, Monroe Eley's first game, and he was running back kicks. On the opening kickoff of the game, he caught the ball, sprinted up field, was tackled and broke his leg.

Under new head coach Cal Murphy in that 1975 season we won the next three in a row, and I almost thought things were going to be fine. But Montreal beat us narrowly and we lost badly in Regina. The team's slide appeared to be continuing if not picking up momentum. The lowest ebb was the next game on October 4, 1975. The last 15 minutes of that Saturday night game against Calgary made me feel as if everything was coming apart for good.

Granted, we'd had a bad summer with the Hunsperger assault charge, then the fans were all over us for getting rid of Musso, then I had to fire the man I considered a friend, a mentor and one of the most knowledgeable people in football. And finally, we were stinking the house out.

We had 17,000 fans at the start of the game – a small house. In the last quarter, there were no more than 5,000 people left. But what I remember most – and it is something I'll never forget – in the last 15 minutes, they all stopped booing. Total silence. It was eerie, and it was profoundly depressing. Five thousand fans too tired to boo, too tired to get up and get out of the rain. We lost 38–12. I had never felt so depressed or so completely demoralized in my life. It was a dank, dismal omen.

Things got worse.

In the early 1970s, the club wasn't making money and had seriously depleted the $3 million rainy-day fund established in the heady days of the Grey Cup win. By 1975, the money was gone, and it was pouring. The directors knew the club was headed for bankruptcy. Our fan base had eroded gradually from the high 20,000s and low 30,000s to half that many in the stands. It was a disaster.

We finished the year 6–10 with the team playing .500 football the rest of the way for Cal Murphy. That left us in fifth place – out of the playoffs but good enough to get Cal and I contract extensions. Still the club was bankrupt.

I faced a real challenge – how to resuscitate a moribund and broke organization and rebuild a mediocre football team. Jack Farley and I went cap in hand to the league for money and to the bank seeking ways of generating operating capital until we could get a new stadium built and solve our problems.

At the Grey Cup in Calgary that year, it was hard to stay in the spirit.

In those days, every club had to run a hospitality suite. We were in dire straits, but we had to put up a front. We got a big, two-bedroom suite to cut costs with Kay and me in one bedroom and Wes Munsie, one of our directors, in the other. The living space between doubled as the hospitality suite.

One night, Chunky Woodward invited Kay and me over to his suite at the Westin for dinner, and we left our place filled with people telling Munsie to make sure and lock everything if he went out. There was a lot of liquor.

"Not a problem," he said.

We left, went for dinner and returned late in the evening.

I remember getting off the elevator and at the far end of the hall I could see that our suite door was open. Jesus! You don't do that at the Grey Cup. That's an invitation to anybody walking the halls to come in. As we got closer, I could see a beer case propping open the door. There was a collection of doorknobs, handles and hardware scattered about on the carpet. The handle and the locking mechanism were missing from the door. A dull roar emanated from the inside.

I looked in horrified. Not one face did I recognize.

Well, there was one: Klondike Mike from Edmonton, the little guy dressed like a prospector with the beard and fully loaded donkey. He was standing in the suite right next to a table of hors d'oeuvres. Mike and his animal both stared at me as if I were the intruder. There was donkey shit on the floor.

I blew my stack.

Kay said it was funny later, but it wasn't funny at the time.

I was yelling, "You get your ass out of here!" I wasn't even thinking.

Everyone stood around, frozen in mid-sentence. Utter silence. I could hear their brain cells working: "Who is this guy?" A few giggles.

I picked up the phone and said loudly, "Hotel security."

Everyone cleared out.

Kay said not to worry about the carpet. "It's those little meatballs, not donkey doo."

I learned later that our president, Doug Johnson, had called maintenance to fix the broken door handle as he left. In the lobby, he told Klondike Mike to go on up to the suite. The repair man, meanwhile, had taken apart the lock and gone for parts, propping the door open as he left. While he was gone, the suite filled up with people who assumed, like Mike, that Johnson would be right back. It being Grey Cup, they helped themselves to drinks – until I arrived.

The maintenance man returned and continued to work on the lock while Kay and I went to bed. She woke me about four o'clock in the morning with a nudge. "I think those people are back in the suite."

Sure enough, I could hear the glasses clinking, conversation and laughter.

I threw on a robe and opened the bedroom door. The suite was full of people. Apparently the same thing had happened again – the locksmith had wandered away before finishing the job and those wandering the hallways had come on in.

I turned and told Kay it was a sign; we might as well get in the spirit.

I did a lot of lobbying during that Grey Cup searching for a solution to the team's finances. I didn't find a lot of sympathy but no one really wanted to see the Lions go under. Six of us went for dinner at Hy's Steakhouse trying hard to dispel the doom-and-gloom. Paul Morton, president of the Winnipeg Blue Bombers, spotted us heading into the dining room.

"How can they afford to eat here if the Lions are so broke?" he quipped to his general manager, Earl Lunsford, loud enough for us to hear.

Red-faced, I spun around. "We're paying for it ourselves, if you must know."

Those were embarrassing times. We really scraped the bottom of the barrel. Jack Farley, one of our directors with me that night, said not to worry, there was a group of people in the community who were prepared to buy the team.

"Steal it, you mean," I said. "That might be harsh. But that's how it looks to me."

He didn't argue.

I thought we had the makings of a good ball club but we were so far in debt I worried about paying for training camp. We couldn't depend on season-ticket sales because fan support was almost non-existent. Dark times.

The Executive Box

IN THE END, our lobbying at the 1975 Grey Cup did no good and the league refused to lend us any money. We were forced to go cap-in-hand to our creditors and to be creative financially. The PNE, which owned Empire Stadium, agreed to defer back rent of $157,000. We owed in total more than $300,000. But Jack Farley came up with the boldest idea – selling debentures. Let people in the community own a bit of the club, he said.

The first step was to raise the $300,000 needed immediately to cover the team's deficit. If that worked, we'd take it to the next step. We offered the debentures in multiples of $50, $100, $500 and $1,000. Vic Spencer, an old friend of the club, bought the first block of $5,000 worth. Within three days, we had sold $102,000 and within two weeks we topped $210,0000. The debentures sold like hotcakes as the public scrambled to buy shares in the team. We sold the full $300,000 within two months.

We paid off the bills and approached the PNE for a rent reduction of $250,000 – $100,000 for each of the following two years and a $50,000 reduction in the third year. We also got a five-year sponsorship deal from Labatt's worth $250,000. In 1982, we devised a new debenture program to move into B.C. Place Stadium and purchase the Surrey football training centre. We sold $1.2 million worth in 1982 and repaid them within five years.

Aside from the financial moves the team made, I got the players out into the community, too. In spite of the business crisis and tarnished record, we generated real excitement and hope. It taught me a lot about community marketing – you've got to get out, get involved and support others if you want people to support you.

We traded three players to get Wayne Smith, a mountain of a defensive end from the Ottawa Rough Riders. I talked Ray Nettles into renewing his contract, and we got Ted Dushinski, a veteran defensive halfback from Saskatchewan. I thought we had a really good team coming together when we snared John Schiarra, the UCLA quarterback who had wowed everyone at the Rose Bowl. We sold $100,000 worth of tickets in the two weeks after his signing.

We managed to hit 16,000 season-ticket sales, which was well below the 20,000 high of 1964 but better than 1975's low of 12,400. It was the first increase since the slide began in 1965. In spite of all the business positives and the good vibes coming out of training camp, we missed the playoffs again and finished 5–9–2 – though Schiarra didn't disappoint. He won the Schenley Award for top rookie.

With the season over, I had a year and a half as the general manager under my belt. I was able to look at the whole picture and say, "Okay, what do we need to do? How do I make things better?"

I decided to let Cal Murphy go.

From my point of view, two wet-behind-the-ears rookies were running an organization and it could only afford one – me. I figured it was also easier for him to find work; there were more coaching jobs around than general manager spots.

I made my mind up to make the change before the end of the season. But I held back from firing Cal because I thought it was a mistake – changing horses in mid-stream. I saw that first-hand when Robinson was fired mid-season. Sometimes you have to be patient. Nevertheless, before the season ended, I knew we were not going to get any better under Cal. We had climbed out of the basement, we were showing incremental improvement, but it wasn't coming together and we had problems on the roster he didn't seem able to handle.

Eagle Keys had traded for Bill Baker, a defensive end from Saskatchewan. Eagle was in love with Baker, who was a great player for him in Regina. So Baker came to the Lions with a huge contract, something in the order of $40,000, which is probably what some of the quarterbacks in the league were making. But he played like he had retired. His attitude was dreadful.

We compounded our woes by trading for defensive end Wayne Smith, another malcontent from Ottawa. A pair of disappointments in my book – both had bad, bad attitude. You just couldn't motivate them. They played only when they felt like it.

Firing Cal was difficult and I took a lot of heat for it. He was a hometown boy, he was popular and he wasn't a bad coach. I thought I would survive some of it because I had hired Leo Cahill. Ha, ha! Leo must have been laughing all the way to the bank on that one. I'll never forget those negotiations with him in Toronto, shaking hands on the deal, agreeing to the press conference announcement and then getting the call from his lawyer telling me Leo wasn't coming. What a surprise Christmas present! Leo cut the deal with me and used it to leverage a better contract out of the Toronto Argos. It was not just a personal betrayal in my view, it left me in a professional hole. Still, with Leo off my list and the heat turned up, I made a mistake – well maybe not a mistake, it was a good learning curve for me – but I began interviewing almost anybody who called me.

The first guy to call was Vic Rapp, the offensive coordinator in Edmonton. He'd been sort of promised the Edmonton job and then they brought in Hugh Campbell. We had really good conversations and I told him I'd get back to him after I'd spoken with the others. Probably I should have gone with my gut. Vic struck me from that first call as the man for the job. I made 18 take-offs and landings in 20 days, interviewing coaches in one city or another, at the Senior Bowl, at the Seattle airport…

On the spur of the moment, after interviewing a couple of coaches in New Orleans, I decided to visit my former roommate Urban Henry. I didn't have to be at the Atlanta coaches' convention for several days and I didn't want to hang around the city. Urban had such an illustrious career – with the Rams, with his pal, offensive guard Jerry Kramer and with the Packers for that year under Vince Lombardi. I saw him play for the Rams when Kay and I went down and had dinner with him.

Urban had gone on to open and close a restaurant, Beverly's Steak House, and a nightclub. He had owned an airplane, a boat, a place on the square in New Orleans, a big house in Franklin, Louisiana, and he had pissed a lot away. Born in tiny Berwick, Louisiana, Urban had partied hard and never married. I talked on the phone with him from time to time.

But I had lost track of him, which is hard to do when you're talking about a renegade six-foot-five, 350-pound guy who called anybody he didn't know or didn't like, "Cleave." As in, "Hi, Cleave, how you doin', Cleave?"

Who was going to correct him?

If he liked you, he called you "Stud."

In New Orleans, I heard he had fallen on tough times. I tried to call him, but when I couldn't reach him I decided to drive over and see if I couldn't track him down. His home wasn't that far from the city and I had a general idea how to get there.

I rented a car at Hertz, asked directions to Morgan City, Urban's last known whereabouts, and headed southwest on highway 90, with the music tuned high and a Diet Pepsi in my hand. It was fitting that I pay him a surprise visit.

During the two-and-a-half-hour drive to Morgan City a lot of old stories ran through my mind: some bad, most of fun times. I had dated Kay while I was rooming with Urban and Tom. Both of them attended our wedding in 1960. Kay grew to love both of them, as I did.

As I drove, I stopped every so often and gave Urban a call. I got lucky. It was a small bait shop and the owner answered the phone. He knew Urban but had not seen him in "quite some time." After answering numerous questions that obviously quelled his concerns and suspicions of a northerner wanting information about a local, he told me Urban lived nearby in Franklin, an hour or so south. He gave me another number.

On the road again, I was soon lost again in reverie. I recalled Urban telling me about the business he, Jerry Kramer and Jimmy Taylor, the great Louisiana State University fullback and Packer All-Pro, started: Packer Diving and Salvage.

Not a lot of people knew much about Urban: for instance, after each season for several years, he returned to Georgia Tech to earn his engineering degree. With his extensive knowledge of diving as well as the use of explosives under water, he became the president and general manager of Packer Diving and Salvage. The three partners, after an initial investment of $5,000 each, had expanded the business into five offices around the Gulf of Mexico. They sold it for a fortune.

I stopped and tried calling the number. A man answered.

"I'm trying to locate a friend of mine, Urban Henry."

Silence.

"I said, I'm looking for Urban Henry."

"Yeah," the man replied with a thick gumbo accent. "What you want Urban for?"

"I'm a friend of his."

"How so?" said the voice.

I explained, and I guess he believed me.

"I got a phone number," he said. "I'm not sure it still works. But this is the last phone number I have for him."

He gave it to me. I phoned. No answer.

Franklin was only another half-hour down the highway, so I continued. I drove into town and stopped at the National Grocery Store and used their phone. To my surprise, Urban answered.

"Urban Henry?"

"Bobby?"

He knew my voice instantly.

"Where the hell are you?" he asked.

"You won't believe this, Urban, but I'm in the National Grocery Store in Franklin, Louisiana."

"The hell you are."

"The hell I am."

"God damn! Why didn't you tell me you were coming?"

"I've been calling you for three days, Urban."

"I've got nine dogs and we been huntin'," he said.

"That's fine, I'll stay overnight in town and I'll see you next time I'm through."

"Don't you move. You stay right there. I'll be there in 15 minutes."

Sure enough, out of the swamp came this monster truck that looked as if the axles were aligned wrong. The windows were cracked, a gun hung in a rack on the rear window. Urban sported a full beard and looked like some mad, giant mountain man from *Deliverance*. He jumped out and bear-hugged me.

"Leave your car there and get in," he said.

With that, he barrelled down the lane and slid the truck to a stop at the back of what he said was a local saloon. He pulled the rifle from the rack.

"What the hell are you doing with the gun?" I asked.

"This bar is so tough you have to have your own gun to go in," Urban gravely drawled.

I didn't know whether to laugh or shit my pants. Don't these guys ever grow up? Why didn't I stay in New Orleans another couple of days?

We went in, he put the gun behind the bar, turned to me with a wink and said, "Didn't want to have it stolen."

We sat and had a couple of Scotches and reminisced.

"Time's up," he said. "Next stop."

We got up and drove through another couple of back alleys and ended up in the back of a general store. He introduced me to the mayor, the chief of police, the community football coach, the high school football coach, a guy off the rigs, all of them sitting around jawing in the back of this general store drinking whisky.

I looked out front, fascinated – it had meat, groceries, vegetables, pots and pans, miscellaneous household goods, a veritable cornucopia. You were on the honour system at the bar or if you wanted a sausage, a steak or something else. You wrote up your own bill.

We sat there and the place filled. You could tell the jungle drums had carried the news – Urban had a friend in town who liked to drink Scotch. We did a tour of Urban's favourite haunts with his best friend, Fred.

Fred owned a large plantation. At one time, his family had grown cotton, then sugar. More recently they struck oil on it. He was worth a fortune but trying to find something for his kids to do because they were desultory twenty-somethings. He flooded 40 acres and created a fresh-water crawfish farm. They ignored it. He was doing all the work and had even invented a machine to remove the meat from the tails.

He took us out on an airboat. We were drunk and it was cold as hell. It was January and we were hurling across the water in this airboat. I was freezing to death and we were passing around a jug of chilled red wine. We stopped every so often and our host put on a large leather gauntlet. He reached down into the water and pulled up a trap.

"Fred, what do you need that big glove for?" I asked.

"Water moccasins."

I laughed uneasily and moved from the side of the boat.

Later, we had a great feed of the crawdads before we headed off to see another of Urban's pals, Preston Foster III, whose brother would become governor. He lived in an antebellum mansion right out of *Gone with the Wind*. His story was the same: cotton, sugar, oil.

Two of Urban's paintings were hanging in the house. One, a magnificent oil, was of Preston's father. "That was the great man himself as he looked when he was alive," Preston said. You'd swear he could walk out of the painting. The other was a beautiful scene of the bayou in autumn. Urban had used subtle colours and delicate shading to capture the green hues and emerald shades of the Spanish moss, the gnarled cypress knees and the murky, weedy water.

As Preston gave us the guided tour, his wife Mary Anne asked me where we were staying.

"I'm going down to Urban's."

Her look said that wasn't wise. "I don't think you want to do that," she said. "You both should stay here tonight."

It was late in the day. I looked at Urban.

"Nonsense." He wouldn't hear of it.

We left and headed back into the swamp along a dirt dyke. We literally ran out of dyke and there was Urban's home, on stilts, in the bayou. It used to be a slave shack, he said, built in the 1800s. Now I understood why Preston's wife gave me that look. I wished we had taken her up on her offer.

There were nine dogs in the shack and Urban had been gone a long time. We could hear them baying and bellowing, "hoo, hoo-o-o, hoo-o-o-o-o-o-o."

"Piss break," Urban yelled, yanking open the door.

They hurled out, howling and splashing into the bayou. They were a motley collection of mangy curs. Obviously fearless, I thought, imagining the denizens of the swamp out there in the gathered gloom. I stepped inside – a holstered .45 Magnum hung on the jamb. I didn't want to contemplate why.

Urban cooked up a bouillabaisse in the large, hearth-like fireplace that dominated the middle of the shack. It was an incredible stew. I had eaten at New Orleans' finest earlier in the week, but Urban's fish soup was to die for.

Two hours later, Urban was outside blowing a moose horn. I'd never heard such a moan. But the mutts came scampering back covered in mud, dirt and debris.

Urban showed me his latest art work and explained he was no longer painting much but playing more with porcelain. He had perfected a technique for creating stamen on flowers. He showed me how he worked with this minuscule file and other tools he had developed. It was amazing – this huge man with small, delicate hands, they were his oddest feature, tiny girl-like hands that easily manipulated the hypodermic needle filled with liquid porcelain making flowers in vibrant colours of orange, lemon and lime. He had ducks, geese and other wild birds in his freezer, wrapped in silk to maintain the vibrancy and texture of the feathers. They were models for his drawing and painting. He was a very interesting man.

Afterwards, he hooked his guitar into the music system and sang and sang. We phoned everyone we knew, Kay a half-dozen times!

I staggered to bed peering through the chinks in the floorboards at flecks of moonlight glinting off inky water. There were alligators down there, I thought.

"Urban, are there any snakes?"

"Naw, don't worry about snakes, Bobby. They won't come in here 'less it gets cold."

I didn't sleep.

Before leaving the shack for the drive to Franklin the next morning, Urban reached up into a rafter and took down a drawing.

"Here, Stud, this is for you."

It was the three famous Green Bay Packer receivers: Boyd Dowler, Ron Kramer and Max McGee. The original sketch, covered in cobwebs, dust and fly specks. I was speechless.

As we drove north from Bayou Salle to Franklin, Urban pointed to some of the local highlights we had missed on our earlier journey. The field, for instance, where he roped a 14-foot alligator, loaded it into a truck and transferred it back to the swamp. "So some dumbass SOB redneck didn't shoot it just for fun."

At the National Grocery Store parking lot, we got out of the truck, hugged and promised to stay in touch. We said we'd get together with Hinton real soon, as well. But that was the last time I saw Urban – a mountain of a man hunched over the steering wheel of a battered truck roaring south toward the bayou with a pack of bawling dogs in the back.

We talked on the phone occasionally after that and we always laughed a lot.

One evening Kay and I threatened to send our 16-year-old son Steve to Louisiana to spend time with Urban. He was a little more boisterous than we wanted and, in a conversation, Urban said, "Send him here for a couple of months. I'll straighten him out."

They would have hit it off great.

But the next morning about 2 a.m. I was wakened by the phone. It was Fred in Franklin.

"Bobby," he said, "our buddy's dead."

Urban had died of a massive heart attack in bed on February 26, 1979. He was 43 years old.

Kay and I made a return visit to Franklin with Jack and Nancy Farley. Preston Foster threw a great party for us at which all the people I'd met with Urban came to celebrate his life. Preston gave me the painting I'd admired, "The Bayou in Autumn," signed "Urban Henry, 1876."

Preston said Urban arrived at the house every so often with his paints and touched it up from time to time. When he finished, Preston said, Urban told him, "We had better age this painting a bit, Stud." That's why he put 1876 instead of 1976. It still hangs proudly in my son Steve's home.

—⚏—

Throughout my time looking for a coach to replace Cal Murphy, every time I talked to Vic Rapp on the phone, it seemed he had a better handle on the job. Every time we spoke, and it was often, I was impressed with the plan he had: Here are my assistant coaches, here are their backgrounds, here is what they bring to the table. Good solid guys and I knew most of them.

Vince Tobin, his defensive coordinator, for instance, would eventually become a head coach in the NFL. From day one, Vic and Vince had researched players who might be available from the NFL because Vince's older brother was the personnel director of the Chicago Bears. They had a pipeline, not just to the Bears, but to talent that might be available and able to play at this level.

As well, Vic had worked in the league with Edmonton for five years and won. He understood what it was going to take to get it done. I think Jackie and Eagle probably knew what it took to win, but they really didn't have a solid plan. They knew where they wanted to be, but they didn't know how to get there. Vic knew how we were going to get there. He knew our personnel intimately because he had played us so many times over the previous years. He had a plan and knew what coaches and players were needed to accomplish it.

Though I felt in my belly Vic was the guy, I wanted to give a shot to everyone I said I'd talk with. By the time I finished interviewing all the other coaches and got back to Vic, he had taken a job at the University of Miami as the offensive coordinator under Lou Saban.

"But Lou knows if you call me, I'm coming to Vancouver," Vic told me, "and that's not a problem. He said he understands what an opportunity it would be. I just didn't want to be sitting here in February and not have a job."

"I understand," I said, "I'm going to make a decision next week."

I made the decision over the weekend and phoned Vic on Sunday but couldn't reach him: he'd gone to the Bahamas. On Monday morning, I called his Florida office.

The secretary said, "I'll get him, he's down the hall."

He took about four or five minutes getting to the phone.

"Oh god, you've made me the happiest man in the world," he said when I told him.

"Well, I'd like you here tomorrow for a press conference. Is that possible?"

"Right," he replied, "I'll be there."

I thought, he's really going to have to rush to the airport, but he made it and we announced his appointment the next day. Surprisingly, I was reminded of hiring Vic years later when I joined the Dallas Cowboys. At dinner with the team scouts, Ron Marciniak mentioned he knew Vic and was there the day I hired him.

"How so?" I asked.

"We were both on the staff at the University of Miami," he explained, sipping his beer. "I had joined Lou Saban a week before Vic arrived. Lou said, 'Ron, look after Vic, make sure he gets settled and gets what he needs for his office,' and this, that and the other thing. It was Vic's first day in the office, and I was showing him around, introducing him to the secretaries. Then I was getting him supplies."

He took another draw on his beer.

"We had this kind of big closet where we kept all our supplies – pencils and pens and, you know, all that sort of stuff. We were in this rickety old building before we moved and in the storeroom there was a big ladder you had to climb up to reach stuff. Vic was holding the ladder."

He paused.

"I was up the top of the ladder and it was really shaky," Marciniak continued, miming as he spoke. "The secretary rushed in suddenly saying, 'Vic, Vic! You've got a long distance call. It's very important!'"

Peals of laughter. He waited a moment for us to quiet down.

"Vic looked up at me and says, 'Ron, I'll be right back.'"

He paused again.

"With that, Vic ran out. He never came back. I could still be atop that rickety ladder."

We nearly fell over laughing.

—⁂—

Vic Rapp arrived in 1977 with very definite ideas. We started right from the first day – boom, boom, boom, boom! No bullshit. This is how we're doing it. He had his staff in there evaluating our football team, evaluating who was available. Just what I wanted. Certainly nowadays that's what I expect when a head coach arrives. But at the time, it was so fresh to me. Here was a guy who knew what he wanted, what he had to do, what we needed to do to be better than we were. He had a good eye for talent, loyalty and commitment. From a staff point of view, by way of passing, he brought in a trainer, Bill Reichelt, who is still with us 30 years later!

Quarterback Jerry Tagge arrived that year. He wasn't especially spectacular, yet he played some spectacular games. "Jerry Tagge and the Cardiac Kids," that's what they called us. Jimmy Young was his favourite target. We were winning games with no time left on the clock. It was exciting, passionate football. We had some great young players. That year we tied Edmonton and Winnipeg for first with a 10–6 record. We were slotted into second, though, because Edmonton beat us at Empire Stadium. That's another game I'll not forget.

We had the ball on their one-yard line. We were headed north, towards the Mountains. We had three cracks to cross the goal line and win the game. It was simple: win the game; take first place. We needed more than a field goal so a touchdown was imperative. We had this big old fullback named Jim Harrison and we gave him the ball three times on the one-yard line. Three times! Three times the old war horse ran at that line, and three times he was denied. It was biblical. He just couldn't breech the Edmonton wall. It held firm. And it cost us first place. Had we finished on top, we would have hosted the Western Final. We might then have had a shot at the cup. As it was, we beat Winnipeg in the last game of the season to gain home-field advantage only for the playoff.

They came back the following week on a miserable cold, windy, wet night for the semifinal with Dieter Brock as their quarterback. They had a great receiver, a big rangy kid, who was really fast with good hands, #70, Mike Holmes. We were leading with the clock ticking down. Winnipeg got the ball and Brock was moving the ball. We were worried. He dropped back and I saw this kid slashing down field on a go pattern. There was nobody near him. Brock unloaded a bomb and the crowd immediately saw the looming disaster – the sprinting receiver, the parabolic arc of a magnificently launched ball, the game on the line, the geometry of defeat … up, up, up went Holmes. Hearts stopped.

Out of nowhere Joe Fourqurean, the left corner, came leaping like Steve Nash to get a finger on the ball and tip it away. I let out a breath. The crowd exploded. We won the game 33–32.

We went to Edmonton the next weekend for the Western Final and got our clocks cleaned. They beat us 38–1.

But we had improved and the fans were excited again. Yet we finished out of the playoffs in 1978 at 7–7–2. We were stuttering but there were highlights. That matters.

—⁓—

John Henry White was a tremendous back who could run, receive and block. I thought he would be great in the CFL. He had signed initially with the Kansas City Chiefs. They released him part way through the NFL season and I thought we had a chance to snare him so I flew to meet his agent, the notorious Howard Slusher, a Beverly Hills lawyer. He had a two-year-old's reputation for being unreasonable and holding his players out of camp. "Holdout Howie" my pro-football colleagues called him; his friends called him "Rusty."

I arrived at LAX about 10:30 in the morning and drove to a restaurant at Redondo Beach. I was on the verandah looking at the ocean vista as the white Silver Cloud Rolls Royce pulled into the parking lot and a short, carrot-topped man swathed in seersucker leveraged himself from behind the wheel and waddled into the restaurant.

Howard proved to be many things. He was exactly the same age and height as me, but 60 pounds heavier – five-foot-five, 245 pounds. He smoked a pipe and his voice squeaked when he got excited about something, anything in fact. He was one of the most powerful men in professional sports and over the years represented an enviable roster of talent – Raiders quarterback Marc Wilson, the San Diego Chargers' Dan Fouts, superstar receiver John Stallworth, outstanding cornerback Mike Haynes, all-star Lynn Swann, the Pittsburgh Steelers' David Woodley … the list went on.

We hit it off. We both enjoyed good food, good wine and good football. We talked over the next 90 minutes about everything except

John Henry White. Finally, he said, "Listen, John Henry would love to play in B.C. but there are NFL teams interested."

Here we go, I thought, there are always NFL teams interested, even when they're only interested in why anyone would be talking to the player. I explained that I thought we could give White a pretty good deal and structure it in the right way for him. We shook hands, agreeing to talk later in the week.

We were close to a deal, and Howard agreed to fly to Vancouver to finish it. I picked him up at the airport and we went to dinner at Hy's Mansion. I brought Kay, my secret weapon. Howard loved the décor, the antique furnishings, the fastidious service and the fine food. Kay charmed him. We completed the deal over dinner, on a napkin.

I dropped him at the airport and he said as we shook hands good-bye, "Don't let anyone know we got along so well. It will ruin my reputation."

John Henry played his entire outstanding, decade-long career with the Lions.

Agents are all different. What most players don't seem to understand is unless you get taken in the first or second round, you don't need an agent. Here's what's going to happen – you'll get exactly between what the guy above you and the guy below you negotiate. That's what every team does. Outside of the exceptional talent, players are slotted onto the salary chart. If you are the third guy in the third round, that's what you are going to get for a signing bonus and a contract. If you are the fifth guy, you'll get that. You're not getting screwed; you're getting market value, and an agent won't change that.

Now, if you are a first- or a second-round choice, you need an agent because of all the outside endorsements and peripheral deals you will be offered. Fourth- and fifth-round players aren't going to get a whiff of that until they become the best special teams player in the NFL. As a player improves in his career, he might need someone to handle his second contract.

That said, I find it easier to negotiate with an agent than with a player. I can talk honestly to an agent about a player's abilities. Sometimes it's hard to tell the player he's not what he thinks he is – you irk him, you get into an argument – it can be a no-win situation.

A lot of them negotiate like linebackers. Al Wilson, an offensive centre, my god, during negotiations he'd leave my office, slam the door, kick things. Lui Passaglia was kind of that way. A bit of a pain. Stubborn – my, oh, my.

With an agent, the emotional element is removed. Most of the time.

As for Howard and me, years later when I was with the Cowboys, he represented one of our starting offensive guards, Crawford Ker. I told Coach Jimmy Johnson of my dealings with Howard since I was handling most of the contracts. He said great. The moment Howard heard I was going to be on the other side of the table, he demanded to deal personally with Jimmy.

I filled in Jimmy on Howard's true personality and said the key was not to be a hard-ass. Howard didn't scare easily, if at all. He grew up in the Brooklyn projects and put himself through school driving a New York cab on the so-called suicide shift, 4 a.m. to 4 p.m. He was tough as nails. At the same time, he loved to be wined, dined and flattered. Don't we all. You truly can get more flies with honey. Jimmy and Rusty got along fine.

By then, of course, the money was insane. The television deal between the networks and the National Football League had gone from pouring $5.3 million US into each team's coffers annually in 1982 to handing each franchise roughly $20 million. At the same time, attendance had ballooned to more than 14 million – adding another $100 million to revenues. Athletes and agents rightly were demanding their end.

I thought Vic and I built a good Lions team around draft picks such as Nick Hebeler, Ron Moorhouse and Mark Houghton. We really beefed up the Canadian contingent, in part, thanks to the football programs at Simon Fraser University and the University of British Columbia.

We took the Canadian draft very seriously – much more seriously, I think, than we had a decade earlier. We also concentrated on the talent that was in western Canada or west of the Mississippi – you can't cover it all, so you zero in on a certain area and do a better job. It was the key to rebuilding the team.

Still, even with John Henry White and Larry Key, another outstanding running back picked up in 1978, the team just couldn't break through and win the Grey Cup. It's good to remember we were facing an Edmonton team with superstar quarterback Warren Moon. No one else beat them either. They won five Grey Cups. We were a good football team; they were a dynastic football team. In 1979 we finished 9–6–1 and got crushed in Calgary at the semifinal 37–2; Edmonton finished 12–2–2, stomping the Stampeders and the Alouettes to carry off their third consecutive cup.

The Lions' financial difficulties continued as a result. We were perennially short of money. The PNE would defer rent and the bank would step in to help, but we were going from loan to loan to season-ticket money. The paucity of playoff games meant there was never any gravy.

At first, the main problem was the on-field product, then it was the on-field product and the stadium. You needed to draw 30,000 to nearly every game. Even when the team played well, people complained unless it was one of those cerulean days when from the stands you could see the snow-capped peaks glistening on the other side of Burrard Inlet. When it was overcast, the fans were snotty. All you heard was whining – why don't we have a better facility? Or comfortable chairs? How about somewhere you don't get rained on or covered in pigeon guano? We were playing entertaining football, but mostly it wasn't an entertaining experience for the fans. Even when the team was doing well, sitting in the decrepit bleachers in the rain or even in the drier sections of the stadium, the physical condition of Empire Stadium detracted enormously from the fun and excitement.

At the same time, we could not get to that next level, even though we excited the fans. We'd play two or three really solid games, then, because of the entertainment value of the football, we'd have a full house. That's when we'd stink out the stadium.

We were always struggling at the gate, struggling financially.

One reason we couldn't beat Edmonton when it mattered in those years is because Vic got hyper. All those years working for the Eskimos and wanting to be head coach, well, he went into those games so wired. The players were affected by the pressure and stress he put on them to win. He'd get so uptight going into the week of preparation, he made everyone else uptight.

One game, he lost it and had to be hauled from the field by the players to prevent him getting into a fist fight with the Edmonton bench. He looked like a Raggedy Andy doll, arms akimbo and legs askew and flailing as a big lineman picked him up and hoisted him to the dressing room.

We went 8–7–1 in 1980, out of the playoffs again, and I knew Vic wasn't going to get it done. But he had done such a good job for us, helped turn it around after taking over from Cal Murphy, it was hard for me to make the decision. There were shafts of sunlight. The provincial government agreed to build a new domed stadium downtown that would seat 60,000. That would be the answer to our financial ailments if we could solve the problems on the field. I thought we were close to doing that. I thought if I stuck with Vic, we might.

Quarterbacks Joe Paopao and sophomore Roy Dewalt gave us strength and depth offensively – both had record years. Ty Grey was a constant big deep threat, and rookie Larry Crawford led the league in interceptions; we were a pretty good football team, a pretty good team. We went 10–6 in 1981, made it to the final by edging past Winnipeg 15–11, only to again have Edmonton eat our hearts 22–16.

In February 1982, as I headed for the CFL league meetings in Toronto, the board of directors presented me with a report on restructuring the club in advance of moving into the new stadium. I read it in my hotel room. Paul Higgins, a very bright guy with Price Waterhouse and president of the Lions, had talked the board into striking a committee composed of former presidents, people I was quite close to. They were charged with the task of coming up with a new corporate structure.

I finished reading the report and called Higgins almost immediately.

"Paul," I said, "I've read that report and it appears to me that you are basically writing a new person into the corporate structure and that person does what I do right now."

He was pretty coy about what he had done. But he did not dissuade me from my conclusion – he wanted my job. I was quite disturbed, obviously, and told him I would be making a formal response to the board.

I called the committee members and asked them what was going on. Most said Higgins led them to believe I agreed with the changes he was proposing and so they had endorsed the report.

"Hey, I feel like I've been duped," Jack Farley told me.

Tom Hinton, one of my closest friends, said the same thing. Ian Barclay, president and CEO of one of the largest forest companies, and Allan Eyre, who owned the Dueck's On Broadway auto dealership, both had been involved with the club for years. Both were equally dismayed at what they said must be the result of a miscommunication.

I told them it was a palace coup.

Higgins had created a new position to be inaugurated once we moved into the new stadium. The position would be called "executive vice president," and as far as I could see from the outlined duties, it made me redundant.

The committee members said my concerns were completely unexpected, given what they had understood.

I sat down with Peter Butler, a good friend who was also the club's lawyer. I probably shouldn't have done that. But Peter and I had a strong personal relationship. I prepared a five-page, single-spaced, hand-written screed to deliver to the board. It read, in part:

After taking over a sinking ship in mid-season 1975... Our public and media relations have improved and the club is now viewed as a stable professional sports franchise in Canada. When I became General Manager, marketing was non-existent. In my opinion, we now do the best job – with the worst facility in the Canadian Football League.

Through the lean years that I have been general manager we have been very competitive on the field. Best record of any B.C. Lion General Manager with a 53.8 per cent win record, second-best attendance average to Jackie Parker. Yes, better than Herb Capozzi.

I called Higgins the day before the board meeting and told him I intended to file my reply to his report. I sent him a copy. He knew he had crossed a boundary he should have respected. He realized the loss of face looming if our disagreement became an open conflict at the board meeting. There seemed to be no way for us to gracefully disengage. To his credit, Higgins stepped down, sparing me the need to file my response.

I think what happened is that Higgins was a wealthy man who had made a lot of money and was enjoying his role with the football club. I'd seen him on airplanes and he would be creating his own depth charts – reference graphs showing each player designated at a particular position, ranked according to his strength – and the like. That's what happens when people watch too much football on television and begin to think, hey, I can do that. Everyone knows how to do it better than the guy who is doing it. Not a chance.

—⁓—

That season, 1982, even with the great Merv Fernandez now in the receiving corps, we ended up 9–7 and out of the playoffs again.

One great game of that season stands out for me – against Edmonton, July 25, 1982, with more than 28,000 in the stands. Usually when we had crowds like that we fell on our faces. We were 3–0 at the time and we won 38–28. It was amazing. Offensively we were outstanding. Harry Holt, our tight end, took a pass from Roy Dewalt and went 80 yards for a touchdown. Larry Key, our running back, had two touchdowns. We put together great drives. Mervyn went 74 yards on a touchdown, and Kevin Konar made an interception and ran it back 35 yards for a touchdown. It was an enormous game for us on a beautiful afternoon in front of a big crowd.

Unfortunately, we didn't do that often enough that season.

I called Vic to my office and told him I was letting him go. I thought it had gone well and he had taken it well until I picked up the newspaper and read him whining about the unfairness. He complained that it was all about selling tickets in the new stadium. Well, yes. We had to make a change because we had to get to the next level. We had to get from third place and out of the playoffs to second place or first place and hosting playoff games. We needed it financially. And as a football team, we needed to win a championship. It was clear we weren't going to do it under him.

Vic had six years kicking the can. That's a pretty good shift. Today, most teams can be brought to a championship level within a three- to five-year time frame. I now understand how to do that and how much it will cost. But in those days, I was still learning. Vic was a good coach. He worked hard, he hired good people. You can't say Vic didn't give it his best shot. He really did, and his coaches did. They worked hard, but they just didn't get it done. They didn't win.

The first phone call I received after I fired Vic was from Don Matthews. Hugh Campbell, before he got the job in Edmonton as head coach, was on my list to replace Cal Murphy. When I interviewed him for the Lions job, Campbell told me about Don because he wanted to hire him as one of his assistants. I was surprised. At that time, in 1977, Matthews was still a high school coach, although he had won two different state championships with two different schools. What I heard about him then from Campbell impressed me. Don flew from Edmonton, where he was the defensive coordinator of the Edmonton Eskimos, to Vancouver to talk to me about the job. We went over everything – coaching, staff, philosophy, player personnel, who we had on staff versus who we needed to win.

He said, "You don't need much here. You have a lot of good players and it's really about fine tuning and attitude." Vic had been a hard, strong, tough coach from the same mould as Wayne Robinson. With Vic you were told to toe the line and you were going to do things his way. You did not screw around with him. I told Don I'd get back to him after I'd interviewed the others I had in mind. This time I restricted the search to about a half-dozen coaches I thought could do the job.

After the interviews, I knew Don was the guy I wanted. He was a guy I could work with. I liked his philosophy. I respected his record – every place he'd coached, he'd won. But the media were down on him. They didn't like him. Some guys, like columnist Jim Taylor, seemed to hate him. He phoned Edmonton when he got wind that Don was in the running and quoted all kinds of anonymous people dissing him.

Taylor and I are pretty good friends, but three days before I made the announcement, he told the world I was going to hire someone else because Don is a jerk – before he even came in the door!

Boy, was he some pissed off when I came out and announced Don Matthews as head coach. From the time Don arrived until I left the Lions, Taylor wouldn't interview him. Amazing.

Radio sportscaster Al Davidson's attack on me was in a similar vein. However, I figured his was motivated more because we sold the football broadcast rights to a competing station than because of any vendetta against Don. Davidson spotted me at a Canucks game and used that as an excuse to lambaste me and scald Don in passing:

> *Although Ackles used to be a goaltender in John Ferguson's days with the PNE Rink Rats, Ackles is an insidious little man. ….Major heads fly every year with Ackles' incompetence, now he hires a coach no one can talk to, or no one wants to talk to – Don Matthews – a waste of time and that's from 99 per cent of all reporters. … Bob Ackles. A twister. A backstabber. A miserable floor-flushing little man. Out of his element. Small time but a general manager of a minor league franchise.*

By the time I got to the office in the morning, the messages were piling up about that broadcast. Tom Larcheid said I had to do something. Our oldest son, Steve, almost got in a fight over it at work when a colleague said, "Your old man must be some jerk."

I called lawyer Peter Butler and had him listen to a tape of Davidson's rant.

Butler called and said it was the funniest thing he'd ever heard. "We could get $50,000 for this." He fired off letters to the station and Davidson, threatening a suit. The station immediately ran for cover and blamed everything on Davidson. Peter said they were begging to settle.

I told him I didn't want a lot of money out of it. I just wanted Davidson to get off my ass. He had been needling me on air for weeks, ever since the Lions pulled their broadcast rights. Kay and I talked about the settlement and we both agreed: people are on our side but if we start to try and kill him financially, they're going to say, get real! We settled for $10,000 plus legal costs.

Davidson, whom we used to see socially, had always told Kay we should go to Spain. He went for a month every year. I didn't have the chutzpah to send him a postcard from Iberia saying, "Hey, Al, your $10,000 really came in handy and did it up nice for us."

———⟋⟋⟋———

Don Matthews did not disappoint me or let me down. He proved he was everything I thought he would be as a head coach – and why he is one of the best and most successful ever.

I have always believed Vic was the right man for the job in 1977 and Don the right man in 1983. There were some similarities to the position Don found himself in and the position Dave Skrien was put into when he took over from Wayne Robinson two decades earlier. Skrien took over that 1960s' team with strong basic talent that had been beaten down too often physically and mentally. In a short period of time, with some tender loving care and very few changes in talent, he transformed the team into a confident, consistent winner and took them to the Grey Cup. He ran into trouble when the players' personalities and egos became too big for such a mild-mannered coach to handle. It was just a matter of time before Dave was looking for another job. In many ways, but for slightly different reasons, Vic Rapp ran into the same problem – he had a good team but couldn't take it to the next level. Don turned out to be an antidote to the attitude issues and a catalyst for excellence.

Without rewriting the roster, Don took the Lions in his first year to an 11–5 record, second-best finish in team history and good enough for first in the West. No one was close. We played Winnipeg in the 1983 Western Final at our new home in B.C. Place Stadium and stomped them 39–21. We should have gone on to win the Grey Cup that year, but we didn't play a full game.

That was a tough loss. We were up 17–3 at the half at home and lost 18–17. It was agonizing. Don shouldered the blame in the eyes of the media and the fans. I don't think that was fair. There are always second-guessers. I was upset too. You're always upset when you lose a game. But if you look back on it, if you watch footage of the game, it was probably our defence that cost us the win. We were up in the first half but our defence couldn't hold them. Yes, in the second half, we didn't score – but we should have held them. I thought Don did a good job in the face of serious off-field distractions, especially with the injuries to his son in a bad car crash only days before the game.

We knew we had a good football team that year in spite of the disappointment. We didn't have to make a lot of changes. In particular, we needed a standout on defence so we traded for all-star defensive end James Parker. It was the biggest trade in Lions history since the Kapp deal.

We finished first again in 1984 with an outstanding 12–3–1 record. If we hadn't lost Dewalt late in the season, we would have gone on to the cup. Instead, we were forced to go with backup quarterback Tim Cowan, a rookie from the University of Washington. Winnipeg exacted revenge and beat us in the Western Final 31–14. With Dewalt it would have been a different ending. It was a horribly disappointing loss. We had to wait.

In the 1985 season the team steamrolled through the league racking up a 13–3 record, beating Winnipeg 42–22 in the Western Final.

The Grey Cup was held in Montreal in the Big O. It had been snowing during the week and we practised at McGill on a couple of occasions with a dusting on the field. I felt pretty confident. This team had already played in a Grey Cup game. We'd won the West three years in a row. The jitters were not an issue.

We had lost the 1983 Grey Cup in Vancouver. But we had improved our football team. I felt we were the best team in the country at the time. We had had an outstanding year. We had stayed healthy. We had good, solid leadership – on and off the field. In the boardroom, Ron Jones, a young entrepreneur whose car dealership was doing well, proved to be an incredible asset. He became one of our best presidents ever, I thought. Overall, I thought we had the best organization in the league and our players were playing well. I didn't think the Hamilton Tiger-Cats had a chance.

Mervyn's leg injury kept him out of the playoffs, but our other receivers stepped up, especially Ned Armour, who was fabulous.

In the Grey Cup game, they carried on. Jim Sandusky made an outstanding play where the ball grazed off another player's helmet, he adjusted, and made the catch and went in for a touchdown – a hell of a play. But just before the half, the Tiger-Cats started to generate offence, and I got that queasy feeling. The Tiger-Cats were a good football team, too. They were not going to hand it to us. We were forced to punt at one point and Lui Passaglia made a hell of a play – the play of the game in my opinion – by pulling down the ball and running for a first down. That really changed the tempo and course of the game. We romped to a 37–24 victory. Each player won $11,000; each Tiger-Cat got $6,000.

After the game, we loaded everyone from the Lions organization onto buses and went to Ruby Foo's for a post-game blow-out party. Later in the week there was a big parade from the Bayshore down Georgia Street through downtown Vancouver and into B.C. Place Stadium. That was a great football team and established Matthews as a great head coach. Later, in 1989, when I was in Dallas, I tried to get him hired there.

I was elated to win the 1985 Grey Cup – my first true championship. Although I was there for the win in 1964, I basked in reflected glory. I was on the inside, sure, as part of the "we" in "we won," but for the most part I shared vicariously in the victory. But in 1985, I felt this was a team I had helped create and I felt as much responsible for the win as any player on the field. I believed I was an important and essential ingredient. I was centre stage.

Back in 1964, as equipment manager, I was part of the team, I was in the locker room and understood what the players actually went through coming in for the game, coming in at half-time, coming in after the game. I was on the bench and helped keep them up and motivated. I was emotionally involved in what was happening on the bench and in the locker room.

By contrast, as general manager in 1985, I was not involved with the players at all really; I was involved with the coaches and understood it from their perspective. There was more of a feeling of accomplishment as a general manager, a sense of pride in what I had been able to assemble. It was different. I had built and moulded this team. I had gone out and recruited. I had negotiated the contracts. I had helped Don and the coaches bring it together, even though I didn't get down on the field. I had hired all the people who put the puzzle together. I felt as responsible for the outcome as Don, his coaches and the players. I saw the big picture – I was aware of all the elements that could impact on the football team in the long run. This was true sunshine.

In spite of the pride and sense of accomplishment at winning, I felt it was fleeting. Nothing lasts forever. "This might be the only time you ever experience this," I told myself. Certainly, a few months later when I boarded that flight to Dallas, I didn't ever expect to hoist a Grey Cup again. I was headed for the National Football League – the pinnacle of major league sports – to prove myself as an executive, vice president of pro-player personnel, for perhaps the most famous franchise on the planet. From here on, I expected the Super Bowl to be the Big Game on my calendar. I was off on an even greater adventure.

America's Team

TEX SCHRAMM, president of the Dallas Cowboys, was a football visionary. I don't say that because he lured me away from the B.C. Lions in the spring of 1986 and hired me as vice president of pro personnel. He had long before established himself as a founding father of modern U.S. professional football. From the merger with the American Football League, to the National Football League's lucrative television contract, to settling the players' strike, Schramm was a true leader. He put money in everyone's pocket. Pete Rozelle, who laid the foundation for what the NFL is today, was his guy. Tex brought Rozelle in to become commissioner. Tex saw the looming problems with salaries and he and Rozelle transformed the league from a collection of gate-driven, economically risky franchises into a conglomerate of television-based platinum mines. The product was no longer just football, it was fashion, footwear and lifestyle – the tiny NFL patch a global guarantee of mega-sales. Schramm, more than anyone, was responsible.

One cable company transmitted live coverage of our training camp in California two hours a day for six weeks to Dallas. All the other stations covered it daily. Home games were covered by 400 writers and broadcasters. Daily tours of the facilities exceeded 500 people. The facilities themselves sprawled over 200 acres and boggled the imagination – a main complex of 80,000 square feet on one floor, a Cowboys weekly newspaper, a dance studio, weight-training centre, spa, three football fields …

I was very fortunate landing in Dallas. It wasn't as if I went to the Cincinnati Bengals. I went to the Cowboys – America's Team. What an eye-opener it was – like a hard, sharp unexpected slap in the face. Tex brought me in because he could see what was happening. Decline. Rot. The organization was aging; the team was stale. The coaching staff needed shaking up. The trouble was that head coach Tom Landry didn't know anyone anymore. Forced to fire an assistant, he came looking for replacement suggestions at the daily 7:30 a.m. staff meeting. I was aghast: a coach who didn't know who was available or who he wanted?

I didn't suspect any of that before I arrived. At the same time, I also didn't realize the size and extent of the Cowboys' mythology, how much the team is revered in Texas or the place of football in that state's culture. But it didn't take me long to learn.

On Friday nights, Kay and I would go to high school games around the city – one early playoff game drew 27,000! That wasn't unusual. At some of the small stadiums seating 5,000 to 10,000, you had to get there by 6 o'clock or you stood someplace off to the side. Both teams would have colourful bands marching around the track pounding out competing fight songs, trading lick for lick. Each school out in force: cheerleaders, parents, grandparents, kin. High school teams in Texas were so big and so well coached, the first time I saw them on TV I thought I was watching a major college game. Wow, high school football! It was hard to imagine as a Canadian. Simply put, Texas is not a round ball state. A Texan might watch baseball or even soccer, but the pebbled pigskin rules.

The B.C. Lions had won a Grey Cup and we were highly respected in the province. We had put together a number of years of entertaining football, come back from the dark days and it was good. But in Dallas, unlike any of the other franchises I had worked for, you quickly learned the Cowboys were unique. They were special. There was a halo around the organization. You were part of something awesome.

The first time I came out of the tunnel onto the field for a Monday night game I was staggered. The roar: it was absolute pandemonium. I like to be on the field for warm-up and then go up to the press box before kickoff. I've done it for decades. I had heard nothing like that noise. That night to hear that crowd, although we were an average football team at the time, was awesome and unbelievable. The fans certainly didn't think this was an average team.

At training camp, however, I had begun to get a sense of the challenge I faced. As I looked at the veterans and returning players, I could only think, "This team is old." We did not seem to have a lot of great players. Like the fans, I believed that the Dallas Cowboys were above the rest. They were the elite. But the team had fallen on hard times and was in a nose-dive.

The toughest thing to deal with was the politics, especially personnel director Gil Brandt's machinations. He wasn't happy when I arrived, even though we had been friends. Brandt was used to being the guru, and his star had been eclipsed. His attitude was, "Hey, we've won Super Bowls; we're 'America's Team.' We're all the stuff people read about. So what if we had a few bad drafts? Things will turn around. We're the Cowboys." He drank his own bath water.

It was a struggle all the time for me. Gil's attitude was cancerous. One of my first problems was getting prospective players in for the coaches to evaluate. You did it on Tuesdays during the season because that's players' day off. The team plays Sunday most weeks. Monday is preparation day for coaches and the players come in to have injuries checked and watch the game tape. They get Tuesday off.

Usually, you bring a try-out into town Monday night or Tuesday morning. They go through the physical workouts in the morning and an on-field 45-minute workout with an assistant coach about lunchtime. I kept running into assistant coaches who said, "Gee, I don't have time today, Bob." We were a very average football team, we were trying to improve, but coaches didn't want to check out new talent? I just didn't get it.

I had got to know Neill Armstrong, who had an office near mine. Neill was a former Winnipeg player, former head coach of the Edmonton Eskimos and former head coach of the Chicago Bears. I asked him. "The coaches don't seem to want to work my guys out. What gives?"

"Let me tell you something," he confided, "but keep this to yourself."

Often when Brandt learned I was bringing someone in, he would run to the assistant coach and indicate (sniff, sniff) the guy had drug problems or else he would say: "You don't want this guy. Character issues."

That's why the coaches didn't want to work out my prospects. Brandt was scuttling me. I had to get around that.

The organization, aside from football and business departments, also operated the Dallas Cowboys Travel Agency. I had got to know one of the agents and I said to her, "You can't tell anybody I'm bringing players in, or who I'm bringing in. The worst thing is if Gil knows because he might look in their file and find something that's negative."

I went individually to the assistant coaches and said to them sotto voce, "Nobody knows so-and-so is coming in; I'd like you to take a look at him about one o'clock today." Not surprisingly, I started having some success.

Coach Landry took notice. "Maybe we should be looking at more of Bob's suggestions."

Still, it was disheartening to have people in your own office discouraging improvements.

—◊—

In Dallas, it bothered me that Tex, Tom and Gil would not admit a mistake. They always were overly concerned about public perception. If they made a draft choice or dealt a player and that was perceived as a mistake, that was a problem. The Cowboys under Tex and Tom and Gil did not make mistakes; they were above that. If you didn't understand, they said it louder: WE ARE ABOVE THAT!

I remember speaking to a newspaper reporter about a big trade. The Cowboys weren't in the mix because a lot of teams didn't want to deal with us; they didn't want anything to do with us. Primarily that was because of the gloating Gil and Tex did after wheedling superstar running back Tony Dorsett away from the Seattle Seahawks. When you run around telling the world you always skin your opposition in a deal, why would anyone want to do business with you?

It was a published story about the trade that brought the attitude home for me. I was quoted making the benign comment, "No, I wasn't aware of that." Later, I got a visit from a grave Tom Landry.

"You should never say that, Bobby. That you were not aware of something. We should always be aware of it."

"Coach," I said, "there are a lot of teams who don't want to deal with us. I wasn't aware of it."

He didn't want to hear that – that meant the Cowboys were out of the loop. He could not conceive of a world that did not revolve around the Cowboys. That was part of his eccentricity. He was taciturn, an aloof man. Undertakers probably have more personality. Every Saturday evening during the season Landry sat at home after dinner by the television, took out his game plan and at 8 p.m. precisely, picked up the phone and dialed his quarterback. No hello. No small talk. Quarterback legend Roger Staubach told me it was weird. Landry simply instructed him to change such and such a play to such and such. Then hung up. No small talk, no chit-chat. Ever.

That was Coach Landry.

The Cowboys weren't in the loop because of their egos. Brandt, in particular, had a rank reputation among some other teams. He made the Seattle Seahawks, to name one, look bad by implying they were fools for trading the 1977 draft rights for Tony Dorsett. The Seahawks wouldn't return calls from Dallas for the longest time, and who could blame them? Why not be gracious if you think you got a steal? My counterpart with the Seahawks, Chuck Allen, was a friend. After I went to Dallas, I asked why I felt such a cold front. He explained that it was nothing personal.

Anytime the Cowboys made a trade they blew their own horn so much they deafened the other team. People stopped hearing them call. Everybody said, "Let's stay away from them." I had to do a lot of fence mending, a lot of bridge repair work. The arrogance of the Cowboys haunted them.

Their egoistic belief that they could do no wrong also coloured how they dealt with players. If they drafted a player in the first round, he was going to be on the roster come hell or high water. It didn't matter whether he could play or not. They'd pay him a lot of money whether or not he was doing the job a first-round draft pick should be doing. They would not reassess. Tex, Tom and Gil, the holy triumvirate, did not make mistakes.

If you err in a draft pick, I say admit it. Don't send good money after bad. Trade him; release him. Sure, give a player two years, but then throw the switch. The Cowboys would wait five years before acting so it didn't appear as if they'd made an error. I saw too many of those situations. Not being able to trade players increased my frustration.

The organization was structured so that Tex, Tom and Gil were running it from the top down and little from below percolated up. Coaches were not involved in personnel decision making. That's wrong. Coaches don't have to dictate personnel decisions, but their perspective is extremely valuable and shouldn't be ignored.

One of my key friends on the coaching staff was Paul Hackett, who joined the Cowboys from the 49ers only a few months before I arrived. Paul was the quarterback, wide-receiver and tight-end coach with San Francisco from 1983 to 1985. Before that, he'd been with the Cleveland Browns as quarterback coach. (His son Nathaniel works with him at Tampa Bay today as offensive quality control coach.) Right off the bat we became friends and often talked about the quixotic way that the Cowboys functioned.

Paul arrived after being with a couple of other organizations thinking, as we all did, that the Cowboys were far ahead of the competition. In reality, their computer system was outdated and little more than a filing system. They were in the Dark Ages as far as utilizing human resources. They had good scouts, for instance, but they didn't listen enough to them either. The scouts had little influence on who should be drafted or even who the team might want to consider.

The politics were ridiculous. I wanted to shake people and say, "Let's just try to find the best guys, sign them or draft them and get on with it." But it seemed to me that there was this knife-in-the-back, you-can't-do-that culture, and that failure was inevitable.

The United States Football League folded the year I arrived, 1986, after three seasons – 1983 through 1985. It had been a media circus. It was founded by a New Orleans art dealer David Dixon, who unveiled the 12 franchises – New Jersey, Los Angeles, Chicago, Detroit, Boston, Tampa, Oakland, Denver, Washington, Philadelphia, Birmingham and

San Diego (eventually switched to Phoenix) – at the infamous 21 Club in New York. Their games were played in the spring and summer so as not to go head to head with the NFL, but their arrival was definitely a gauntlet tossed at the league's feet.

One superstar emerged – Herschel Walker, the Heisman Trophy winner who quit school a year early to suit up for the New Jersey Generals. He didn't help them win the title, but he made a lot of believers out of fans.

Still, the league couldn't pay its bills given the exorbitant player salaries. In its second year, Donald Trump came on board and the league added several new franchises. Mike Rozier, perhaps the best prospect that year, signed with it. Other nascent stars followed – Jim Kelly, Reggie White, Steve Young, Doug Flutie ... But it was a façade buttressed by borrowed cash.

In 1986, the league announced a fall schedule to go head to head with the NFL while its ongoing antitrust lawsuit rolled through the courts. The financial pressures were proving too much. A month before the league was to begin the season, the USFL won the suit. But it was a pyrrhic victory. The league was awarded damages of $1 – upped to $3 under the competition law. More than $160 million in debt, the league folded. As a result, Dallas won the lottery – we landed Herschel Walker.

Walker was probably the best running back in America. We held a huge press conference at California Lutheran University, our Thousand Oaks training camp, to announce his arrival. News helicopters came from Los Angeles. We had more than 200 media to greet Herschel.

But Tony Dorsett believed himself to be one of the best backs in the world – and proven in the NFL, not in some upstart second-tier league, in his opinion. Tony was a blue-chip everything out of Pittsburgh University. He considered himself *the* star in the Cowboy firmament, a tremendous back and a former Heisman Trophy winner, too. The morning after Walker's press conference, Dorsett was really pissed off because some guy from some nowhere league was getting the publicity. He threw a hissy fit and even called his own press conference. Ego, pure ego.

Tony was a good guy, as was Herschel. Both would go on to play together on the team for three years and play reasonably well. That year Dorsett rushed 184 times for 748 yards, which was definitely pretty good, a 4.1 average and five touchdowns. Walker rushed 151 times for 737 yards, a 4.9 average and 12 touchdowns. So Herschel put it in the end zone. Together they rushed for 1,500 yards, which is decent. Walker also caught 76 passes. That's a lot, and he turned those snags into 837 yards. He was probably an even greater offensive threat.

But we didn't win. We were still an average football team.

We started the season well with Danny White as our quarterback. We beat the Giants on opening day, we beat Detroit, we lost to Atlanta, we beat St. Louis (which became Arizona). We beat Denver, Washington, Philadelphia and St. Louis, all teams we had to beat in our division. Then Danny broke his wrist.

Nine games, mid-season, the Giants game in New York – we lost 17–14. Our backup was a young kid who hadn't played much, Steve Pelluer from the University of Washington. He was a number-two quarterback. Period. It wasn't his fault our season fell apart. We dropped our last five games, finished 7–9 and were out of the playoffs. The Cowboys hadn't missed the post-season in years. But the organization remained in denial.

—⚹—

I travelled a lot for the Cowboys that first year and got to see all the teams in pre-season plus the regular season games looking at talent. There were college all-star games, too – the Blue-Gray game, the East–West game, the Senior Bowl in Mobile, the Hula Bowl. I learned an immense amount and met even more people. I met scouts, personnel directors and coaches. Those connections were invaluable. It meant when I called someone, I could put a face on him, he knew me and we already had some rapport. It was an Everest-like learning curve. I loved it.

Kay and I flew first-class to our first Super Bowl in Pasadena, California. There were limousines and parties out of the Arabian Nights. At the game itself, Kay and I sat on the 50-yard line, 15 rows up in the Rose Bowl, with Tex and his wife Marti, Tom and Alecia Landry,

Roger Staubach and his wife Mary Ann ... There were a dozen of us from Dallas.

It was unbelievable: corporate America on parade. There were celebrities everywhere. At the NFL's Tailgate Party, I couldn't believe some of the people I sat with quaffing a beer.

The Grey Cup had that kind of cachet in years past. You could bump into 40 or so top Canadian executives and moguls, the prime minister and premiers attended and there was a similar sense of cultural importance attached to the game. We lost some of that when we expanded into the U.S. and during the downturn of interest in the game in the 1990s. We were lucky if the two competing teams' hometown mayors made a bet for the media. Fortunately, that's changed. The performance of the host cities of Vancouver in 2005 and Winnipeg in 2006 has gone a long way to restoring the shine. They did a great job and Cup week was a huge success in both.

—⁓—

Dick Mansperger, the head scout, was the key to the Cowboys draft operation. For my first NFL draft in 1987, I studied how he did things.

Each NFL team belongs to a scouting combine – a cooperative of about a dozen scouts who scrutinize every college player in America. They produce a thick book along with a printout on every school. Maybe Chappaquiddick College has a football team. Maybe they have 12 graduating seniors that year. The combine takes the time to go look at them and talk to the coach. Each player is assigned a rating number and that tells you whether they are a prospect, a suspect or a reject.

We have a workout camp in the CFL that all of the teams' staff and all the top seniors attend. The players get weighed, measured and videotaped running through various drills. It's like you're going to shove a fork in them to see if they are ready. It's amazing.

In the NFL, teams annually gathered in Indianapolis at combine workouts for five or six days to scrutinize some 325 to 350 of the best college players. One of the good things was you got to see different position groupings working out with each other. You looked at offensive linemen; then you saw the defensive linemen or receivers.

They are totally different athletes, so it's much better to see them in a situation where you can compare them with their peers performing together rather than in a normal playing or practice situation.

Every team uses the combine report to confirm its own scouting program. A team's area scouts all have an opinion. If there's a suspect in Chappaquiddick College according to the combine, your area scout will head over and have a look, if he hasn't already identified the player. He's not a prospect, usually, because everybody's heard about or identified the exceptional talent, but a suspect.

If you are the general manager or the personnel director, you survey the schools in the combine report and highlight players your scouts didn't notice – here's a guy we maybe should see. Or you use it to cross a school off a scout's itinerary – don't bother, they haven't got anybody. But everyone keeps an ear tuned.

"Gee," you hear over beers, "somebody went in to Chappaquiddick."

Someone else says they heard two guys had been in there. What's happening? Why are guys going in there? Now the scout makes a couple of phone calls and you say, "Hmmm, you know what, we better get some tape and look at this kid, then see if we have to go in there or not."

You have to be aware of what talent is out there. You don't want to be surprised on draft day when John Smith from Chappaquiddick appears on the board as a Washington Redskins pick in the third round and no one on staff knows who he is. It happens every year.

You've got to count on your area scouts to flush out the suspects and the prospects. But once they're flushed, that's when your coaching staff should be brought in to evaluate them. Gil should have allowed the coaches to go in more often and access the players. That didn't happen enough and that hobbled the Cowboys.

Why is that? Why would he not say, "Here's the top five or 10 defensive backs. We're looking for a defensive back, so why don't we have our secondary coach look at these guys and see what he thinks about them? He's going to have to coach them." I just shook my head in disbelief. The Cowboys were running an antiquated program and were fettered by bad attitudes.

Paul Hackett, several of the scouts and I constantly urged change. If we need a guy for a specific position, why not have the position coach weigh in with his opinion? We were having a lot of internal problems. Our organizational structure needed to be revamped.

Yet the Cowboys had developed some programs that were unique and worthwhile. In particular, Dallas had a player grading system that was as brilliant as it was arcane. I had to go to classroom sessions during my first training camp to learn its Byzantine intricacies. Here is a sample:

9A1 *No weaknesses, start first game, All Pro.*
2 *No weaknesses, start first game, Pro Bowl.*
8B3 *No weaknesses, start during rookie year, All Pro eventually.*
4 *No weaknesses, start during rookie year, Pro Bowl eventually.*
6D10 *No weaknesses, will overcome inconsistencies to start*
for contender.
5E22 *One weakness, back up for contender, probably never start.*
5E25 *One weakness, "star or bust," fit anywhere in sequence list.*

Free Agents
6D16 *No weaknesses, may start for non-contender, little help to contender.*
5E26 *One weakness, may start for non-contender, little help to contender.*
6D19 *No weaknesses, specialist (K, P, RSP, RSK, LS, H)*
for non-contender.
3H41 *FA: athletic ability, character and competitiveness strong points.*
3H47 *FA: size strong point.*

Everything was broken down in great detail. Complicated as it was, once you learned it, you could read off the number and know exactly what you needed to know about a player. If everyone gave that same number to a player, an 8B3, for instance, you knew it fit him to a tee, and in your mind's eye you could see exactly what he would look like and how he would perform. You could picture him and you knew exactly what he was going to do – just from the number.

Devised by scout Bob Griffin, who was a baseball fan and metrics nut, the system was very good but you had to work with it all the time to really understand it. Later, Coach Jimmy Johnson arrived with his new staff and they were flabbergasted. Once they comprehended it, it was like a light went on. They kept it.

The system evaluates and rates the player on the following criteria: character, quickness and control, competitiveness, mental alertness, strength and explosion, speed, strong points and weak points. Here is the report on a lineman taken as an offensive tackle in the fourth round:

Does not have a toned look – wide hips – developed buttocks – long arms – big feet…Bench 395, squat 505, power clean 325, vertical jump (29) … He lacks "self discipline," he cannot control his weight … he is a team leader … he does not blow his assignments.

He is a very mild-mannered young man! He has a passive personality! … If I did not view the East–West practice and game tapes I would not 'feel' he had the (mental toughness) to be a viable NFL prospect! …

He ran a very disappointing time at Indy (5.57)! He plays faster than this time! During the spring (at 336 pounds) he ran 5.37! He can run for a man of his size! He runs like 'an athlete'! … very coachable … He will 'battle a weight problem' throughout his NFL career! He is not a 'grinder'!

Scouts have a time speed and a play speed. Some guys can run fast, lift weights, and in their shorts do all the tests and look marvellous. But put them in a game and they can't play at that level. Here is the summary on the lineman:

If I did not study the East–West tapes (practice and the game) – the very best grade I could have possibly given him (as a college player – only) would have been (6D17) [No weaknesses, backup for contender, can't improve] – his college play (not his physical prowess) would not qualify him to be a prospect for a "contending team"! I was impressed by his play during the East–West practice and game tapes that I evaluated! Based on his "very improved play as a tougher player and a better technique player," I feel that he can play with a contending

team (with a grade above 6D13)! Dallas wants Big (Offensive Line-
men), but, he would be a much better player at (325) than at (356)!
Solid draft choice for Dallas – Rounds (3-4).

Grade 6D13   No weaknesses, spot play for a contender,
*   probably never start.*

We also used Mike Gidding's intelligence on players who had been
through a draft or were free agents, whether they were on a roster or
just becoming available. Mike had been a good player and a coach. I
nearly hired him years earlier when I was looking to replace Cal Murphy as coach of the B.C. Lions in late 1976. But Mike had a temper,
which is why he never got to the top of my list. I hired Vic Rapp – a
guy with a temper! But Vic controlled it other than a time or two.

Mike ran Pro Personnel Scouting, in which he compiled data on
any player you could think of: invaluable metrics, and not just how
fast an athlete runs the 40, but height, weight, body mass and a psych
report. He even included salary expectations, what players of that calibre were earning, etc. It was like having another guy in your office. It
was expensive information but worth every dollar.

I was preparing for training camp in 1987 when Tex called me
into his office. Tex was the chairman of the competition committee
and knew everything that was happening behind the scenes. He was
also discreet.

"Bobby," he said, "I think we should bring some extra guys into
training camp this year. I do believe we might see a strike."

We did.

The teams agreed that during training camp if they released a
player, that player could sign a one-page agreement for $1,000 that in
the event of a strike, he could come back. So that meant the coaches
ranked not only a starting lineup and regular backups, but they identified a potential strike team as well by selecting late cuts as players
we'd want.

Tex was shrewd. Some of the veterans whose contracts he negotiated,
knowing the strike was imminent, had signed deals with significant
amounts of money deferred. In order to qualify to receive the money

in their contract, the players were bound to play – even in a strike situation. They were outraged when they realized it. They should have seen it coming though; the conflict was inevitable.

We played on a Sunday, the day the players hit the bricks, and by Monday I had roughly 60 players in town under contract. I thought the strike team, under quarterback Kevin Sweeney, played a lot better than our regular team. We were 3–1 in strike play and the other team was a laugh.

The Washington Redskins and a couple of other clubs did a pretty good job fielding strike teams, too. It was a very unsettled time. The players picketed and called the strike players scabs. There were a lot of hard feelings because in the eyes of the players this was a counterfeit team wearing their uniforms playing in Texas Stadium. There was a lot of anger.

Coach Tom Landry didn't play the handful of veterans forced to suit up in the first games. They sat on the bench or stood sullenly on the sidelines. If they refused to dress, they forfeited large sums of money. They hated it. Worse, we got in a tight game and Landry forced them to play. It was the only game we lost, and the fans booed the shit out of them. It was a horrible day.

Still, those games counted in the regular season schedule when we came back. The strike did get settled pretty quickly. It was in no one's interest to have a prolonged walkout.

In my third season with the Cowboys, the effects of the strike and the mediocre on-field product took their toll on the box office. For the first time in anyone's memory, the Cowboys announced cutbacks. We were hemorrhaging money and the Texas economy was stagnant. Owner Bum Bright worried he might lose everything. Trucking, banking, oil – all Bum's investments – were in the dumps and he was petrified the Cowboys would drag him down. A self-made man, he had visions of losing it all. He told Tex to trim costs and the first place Tex cut was the liquor budget at training camp.

Normally, Gil had visiting college coaches come to camp and he'd take them to the local Red Barn liquor store.

"You like wine?" he'd say.

The coach would say, "Sure."

"What colour?"

Gil would buy a case or two of the most expensive wine to impress the coach. Back at the dormitory, they'd drink a bottle or two.

Billy Hicks, who was in charge of training camp, was my roommate. Tex told him to change the signing authority at the Red Barn as a result of the new austerity measures. Hicks was responsible for the bills from now on. But Hicks had been afraid to tell Gil he could no longer sign.

We were in our room and the phone rang. It was Brandt for Hicks. He was standing at the cash register at the Red Barn with a cart full of hooch and they wouldn't let him charge it.

Hicks didn't know what to do. He put his hand over the phone. "Bobby? What should I tell him? He'll go berserk!"

I told him, "Tell him it's okay this time, but from now on everything has to be approved first."

Brandt didn't take it well, but he didn't squawk too loudly, either.

—⁂—

Coach Tom Landry announced at the staff meeting on February 23 – a Thursday morning – that he'd finished his interviews for the new defensive line coach and would be making a decision over the weekend. If we had anything to add about the candidates, he said to let him know before four o'clock.

Landry was a Second World War bombing pilot and he flew to his vacation home in Austin most weekends during the off-season in his twin-engine plane. He popped by my office about 3:30 and said he just wanted to pick my brain a bit more about the coach I suggested – Don Matthews. When he left, I had the distinct feeling Don had the job and was the new defensive line coach of the Dallas Cowboys.

Great! It would be Don's stepping stone to a head coaching job in the NFL and no one was more deserving. At least, that's what I thought.

About seven o'clock, I stopped to say goodnight to Tex and let him know I was headed home. Bum was shopping the Cowboys, and I wondered if he'd heard anything.

"Naw," he drawled. "Nothing. Bum don't tell me nothing. How about giving your buddy another call in Vancouver?"

"Jimmy Pattison?"

"Yeah."

I chuckled, as he was hardly my bosom pal. I had called the B.C. billionaire a few months earlier and told him the Cowboys were on the auction block and would he be interested. He sent a couple of his lieutenants down to have a look. But nothing had come of it.

"I'll give him another call in the morning if you want."

"Sure," Tex said. "Why not?"

"Goodnight, Tex."

"See ya, Bobby."

—◆—

Kay and I were eating dinner in the TV room. The phone rang. It was Joe Bailey, one of our vice presidents, calling from New York where he was in meetings at the league office.

"Is anything going on?" he asked. He had obviously heard something.

"No, what about you?"

"Nothing. No, nothing."

Kay hollered.

"Hang on, Joe."

"They've just broken into the program, Bobby," Kay called. "They'll be doing a half-hour special later on the sale of the Dallas Cowboys."

It was nearly 10 o'clock – on a Thursday. Tex didn't know at seven o'clock; Tom didn't know before he flew to Austin. I still didn't know.

"He's apparently sold the team, Joe," I said into the phone.

"Jerry Jones," Kay shouted.

"Jerry Jones," I repeated.

"How much?" he asked.

"A reputed $140 million," Kay called.

I told him.

"Holy shit," Joe muttered. "I've got to make some calls." He hung up.

The television news was right on top of it. The promised half-hour special feature on the new owner, Jerry Jones, and the incoming coach,

Jimmy Johnson, was great. Kay and I were amazed. What did it all mean? Change to be sure. Big change.

— ⁓ —

I arrived at the office about seven o'clock the next morning and the Cowboys' parking lot was teeming with people. Security guards kept everyone out of the complex. I tried to find out what was happening, but apparently Jerry and Bum were still working on the deal.

By Saturday they had it resolved and a press conference was arranged in our 200-seat theatre for later that night. It was crammed and claustrophobic. You couldn't get into that room. I'll bet there were at least 25 ENG cameras. Crews from Los Angeles, New York, London … But Jerry would keep them waiting until about 10 p.m.

Jerry had flown his private jet to Austin to personally fire Tom Landry. It must have felt a bit like evicting *Bonanza*'s Ben Cartwright from the Ponderosa Ranch. It took Jerry longer than expected to get back, which is why the media conference was delayed. None of it should have been necessary. Bum Bright ought to have told Tex and Tom this was going down. It was a classless thing to do.

At the media show, which was carried live on radio state-wide, Tex was shuffled to the side and Jerry took centre stage. You could tell he relished every second of the limelight. It was all about him.

— ⁓ —

Tom Landry came into the office on Sunday and I helped him pack his things. On Monday, returning players arrived for a mini-camp. Tom came in again and broke the news to them personally. It was a teary goodbye. We sent the athletes home and cancelled the camp. The assistant coaches were told they were finished.

Later, Coach Landry sent me a goodbye letter for my resume. It began, "To whom it may concern …"

He really was not a very warm man.

— ⁓ —

On Tuesday, we were back in the press theatre for another carnival-like media event: Coach Jimmy Johnson had arrived in Dallas. There might have been even more cameras to record the event than we squeezed into the room to introduce the new owner.

I introduced myself to Jimmy afterwards and we hit it off.

This was his first NFL job after coaching the national champion University of Miami team, and Jimmy was bringing in his own staff. They would arrive in the next week or so. I had five days with him, one on one, talking about free agency and things he didn't know about that were integral to understanding how the NFL functioned.

Free agency was a concept that grew out of the players' strike as a way of giving the players something in the run-up to a league-wide salary cap. It was a complicated arrangement but basically it allowed teams to protect a certain number of players and the rest were allowed to sell their services to the highest bidder. Most of the really good players left unprotected already had been signed. But, as I explained to Jimmy, Dallas had not signed anyone because while the team was up for sale Bum would not authorize any new contracts. We needed to make some moves quickly.

One of the players we had to move on was safety Ray Horton. He was in his late 20s but still had a few years left, I told Jimmy, and we could get him for a decent price. Trouble was, he was heading for Hawaii for a holiday and I wanted to get the deal signed before he left. Deals like that have a way of going south.

"I'm going to fly to Seattle and meet him at the airport to get the deal signed."

Jimmy agreed.

The next morning, he looked at me as if I were an apparition. "I thought you were going to Seattle to sign Horton?"

"Yeah," I nodded. "I flew there late afternoon, met him, signed the deal and flew back on the red-eye."

He grinned. Jimmy, I came to learn, liked people who worked hard and were loyal. It secured my future with him.

—⚬⚬—

Jerry Jones held his first staff meeting a week or so after he arrived and promised no more coaching-staff style wholesale firings. He had axed all of the coaches on his arrival and a lot of people on the business side of the Cowboys thought he planned to do the same in their area. Most didn't realize that was the custom in football – the assistants are usually fired with the coach. But Jerry at least moved to ease those fears. He would not guarantee lifetime employment but he at least made those who were anxious feel better. He said he needed those of us left on the football side to teach him about pro football and also to get the Cowboys back on track.

Funny, Jerry eventually fired everyone or almost everyone in the room within a few months. But it wasn't wholesale: he mainly did it one at a time. Most of the football people were gone quickly. Some left of their own accord. Joe Bailey, vice president of administration, went with Tex to the World League of American Football. I was one of the very few who stayed.

I didn't have a green card so my status in the U.S. was precarious and dependent on my job. I decided I wasn't going to stand behind the door or hide in my office. Right from the get-go, I attended all of Jimmy's staff meetings. In fact, Dave Wannstedt said to me after a while that I was the only person Jimmy had ever allowed to sit at his right hand. He didn't allow anyone to sit in that spot for some reason.

I did the same with Jerry. In fact, several weeks after that first staff meeting, I got a chance to sit with him and talk about negotiations with Troy Aikman, our number-one draft pick, and his agent, Leigh Steinberg. Jerry said they sat up until 5 a.m. talking. It sounded good.

Steinberg was the model of the good agent in the Tom Cruise movie *Jerry Maguire*. You could trust him. His book, *Winning with Integrity*[1], is filled with the kind of advice I'd dispense, especially with its emphasis on core values.

We finished and I asked Jerry if he saw me fitting into his organization and if so, where?

"Absolutely, Bobby," he said. "Right where you are – pro personnel."

"I'll work my butt off for you, Jerry," I said, shaking his hand.

––––—∿—––––

1 *Winning with Integrity: Getting What You're Worth Without Selling Your Soul*, by Leigh Steinberg and Michael D'Orso (Random House: New York, 1998).

Jerry and Jimmy were a very funny tag team, a true odd couple. They were the same age, 47. Both were offensive guards for the 1964 national champion Razorbacks during their sophomore year at the University of Arkansas, where Jones studied business and Johnson psychology, though Jimmy insisted they were never buddies. They roomed together because of where their names came in the alphabet. When Jerry bought the team, Jimmy was the only coach he wanted. They were a strange pair. I reported to Jerry about money and to Jimmy about personnel.

Jimmy and I worked very closely together. He changed the culture of the Cowboys. He flattened the hierarchy and opened up the process. A lot more opinions were expressed and much better choices were made because more opinions were canvassed. We now had more eyes looking at people and talent. That was good.

Make no mistake, Jimmy made the final decisions. But the process was more transparent. It wasn't Gil Brandt scrubbing some guy's chances by insinuating a drug habit or a character flaw. Jimmy didn't stand for innuendo. If you said something about a guy, Jimmy wanted the evidence.

There were also revelations. Brandt always talked about Jimmy as if he were his best friend, "Oh, I stay at Jimmy's house when I go south to Florida."

Everybody thought that Brandt and Jimmy were tight. They weren't. Brandt disappeared around the time the ownership changed and no one knew why. The rumour was he was lying low because he was part of the deal with Jerry Jones. He wasn't.

"Everybody thinks Gil and I are close," Jimmy told me. "We're not close."

He said Gil would come to the University of Miami and be seen on the sidelines at his games because they were national champions and always on television. Brandt was a good friend of the president of the university. He'd come, strut around practice for a few minutes, back and forth, and then head to dinner with the president, Jimmy said.

I found out that was Brandt's modus operandi. He'd drop in, make a big splash, be seen by the coaches and the players – "Gil Brandt of the Dallas Cowboys, harrumph, harrumph" – go to the game, appear on TV and have dinner with the president. He was a likeable guy if you didn't work with him.

My secretary, a Greek woman, Tula Johnapolus, who was with the Cowboys for years, told stories about how she would quit or Gil would fire her every two months when she was assigned to him. She was a great old gal and told me he would yell at her up one side and down the other if she made a mistake. He blamed her for everything. But Gil didn't make mistakes.

We had first pick in the draft that year but it didn't require a genius to figure out what to do. Aikman was sitting there. Talk about being in the right place at the right time. What luck! Jimmy always said he didn't believe in luck. But how would you like to be a rookie coach coming into the NFL and there's Troy Aikman waiting for you? If that's not luck, what is?

I don't think there is any question that Jimmy's first truly big decision was that October – to trade Herschel Walker. Jerry, Jimmy and I worked on the deal for the Cowboys while Minnesota president and general manager Mike Lynn alone handled their end of it (apparently without telling anyone else) and then, of course, there was Herschel's agent, Peter Johnson. At the time, Johnson was perhaps the most influential agent in the U.S.

The genesis of the deal was a Cleveland Browns game. They lost their big running back, Kevin Mack, during a Monday night telecast. Everyone in the league who was watching knew immediately as they watched him go down that the Browns would have to replace their Mack Truck or abandon their drive for the Super Bowl. They were a favourite and weren't going to throw in the towel. I knew they'd be calling us, so I phoned Jimmy and asked him if he would trade Herschel.

"In a New York minute," he replied.

Sure enough, the next morning about 10 o'clock, Jimmy got a call from the Browns. But they insisted they needed a decision before the end of the day.

"Anyone else who might have an interest?" he asked me after he got off the phone.

We reviewed the rosters of the other NFL teams that were posted on my office wall. Minnesota had an undersized running back, Darrin Nelson. A good running back, but he was a little guy. The Vikings could use a power back like Herschel, I said.

Jimmy picked up the phone and called Lynn.

"We've had an expression of interest in Herschel Walker," he said. "We thought the Vikings might be interested in him, too. So we thought we'd give you a call."

You could hear Lynn practically salivating.

"Oh, yeah," he said after a long moment's silence. "We might have an interest in him."

"You might," Jimmy said, grinning at me. "Well, here's the thing. We've got to respond to the offer we have by the end of the day. So if you're interested, you'll have to get back to us before then … Great. We'll watch for it."

Lynn faxed us an offer within 40 minutes. It was filled with dates and it appeared complicated. I called Joel Bussert, head of player personnel at the league office, and asked him about it. He wasn't sure so I sent him the paperwork. In essence, every player offered in exchange for Herschel was also attached to a draft choice or two. We could take the player or the draft choices. The dates had to do with when the new contracts had to be registered and marked the deadline by which we had to make up our mind on each athlete. It appeared as if we could take the player, play him for the remainder of the season and then release him if we didn't like him and pick up the Viking draft choice. It was a hell of a deal. I couldn't understand why Minnesota was being so generous.

We tried to squeeze more out of them.

"You guys are worse than I am," Lynn sighed.

In the end, the deal didn't change much from his initial proposal. It was one of the biggest trades in NFL history. I called Herschel and told him to come in.

"We've traded you to Minnesota," I said.

Herschel was stunned. "What?"

"We've traded you to Minnesota," I repeated.

He left the office and called his agent, Peter Johnson, who was immediately on the phone to me. Johnson launched right in. "This deal wasn't going to be the Cowboys get a handful of players, the Vikings get Herschel and the greatest running back in the game gets a plane ticket," he said: "No siree, Herschel wants his end."

Any trade deal is contingent on the player reporting to the other team and passing the physical exam. That's a key proviso. We had done the paperwork, but Johnson said Herschel wouldn't report. The deal now was suddenly transformed into a tripartite negotiation.

In the end, Jerry Jones tossed in quite a bit and Minnesota's Mike Lynn tossed in quite a bit extra, too. Jerry came up with another $1 million, 10 first-class airline tickets, the use of a Mercedes Benz, the use of a mansion ... The deal got done.

Peter Johnson was a tough negotiator, but he was not going to see the package collapse because it was still advantageous for his client. Herschel was going to go to a team that had a real shot at the Super Bowl. Dallas was going nowhere. We won one game that year.

The deal appeared set when Minnesota's Nelson said he wouldn't report. He didn't want to come to us because we didn't have a chance in the playoffs. So, I made a deal with the San Diego Chargers to send him there. But the Walker trade was contingent on none of the Minnesota players being flipped. So I had to get permission from Lynn to make the trade. He agreed, but he wanted the draft pick that was involved. We were going to get a fifth-round pick from San Diego, and I was going to give them Nelson.

"Wait a minute," Lynn said, "we'll take the fifth-round pick; you keep the sixth-round pick we were getting."

Although the deal involved six players and 12 draft picks initially, by the time Jimmy had finished wheeling and dealing, 15 teams and 55 players were connected to the trade. We immediately got linebacker Jesse Solomon, linebacker David Howard, cornerback Issiac Holt and defensive end Alex Stewart. But Emmitt Smith, safety Darren Woodson and defensive tackle Russell Maryland and others would arrive in Dallas as a result of the trade.

Minnesota never seemed to recognize we didn't care about the players. Jimmy wanted the draft picks.

"We did not mind sacrificing a few wins to upgrade the talent," Jimmy explained to Jerry later. "I looked at it this way. When you're at the bottom and you don't have any real prospects of getting better, you need to do something, even if it's wrong."

Jerry immediately sent his private jet to Minnesota to pick up the players.

Linebacker Jesse Solomon turned out to be eccentric, to say the least. I came across him and Jerry Jones in the washroom arguing over his contract. Solomon was sitting on the throne saying he wasn't going to sign it until Monday come hell or high water.

Jerry, practically spitting, stalked away fuming.

I followed in his wake telling Jerry he was a lucky son of a bitch. Jerry had negotiated the deal himself and it was way too rich. I let him go. As I sat in my office wondering if we could still get out of it, Jerry's son Stephen arrived. He had been made a Cowboys vice president at 24 when his dad took over the team.

"Why'd you let Jerry cut that deal? Why the hell would you let him do that?" Stephen asked.

"I didn't let him, Stephen," I said. "He owns the team. I told him he wasn't worth the money."

The next day, Solomon told the world he still had not signed and was sniffing at the latest offer. Other players hit the roof when they heard how much Jerry had put on the table. By the end of the weekend, Jerry and Jesse were on the phone going back and forth, back and forth. About 12:30 a.m., Jesse called me.

"Bob, what should I do?"

"Jesse, sign the fucking contract!"

"Okay," he said. "When do I show up for the physical?"

I remember him arriving to sign the contract. He was very subdued. He would not shake hands. I couldn't ever remember a time a player wouldn't shake hands, no matter how acerbic the negotiations. I eventually traded him to New England, who flipped him to Tampa Bay. He came to see me years later when I was with the Miami Dolphins. He was a completely different guy. A good guy. But in those days when he was playing – god, he was goofy.

Defensive end Stewart stayed only for a cup of coffee. He looked like Tarzan and played like Jane. Howard and Holt played well for us during the rest of the season, as did Solomon, but we didn't fall in love with them – we wanted those draft picks.

That Christmas, Jimmy gave me a pair of hand-tooled ostrich cowboy boots. Beautiful. He was the complete opposite of Landry. Warm, personal, engaging, emotional.

—⟋⟍—

We flew to the Super Bowl in New Orleans on Jerry's private plane. It was fabulous. We stayed at the Sorrento Hotel in the French Quarter. Actor Don Johnson was next door and we sat on the balcony watching him entertain his fans on Bourbon Street. San Francisco slaughtered Denver 55–10.

It was the first Super Bowl we had attended since Pasadena because of cutbacks under Bum Bright. The first of many, it turned out.

In 1991, there wasn't any room on Jerry's plane and we flew with Reece Overcash, Jr., who ran the Associates Corp. of America, the financing arm of Ford, and his wife. We became good friends and because he was on the Warner Bros. board, they often had screening parties at his board room. One night I sat beside Ross Perot munching popcorn and eating hotdogs. That year we stayed on the beach in Tampa with Jimmy and Rhonda, and Dave and Jan Wannstedt. It was great fun.

We flew to the 1992 Super Bowl with Reece as well. That year was memorable because we took our good friends Anne and Maurice Favell. Maurice was dying of cancer and it was a last wish for him. I arranged to have him accredited as "Columnist for the *Kerrisdale Courier*" – an old-time, now-defunct Vancouver paper. At super-agent Leigh Steinberg's party, Maurice got a chance to mingle with Warren Moon and Troy Aikman. He chatted with Donald Trump and Marla Maples. Gordon Forbes, NFL columnist for *USA Today*, talked with him for an hour. He cherished those memories in his final months, the pictures beside his bed.

—⟋⟍—

We had to advise Minnesota by February 1, 1990, whether we were going to keep the players or take the draft picks. We had no intention of keeping the players.

After the owners' meeting at the New Orleans Super Bowl, Mike Lynn, Jeff Diamond of the Vikings and Jerry sat at the end of a long banquet table, while Jimmy and I sat at the other end out of earshot. They talked quietly for a few minutes.

Lynn had a perpetual George Hamilton, I'm-just-in-off-the-golf-course tan even though he lived in Minnesota. I could see the colour vanishing from his face. He was a handsome man, just too smart for his own good. It was dawning on him that the trade had never been about the players – it had been about draft picks. He was snookered.

Jerry turned and called to me, "Bobby, do you have those letters?"

I opened up my briefcase and took out the sheaf of correspondence. I had a letter covering each player, copies for Lynn and copies for the league. Jimmy couldn't keep the smile off his face. Lynn was mute as he accepted the letters. He had outsmarted himself royally. He'd figured we'd fall in love with the players and he would keep his draft picks.

He had not told his head coach, Jerry Burns, or the team's two personnel administrators, Jerry Reichow and Frank Gilliam, before consummating the deal. They were flabbergasted. Lynn had the right to make it, but he was a non-football executive and he should have run it past them. If he had, they would have said let's try and get Herschel but don't give up all this; we can get him for half that. They might have succeeded, too.

We were the big winners. The Cowboys reaped three Super Bowls as a result of the players harvested from the deal. Herschel didn't get as much as we got, but Peter Johnson got him a lot of extras and more money. Minnesota was the big loser. They got a player who played okay but didn't lead them to the promised land. They went to the playoffs but Herschel couldn't carry them to the championship.

In the end, he played only two-and-a-half years with the Vikings and never notched a 1,000-yard season.

Minnesota fans and the media dumped all over Mike Lynn, and it eventually cost him his job. He went on to become head of the World League of American Football.

It remains one of the biggest and all-time great sports trades.

—▨—

Jimmy went 1–15 his first year, 1989. Everybody said we were going to ruin Aikman because you shouldn't throw a rookie quarterback to the NFL wolves. The press talked of Steve Bartkowski, chosen by the Atlanta Falcons as their number-one pick in 1975 and turned into a starter. He suffered through a couple of tough years before the battering took its toll. But, Jimmy pointed to Dan Marino, the Dolphins' first-round pick in 1983, who went on to win rookie of the year honours and to become the first rookie pivot to start in the Pro Bowl.

In camp, Aikman joined quarterbacks Steve Pelluer, Danny White, the 14-year veteran who had been our starter, and Scott Secules, a sophomore. Jimmy said any of them might start. He went with Troy, who went on to become a Hall of Famer.

At one game on the sidelines, retired Cowboys' quarterback great Roger Staubach came over to tell me he had met Ian Barclay, a former B.C. Lions director. Barclay thought the world of me, Roger said. I had to laugh, thinking of the report he had helped author. He also told me I had a great challenge ahead of me to turn the Cowboys around. Roger had been around the organization under Tex and Tom Landry, but I got to know him surprisingly better after Jimmy and Jerry arrived. He and Jerry became very close.

In the supplemental draft in June 1989, we took quarterback Steve Walsh. Other teams said we were out of our minds. But Jimmy had Walsh at the University of Miami and he knew what he could do for us. He also knew his worth down the road as trade bait. Although he was our backup, Steve chalked up our only win that year – at Washington, 13–3. That first win under Jimmy, you'd have thought we'd won the Super Bowl. Jerry Jones was walking on air.

The next year we traded Steve to the New Orleans Saints for a first- and third-round draft pick in 1991 and a conditional second-round pick in 1992. Jimmy had armed himself with more choices and picks. Utilizing the bounty from the Herschel Walker and Steve Walsh trades, he built his Super Bowl team. His long-range perspective and the way he always considered the big picture were an education for me. There is no easy road. To build a good team you've got to spend the time to come up with the information to make proper decisions on draft day. And the proper decisions really aren't made on draft day. They're made in the six months leading up to the draft. They are a result of hard work, not luck. You make your own luck in Jimmy's book. I learned so much from him. He was the master. The first year, I didn't play a great role but in subsequent drafts I pulled everything together and oversaw all the research. Like everyone else on the football side of the operation, however, Jimmy listened to my point of view and then made his decision.

—⁓—

Jerry changed everything in the Cowboys organization. He didn't just come in and say we're getting rid of this. He brought his own financial guy in and fired the accountant who had been there for 25 years. The new whiz examined every department and began letting people go. Why do we have five people when we could do it with three? He pared the organization back.

Jerry said to me, "You, Stephen, Jimmy and I, with half a dozen good secretaries, could run this whole operation."

That was his mentality. He'd run his own business and he was very close to the bone. For a year or so we were pretty thin, but now they're like every other NFL team. They have so much money they just keep growing and growing.

After his first draft, Jimmy fired Gil Brandt. He walked into my office and said, "Why don't you move over there. I want you to run the whole personnel department, contracts and all that. Everything."

It was quite a change. Under the previous management, Joe Bailey had done the contracts, Gil did college scouting and I did pro personnel. That was combined and I handled everything to do with football operations. I worked with Jimmy, but I also reported to Jerry on contractual issues.

We didn't change our scouting system, but we integrated the assistant coaches into the process. We began with the combine report on roughly 14,000 college players; our scouts whittled that down to maybe 2,000 suspects and prospects, and we would streamline that 2,000 to maybe 400 players on our board for draft day – the 400 we thought might be able to play in the NFL. Of those, our coaches would evaluate maybe 200, the players we were really interested in drafting. It was a process of elimination.

Jimmy sat with each individual area scout and went through a large binder containing a page of data on each player under consideration. For each top player, there could be five or six assessments – the combine report, the area scout's perspective, the regional scout's view, a cross-over double check by another regional scout, and the national scout's opinion. Jimmy listened and highlighted his copy of the final report on the player. Occasionally, he would remove a page from the binder. In his mind, that guy couldn't play for us.

Jimmy didn't do his review with all the scouts present. He talked to them one at a time. Some people are quiet and some are animated, he explained. If one scout was more animated about a player from his area than another scout, in a group meeting the animated person will win out because he is naturally more adamant that his guy can play. Jimmy said he needed to hear everyone's point of view, not just those adept at group dynamics. He was exceptionally thoughtful about everything he did – even his temper tantrums.

As we got closer to the draft, Jimmy would have everyone in the room with a wallboard grid covered with index cards. Each player had an individual card. They were arranged by position and draft round.

On the top tier, round one, there were 16 to 18 players whose grades said they were first-round material. There were 28 or 29 picks in the first round that year, but in our opinion, only 16 or 18 of the prospects were truly first-round material. Next, we had the second-round players and there might be 35 of those. As we moved down the grid to the later rounds, there were more and more players.

Every day for about six weeks, Jimmy and the rest of us sat in the room and moved the cards around and talked about the players until we had them in what we all thought was the right order. If we didn't have enough information, we sent someone to take another look. It was a very expensive and protracted process to narrow the choices down to the guys we wanted to consider for the draft.

Once we went through that board, position by position, and we had everyone in position with their number, we created another list of names – the best players. Who is the best player on that list? There is the player with the highest grade. Is he the best player? You argue that. You finally decide that, okay, here's the best player, you move him over to first place; he's number one. Then who's the second-best player?

It might take you two hours to get the best player up there. Then you do the next. And so on. Then you colour code the cards: he's the best player but he has a character issue, an injury, a drug problem, or an attitude.

You leave flagged players on the list even though it means you are probably not going to take them. You leave them up there so you can assign them to one of the other teams if he's taken and you know why you weren't interested.

Jimmy was a specialist in psychology so he always thought he could handle players who had a problem or two. But I gave him credit, if they didn't change – snap – they were gone. Jimmy had no trouble admitting he had made a mistake. Mistakes? We all make them. That was his attitude. Fix them and get on with it.

It was refreshing after three years of the old Cowboy system. His draft preparation process was so thorough we ended up with some amazing talent that left everyone scratching their heads. How did we know about these guys? How did we find guys like Leon Lett, Tony Tolbert … ? Hard work.

Jimmy also could say, other coaches won't look at that guy, but I can make him a player. Most of the time, he could. From where I sat, he was worth every penny Jerry paid him, and Jerry paid him well. That year, 1990, Jimmy got $1.433 million. Dan Reeves at Denver was pulling down $985,000, while a lot of NFL coaches were earning between $300,000 and $500,000. Marty Schottenheimer was getting $593,000, John Robinson $537,000. Don Shula raked in $1,090,000. That's a lot of money, sure, but you figure one guy, Jimmy Johnson, was earning a million and a half. Nearly half a million more than the next closest guy – and he was worth it.

Jimmy hated training camp at Thousand Oaks because it was always cool in the morning on the coast. It took hours for the sun to burn off the haze and really warm the air. By the afternoon it was quite hot. But Jimmy didn't like it, so he moved the training facilities to Austin and it was hot, hot, hot. Jimmy loved that.

We also began to draw 5,000 to 6,000 people to practice, which wasn't necessarily a good thing. For one, Jimmy and Jerry were prone to arguing on the field. Trainer Kevin O'Neal, Tony Wise, Dave Wannstedt and two or three others on staff came to me and said I had to do something about this.

My routine was to go out and join Jimmy as the team started to warm up. On this particular day, we were talking about what was happening around the league, whether anyone was looking to move a player, things like that.

Jerry drove up in his golf cart, got out and walked towards us. Jimmy immediately walked down the field and made as if he needed to discuss something with one of the coaches. Jerry followed, trailing about 25 yards. Jimmy stopped to talk to the defensive line coach, but when he saw Jerry get within 10 or 12 yards, Jimmy briskly walked away, heading for the receiver coach. He stopped there and the same scene ensued. Jerry approached and got within 10 or 12 yards, Jimmy scurried away to another group on the field.

It didn't take long for the press and the spectators to realize what was going on. There was a ton of media. And it was comical. But eventually Jerry caught up with him and he and Jimmy just had it out with each other. It was very ugly.

A day or so later, I talked to Jerry on the field. I told him that I thought he had something special in Jimmy Johnson. My philosophy is the most important individual in professional football is the head coach, I said. I emphasized that with Jerry. If the job is going to get done, he's the guy that's going to get it done. We can all do our parts and help, but he is essential. If you look around the NFL, there are a lot of guys who can't get the job done and who never get the job done. That's why there are so many changes in head coaches.

At one time they would give a coach five years. Not anymore. They know within two years whether a guy is going to be a winner. And really, it's a gut feeling. You're all working towards putting it all together and if you are observant enough you can see what's happening and the progress you're making. Jimmy was definitely making progress with the Cowboys in his second year.

I told Jerry he really had a chance to be part of something special. Jimmy could see the big picture, and a lot of guys don't. The dividends of the Herschel Walker and Steve Walsh trades were coming through.

Jerry and I stood on the field for 20 to 30 minutes. Kay thinks that was the beginning of the end for me with Jerry. I had declared myself Jimmy's guy and Jerry couldn't abide that. I thought I was a Dallas Cowboys guy. Their relationship hadn't exploded, but the timer was ticking.

—⚏—

In the pre-season, Jerry, Stephen, Jimmy and I were having a beer in Jerry's office. His secretary poked her head in the door and said, "Charlie Pride is here to see you, Jerry."

"Have him come in," Jerry said as we all turned to see the country singing legend.

Charlie joined us and we shared a few laughs. He had tickets in front of Kay at the games. She told me he and his family came to most games and were totally nice people. But Charlie explained he was waiting for his tickets this year and when they didn't arrive, he called Gil Brandt. Charlie said that Gil had initially arranged for him to buy his tickets, and he'd been buying them for 15 years.

"Mr. Jones, I've been a great Cowboys fan for years and I've had these tickets for years. I've always bought them. I said, 'Gil, the tickets I've been buying for 15 years through you.' He said, 'Oh those weren't your tickets; those were my tickets.'"

Jerry blanched. The rest of us looked at our shoes.

"I just wanted to come in here and say I'm still a Cowboys fan, buddy," Charlie said, "but I'd like to purchase those tickets again."

Jerry assured him he'd straighten it out. Kay told me Charlie and his family were back in their seats that season.

—⚏—

We began to see improvements in Jimmy's second season. We went 7–9 in the NFL's toughest division, the NFC East. So to win seven games in your second year when you've never coached in the NFL before – that's astounding. By the third year, we were 11–5 and in second place in the NFC East. We beat Philly 25–13 in Philadelphia to clinch our first playoff berth, the first playoff since I came to Dallas in 1986. Was the plane ride home ever nice!

The 1991 NFL season was my most enjoyable in my six years with the Dallas Cowboys. We had put together a competitive team headed in the right direction. Since joining the Cowboys in 1986 all the hard work was starting to pay off.

We played the first NFL playoff game of my career in Chicago. We faced the Bears on a frigid Sunday. Four times the Bears knocked on our goal line but crossed only once. They looked like a tired football club and we held Neal Anderson to only 34 yards rushing. I thought Bill Bates made the key play with an interception late in the game that stopped their drive. It was an upset win, 17–13, and a poor performance by Mike Ditka's team.

(The evening was memorable, too, because George Wendt, who played Norm Peterson on the sitcom *Cheers*, a quintessential Chicago fan, came to our locker room and said hello. I remember he had the good grace to take off his Bears jacket before coming in.)

We went into Detroit the following week with the belief that, who knows, we might possibly take another step towards a Super Bowl. It was not to be. We lost to the Lions – a very disappointing loss, 38–6. Their quarterback Erik Kramer hit wide-receiver Willie Green for a touchdown and Detroit romped the rest of the way. They were up 17–6 at the half. I still remember Barry Sanders, their great back, making a half-field dash, 47 yards through the heart of our defence, in the fourth quarter for a touchdown. It was a hell of a run.

In the locker room afterwards, Jimmy surprised everyone. The room was extremely quiet. Morose even. You didn't want to shuffle your feet or sip a soda for fear of disturbing the mood. Jimmy stood in the middle of the room. It fell silent.

As a team, we had arrived with visions of the Super Bowl dancing in our heads. We were massacred 38–6. We were not in the game from that opening strike. Everyone expected Jimmy to explode. He was such a volatile guy. We all expected him to rant and rave. At the end of a game, a loss is so demoralizing, so depressing. A playoff loss magnifies that by its sheer impact. It's abrupt, it's the end, it's final. And there's nothing you can do until next year.

We expected Jimmy to tee off on a tirade about it. He didn't. Jimmy was somber. He spoke quietly, not loudly. Some coaches might have turned the moment into something maudlin, sentimental and false. They would have unpacked the clichés – "We've faced a lot of adversity blah, blah, blah." Not Jimmy.

Amid the topsy-turvy of used towels, sweat-soaked pads, jerseys, pants, scuffed helmets and the closely assembled mass of battered, exhausted human flesh, Jimmy remained silent for an eternity. When he did speak, he spoke with the solemnity of a man in a chapel.

The season had come to an end too soon, especially for a team with such promise, such potential for greatness. He looked around the room slowly, acknowledging this beaten warrior and then another with a nod, not saying anything, just catching each man's eye. Looking into the faces etched with overwhelming feelings of failure, he asked each of them to recognize their own achievement and their achievement as a team. "You went into Soldier Field and beat the Bears! This is only the beginning. This moment," he said, "this moment, remember it. It is not an ending; it is not a defeat. It is another step on the road that leads inexorably to the Super Bowl and greatness as a football team. You are on that road."

I won't forget the speech. To me, that talk planted firmly in the minds of those players the unshakeable belief that they were a good team, and they could be a great football team. From that moment forward they began to honestly believe in themselves. Jimmy's speech was awe inspiring and set the tone for the Cowboys' first Super Bowl win the following season. And it came after a loss.

Jimmy was the master: he knew when to set the standard and the mark and he knew when he had to be vocal. He would make an example of a guy just to make everyone sit up and take notice. In the doldrums of training camp, he would do something that would make everyone think, "Oh, I better pick it up or I'll get my ass in trouble." He was a volatile guy who controlled his emotions. He was the master.

—ᴍ—

Immediately after the playoff run I began preparing for the player draft and Plan B-Free Agency deals. There is not much time off between football seasons.

I kept waiting for Jerry to arrive with my playoff share, which was an agreed on amount. It did not happen. He had not mentioned anything about a share for the scouting staff, either. I had a relatively close working relationship with Jerry, so I brought it up with him on my way home at the end of a day.

He stated he did not intend to pay the playoff shares.

I indicated all NFL teams pay their scouts and personnel people playoff shares or a portion of a playoff share. "You're not being fair," I said.

Jerry shot back, "Life's not fair."

End of conversation.

—◦◦◦—

I joined the coaches, scouts and personnel staff in Mobile, Alabama, for the Annual Senior Bowl College All-Star Game. The game pits the best in the country against each other and it is an important showcase. You have a chance to evaluate the players at twice-a-day practices under the very best coaches – each team is coached by a top NFL team's staff. You can visit with the players and get a feel for their personalities and characters. It also gives the management, coaches and scouts an opportunity to let their hair down and have some fun.

Jerry, Jimmy, Stephen and I, along with numerous others from our staff and anyone who wanted to get in on the action, would meet in the bar after the last practice of the day. On the first day, I received a telephone call from Murray Pezim, then owner of the B.C. Lions, asking me to let him put my name forward for the vacant CFL commissioner's position.

He had called during our playoff preparation and I told him I would not even consider it until after our season ended. But here he was on the phone again. I really did not have an interest in the commissioner's job, but as a favour to Murray I agreed to talk with the steering committee. Kay very much opposed my even considering the move.

I told Jerry about the phone call. He said he wished someone would offer him a commissioner's position. He gave me his blessing and encouragement. As usual, Jerry and I closed the bar and as we headed to the elevator, he put his hand on my shoulder and said, "Bob, I want you to be with the Cowboys. We need you to be with the Cowboys, but go check out the CFL job."

Later in the week, Jerry asked me if I wanted to join Jimmy, Stephen and him after the practice for the flight back to Dallas on his private jet. That was a non-question. Of course, I said.

Upon arriving at Love Field in Dallas, we were all a little inebriated. Jerry reiterated what he had told me at the hotel: the Cowboys and Jerry Jones needed Bob Ackles. Kay picked me up and he said the same to her. She and I talked about the future as we drove home. It seemed bright. Life was good.

—⁂—

Over the following weeks, I had a couple of conversations with Jerry and Jimmy about the importance of scouting if we wanted to build a dynasty. I emphasized again with Jerry that sharing playoff bonus money with the personnel staff was expected. He bristled. I probably should not have brought it to his attention again, I figured.

On February 18, I flew to Toronto to meet with the CFL selection committee about the commissioner's job. I didn't get it. I probably dodged a bullet.

—⁂—

At the end of April 1992, I found Jimmy and Jerry nose to nose. I thought they were going to start swinging. Both were raging. The draft was due to start within the hour. We didn't need these two going at it. Jerry stormed past me.

"You okay?" I asked Jimmy.

"Yeah. He's an asshole!" he snapped, indicating Jerry's disappearing back. "When the cameras are on our table he wants to lean over and have it look like he's making the call. Fuck him."

Jimmy saw himself as the architect of a football team that was destined to be one of the best in NFL history. He didn't want to share the credit.

"Jimmy, he owns the team."

"Fuck him."

He stormed away towards the parking lot. I wasn't sure he was coming back. I went back to our draft room and waited. Eventually I told Dave Wannstedt to go get him. He talked Jimmy into returning. They made it look good for the TV cameras, but they didn't so much sort out their differences as agree to bury the hatchet for the moment.

That year we drafted Emmitt Smith. Joe Brodsky was the coach who brought him to us. He looked at every game Emmitt played in high school and college. He knew this kid inside out. Jimmy asked him what he thought and Brodsky virtually stood on the table. Emmitt Smith! Emmitt Smith! Emmitt Smith! He was so high on Emmitt, he said there was no way we could choose anyone else. This guy will be the best in the league, he predicted.

Hmmm. Emmitt was kind of small. Not as speedy a guy as you might want. He was not a 4.3 guy. But Joe was emphatic: this is the guy. And he did turn out to be the best. I think Jimmy was lucky that Emmitt appeared when he did. I remember calling Emmitt at home just before we put him up on the board.

"This is Bob Ackles, player personnel director of the Dallas Cowboys. Emmitt, how would you like to be a Dallas Cowboy?" I asked.

"I'd love to be a Dallas Cowboy," Emmitt said.

I asked for his agent's number, rang off and told Jimmy to give him a call. Emmitt was a product of the Walker trade. It was beginning to pay big dividends. He rushed 241 times for 937 yards and scored 11 touchdowns as a rookie. He was as good as Brodsky predicted.

Aikman also began maturing. In his sophomore year, he made 399 attempts and 226 completions for a respectable 57 per cent completion rate, 2,579 yards, 11 touchdowns and 18 interceptions. That's a 2.8 touchdown ratio and a 4.5 turnover rate. We were still throwing too many interceptions, but Troy was starting to develop.

We had a couple of decent receivers. Michael Irvin only caught 20 balls that year because of an injury. But Kelvin Martin caught 64. Jay Novachek was a plan B free agent I signed and he turned out to be the best receiving tight end in the NFL. Arizona let him go and I snatched him as quick as I could. Why is that team in last place all the time? Dumb things like that. Novachek had a bit of a back problem but his biggest problem with the Cardinals according to the word on the street, was that the owner, Bill Bidwill, Sr., didn't like him. We signed him and he was a draft horse in the Cowboys' runs to the Super Bowl.

But Jerry and Jimmy were having ego problems. They were head-butting all the time. The business side of the Dallas Cowboys was coming together as fast as the football team, and Jerry wanted some of the credit. He did as good a job on the business side as Jimmy did on the football side.

But people liked Jimmy more. Jimmy is a genuine guy. If he takes you into his circle, you're going to have a good time. He's sincere; he's doing it because he likes you. You'll have a good time with Jerry, too, but Jerry usually does it for a reason. He wants something. That's why he dishes up steak and lobster. He's a likeable guy. He just tries too hard. And he so wanted to be the general manager that he finally gave himself the title – owner, president and general manager.

For some time now, the media were aware that Jimmy and Jerry were butting heads. Everyone knew Jerry owned the franchise, but Jimmy assumed all the credit for putting together the outstanding team. Rightly so, I thought. I guess I was too much of a Jimmy guy and not enough of a Jerry guy.

On May 21, 1992, a month after the draft, I got the call to come see Jerry in his office. No sooner had I settled into the couch than the meeting ended abruptly. "You're outta here."

I was certainly angry when I left his office. I really could have given him that shot in the head. But again, sometimes things happen in life that allow you to keep things in perspective. Jack Mills, an agent, was waiting to see me about Chad Hennings.

In 1988 the Cowboys had taken a gamble and drafted Chad, a great big defensive lineman, in the penultimate round. He was in the Air Force and wasn't going to be able to play for us until he got out. That's why no one else had taken him. We signed Chad to a contract, gave him a little bonus, and then suspended him until his discharge. That way his rights remained with us and he didn't become a free agent.

Chad served four years as the pilot of an A-10 Thunderbolt. Dubbed "the Warthog," the Thunderbolt was a specially designed jet for destroying tanks, armoured vehicles and providing close support for ground troops. Chad flew sorties in Gulf War One. During Operation Provide Comfort in Northern Iraq, he earned two medals and a humanitarian award for flying 45 relief missions to support Kurdish refugees. He was a courageous and inspirational young man. At 27, he was starting a promising professional football career that would span nine seasons!

Jack, his agent, had come to renegotiate Chad's contract, as the 1988 deal was long out of date. Beside Chad's experience, my own situation didn't seem quite so catastrophic.

"You sure you're okay, Bob?" Jack asked.

"Just fine, Jack."

I called Jerry, explained the situation to him and said Jack was coming over.

"You understood what I said, didn't you?" Jerry growled. "You're still outta here."

"Yes, Jerry, I understood," I replied.

I hung up. Jack shook my hand and headed over to see Jerry. I called Kay.

I really should have stopped talking about the scouts and their playoff share. That night was Johnny Carson's last stand. Robin Williams and Bette Midler were the final guests. Kay and I decided to take a holiday.

NFL Menagerie: Cardinals and Eagles

Phoenix, Arizona
June 10, 1992

SITTING IN a Phoenix hotel registered under an assumed name didn't bode well. But there I was. I had been mulling several options in the wake of being fired. I even toyed with the idea of becoming a player agent. I was still considering it when Arizona Cardinals General Manager Larry Wilson called. I didn't know him well. He had been a great player with the team when it was still in St. Louis and I had chatted with him a couple of times at league meetings.

"I'd like to talk to you about something," he told me on the phone, "but this has to be kept extremely confidential. I can't even tell you on the phone what it's about. But if you could come to Phoenix, we can talk about it."

It sounded like something out of Dashiell Hammett. Now Kay and I were checked in as Bob and Kay Francis, Kay's maiden name.

We met Larry and his wife Nancy for dinner and we learned a little more. Larry wanted to fire the team's director of college scouting and hire me. George Boone had been with the club for years. He was a surrogate father and mentor to Bill Bidwill, Jr., the owner's son who worked in the scouting department. Cardinal draft picks had been the butt of jokes in player personnel circles for years for producing seven consecutive losing seasons.

If I were interested in taking over, Larry said, we'd have lunch the next day with the owner, Bill, Sr.

I said sure.

Bidwill, Sr., was a different kind of a guy. He seemed introverted to me, occupying his own space and looking at things from a unique perspective, to say the least. He, Larry and I had a nice lunch but really didn't talk much about the Cardinals or what was being contemplated. After Bill left, Larry drove Kay and me to the airport.

"I'll be in touch," he said. "But secrecy is imperative … if word ever leaks out anywhere, the whole deal is off. Bill's favourite saying is 'loose lips sink ships.' He lives by that. He doesn't want people outside the organization knowing anything."

Right, loose lips sink ships. Strange.

Larry called a week later and said I had the job.

I flew to Phoenix, Larry picked me up at the airport and told me to come into the office about 10 the next morning – they still hadn't fired George Boone!

Larry greeted me the following day and quickly left to go fire George, who apparently had been on vacation. Larry came back and led me downstairs to meet the media. Very strange.

Bill Jr. never did get over the way they treated Boone and didn't want anything to do with me. In spite of the intrigue and weird behaviour, I enjoyed working with Larry and the Cardinals' head coach, Joe Bugle. I thought Joe had one of the best coaching staffs I had seen. A couple went on to become head coaches and coordinators. Yet the Cardinals had difficulty winning.

We were in the toughest conference at the time, the NFC East – Dallas, the Giants, Washington, Philadelphia and us. So the Cardinals were always struggling. They had moved from St. Louis to Arizona in 1988. But someone gave them bad intelligence about the local market.

Bidwill set ticket prices too high and turned everybody off before they even had time to have a honeymoon with the team. The stadium at Arizona State University, where the team initially played, was terrible. One side was in the sun, so you had a tough time selling tickets because it was a broiler. People stood under the stands until kickoff, ran out, watched the first half and then disappeared again until second-half kickoff. Worse, we didn't have a great team. Season-ticket sales had fallen to 21,000 from 55,000, the second-lowest in the NFL, ahead of only New England at the time.

It was also an odd organization in the sense that it reflected Bidwill's personality and style, and he took advice from people who seemed to me to be eccentric. I was not sure the Cardinals could ever win the Super Bowl under his ownership. Bidwill had been in football all his life, but he didn't have a clue. How does that happen? He didn't have any football common sense. He didn't seem to have a huge ego. He was sort of a hermit who sat in his office, a sprawling office, piled with stuff. He'd pop into my office once in a while and tell a joke. But usually his jokes weren't particularly funny.

One of his main advisors was Benny Greenberg, who had been with him for years. Benny was probably worth $25 to $30 million. He was into his 70s and still managed the video for the Cardinals. In St. Louis, he owned a camera store and did the film work for the team when it was there. Around the league they joked that our video was the worst because it went the way of Benny's eyesight. He also owned a lot of real estate downtown, which was the source of his fortune.

Benny had Bidwill's ear. When the team moved, Benny moved with it. The coaches used to quip that Benny ran the franchise; if Benny doesn't like you ... watch out. Whenever Bidwill was going to fire somebody, he talked to Benny first. He was a good old guy, but he didn't know shit about football. Still, Benny and his wife and Kay and I got along just great. As far as I could see, one of Bidwill's key lawyers was the same – thick about football. But he had Bidwill's other ear.

Dick Mallory, Bidwill's lawyer in Phoenix, returned from a Super Bowl where he met Roger Staubach. Roger, who was my friend, told him apparently that I was one of the best football men in the country. What else? After being treated like chopped liver, I immediately became steak in his eyes. This guy thought I was something special because Roger told him so. Roger and I were friends, you know; how superficial is that? It was a strange, strange situation.

The first Monday night game of the new 1992 season – my 40th in professional football – Kay and I were upset to watch the Dallas Cowboys so handily thrash the Washington Redskins 23–10. Emmitt Smith had a fantastic game – his fourth consecutive 100-yard-plus effort.

God, he could run. Michael Irvin played up to par, which means magnificently. Aikman dominated … All night long, the Cowboys were in Redskins quarterback Mark Rypien's face, sacking him twice and putting him on his back more often. Washington gained only 75 yards rushing. And there – wow – safety Ray Horton shutting down Washington's last-ditch effort, breaking up the play in the end zone. It was an impressive performance. They were a great team.

Kay and I felt we should be in Dallas reaping the benefits belonging to a team on the way to the Super Bowl. We weren't unhappy in Phoenix. It just didn't seem *fair*. Here we were with a so-so team. Most of the Cowboys were players I helped sign. Ray Horton was the first guy we signed as a Plan B free agent, right after Jimmy arrived. We signed the contracts in the Seattle airport as he and his family headed to Hawaii. Now Kay and I were starting again.

Right off the bat with the Cardinals, three losses – including one in Dallas (ouch!), 31–20, one to the Eagles, 31–14, and one in Tampa Bay, 23–7. We never did get on track. We finished the season an abysmal 4–12.

We should have done better. The Cowboys won the Super Bowl as Kay and I knew they would. Bidwill took three weeks deciding to give Larry Wilson and Joe Bugle new contracts. But he did the right thing in spite of pressure from the media and fans to dump Joe after such a dismal season. They wanted him to hire Dan Reeves or Mike Ditka, who had won Super Bowls and were available.

Kay and I moved into our new home thinking we might have to move again if things didn't settle down with Bidwill. During a losing spell, you need a winning tradition to fall back on. We had it in Dallas. It was a problem here. Show me a team that can't turn it around and I'll show you a team that keeps changing personnel. We needed players and we needed time to let the young guys stay, grow and improve. Trouble is, when you are losing, you don't have time – everybody wants it now.

My first full draft with the Cardinals in 1993 was a huge success. Most people in the NFL considered the Cardinals to have made the best moves in the league that year. Our preparation was exceptionally good thanks to the work of our scouts and assistant coaches.

We drafted four of the top 32 players we had identified and placed

The Miami Dolphins' War Room, 1998. Drafting players with Jimmy was always exciting; this photo shows the calm side, searching for a gem. Left to right: Me, Jimmy Johnson, Tom Bratz, Tom Heckert and Scout Anthony Hunt; in rear, Trainer Kevin O'Neill, and Jimmy's lawyer and good friend Nick Christin.

Heading to the Bahamas, Spring 1998. Jimmy was always generous with his friends, some of whom are gathered here on Jimmy's 53-foot Ocean, *Three Rings* (named for his three championship rings as head coach, two Super Bowls and one National Collegiate Championship).

Beginning of pre-game warm-up at Pro Player Stadium, Miami, in 1999 with Fred Owens, one of my two former high-school football coaches. Fred and his wife Ann gave me a place to live for my senior year of high school.

Fun in Las Vegas in the kitchen at Gallagher's Restaurant, New York New York Hotel, 1998. We always stayed at Caesars and hit some other spots. Back row left to right: Dave and Jan Wannstedt (Head Coach, Chicago Bears), Rhonda and Jimmy Johnson (Head Coach, Miami Dolphins). Front row left to right: Nancy and Norv Turner (Head Coach, Washington Redskins), Kay and Bob Ackles (Director of Football Operations, Miami Dolphins).

My induction into the Canadian Football Hall of Fame in September 2002. With four great guys, and pretty good players as well. Left to right: Bob Ackles, Roger Aldag, Paul Bennett, Les Browne, Ray Elgaard.

My induction into the British Columbia Sports Hall of Fame in 2004. Left to right: (rear) Robert Ackles, Theresa Ackles, Scott Ackles, Steve Ackles, Kyle Ackles, (front) Ashley Ackles, Bob Ackles, Kay Ackles, Sherri Ackles.

A day of relaxation with Kay on Jimmy Johnson's boat, June 1997. Always a great day of cruising, fishing and snorkeling.

A proud father with his two sons. Steve, Scott and me.

These are the nicest young people I know: our grandchildren in 2004. Left to right: Robert Ackles (holding Kasey Ackles), Kyle Ackles, Robyn Ackles, Ashley Ackles (holding Robyn).

My hobbies – oil painting, photography, book collecting and reading – and there's never enough time to enjoy them. This is a self-portrait of me painting in our home in Las Vegas where I attended the UNLV Fine Arts Program in 2001.

On our 40-foot boat *Waterbuoy* in the Gulf Islands, British Columbia. Two days on the water is as good as a week in Maui. Kay does all the docking and I am the deck hand; she does a better job than most men I see and with no bow thrusters.

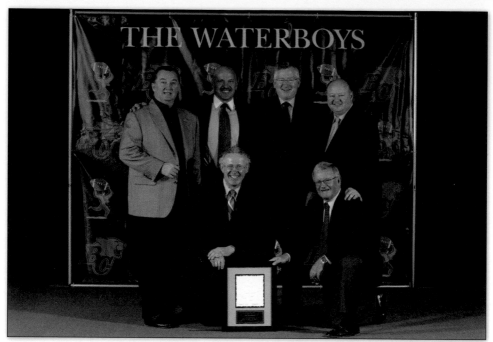

The Founders of the Waterboys, a group of business leaders that did community outreach on behalf of the BC Lions in Vancouver. Here, minus Jamie Pitblado, at the Commissioner's Ring presentation to the group. Left to right (back): Moray Keith, George Chayka, Tom Malone, Dennis Skulsky. Left to right (front): Tom Wright (CFL Commissioner 2002–2007) and Bob Ackles.

At the Marina in Vancouver in 2005 with three of my best friends, all past-presidents of the then-community-owned BC Lions. Left to right: Bob Ackles, Ron Jones, Norm Fieldgate and Jack Farley.

Pre-game discussion with Oakland Raiders owner Al Davis, Oakland Coliseum, California, September 1996. Al Davis and Bill Parcells are people that I would like to have worked with.

Two legends at a legendary stadium, Sunday, September 14, 1997, during the pre-game warm-up at Lambeau Field in Green Bay, Wisconsin: George Blanda, Quarterback and Kicker extraordinaire, and Jerry Kramer, Offensive Guard for the Green Bay Packers, during their championship years.

Media Conference following the first XFL game held in Las Vegas, February 3, 2001. Left to right: Dick Ebersol, President of NBC Sports; Dick Butkus, Hall-of-Fame Middle Line Backer; me; Pat Christenson, Director of the Thomas and Mack Centre; Vince McMahon, Owner XFL. The Las Vegas Outlaws beat the New York/New Jersey Hitmen 19-0 to a sold-out stadium.

What the game is all about, but certainly not what life is all about. Life is about the friendships, relationships and family. The two men I work closest with I count as good friends: BC Lions Owner, David Braley, and Head Coach Wally Buono, immediately after the Lions' fifth Grey Cup win (my third) on Sunday, November 19, 2006.

on our board, trading up on two occasions to get players we wanted – Garrison Hearst, a running back, and Ernest Dye, an offensive tackle. We also took Ben Coleman, another offensive tackle, and Ronald Moore, a second running back.

ESPN had a crew in our draft room and their commentators had the highest praise for our performance. Joe Theismann said at the close of their program there was no doubt Phoenix had the best draft. His opinion echoed around the country. Ron Wolfe, Green Bay Packer GM, said Phoenix kicked butt in the draft. *The Dallas Morning News*, *Chicago Tribune* and *Houston Post* gave us alone an A+ for our picks. The accolades were great.

As for our owners, the Bidwills, not a word. They didn't say we'd done a good job. Nothing.

Bill Jr. came into my office two or three days after the draft and looked at my board, which now sported draft tags. "It's pretty easy to have a good draft when you have all those high picks," he said.

I chortled.

"As long as you have the players in the right order and are prepared to go up and get them or wait until they fall to you," I replied.

I thought to myself, this kid is an asshole. He really doesn't know what it's all about or what it takes.

During a pre-season game against the Rams, both John Shaw and Jay Zymgunt, the Rams' president and vice president at the time, were still talking about our performance at the draft. Bill Bidwill, Sr., arrived and got involved in the conversation.

"Our scouts were really impressed, Bill," John said.

Bill scoffed, "Anyone can have a great one when you have high draft picks."

I was right: they really had no idea.

—ᘑ—

At the combine meetings in Tulsa that December, I got a call from Bidwill telling me Larry Wilson was stepping down. It was a shock. Bidwill said Larry would remain in some honourary capacity. Larry was the only great player who remained connected with the team. I was happy to hear that.

Bidwill didn't cultivate alumni. I thought that strange, too, especially given the role I knew former players can fulfill. Norm Fieldgate and his wife were an incredible force with the B.C. Lions, embodying a sense of abiding spirit and tradition. Former players felt welcome to stay around. It was great for the fans, it helped boost morale, it aided ticket sales, it made sense.

There was talk that Eric Widmark, director of pro personnel, or I might get the general manager's job. There was even speculation Joe Bugle was in the running. I thought most of it was hot air.

At the Senior Bowl in January 1994, the coaching and scouting staff met daily for breakfast in the coffee shop. Bidwill joined us but didn't contribute much; he just sat glumly. I had a big table reserved. Between bites of toast and swallows of coffee, we'd go around the table and hear a one- or two-line report from the scout or coach on each player they had seen the previous day in practice. Everybody got a daily update and a new assignment.

After breakfast the second morning, Bidwill said, "Bobby, can I see you for a few minutes?"

"Sure, Mr. Bidwill."

We sat at the table when everyone left and he said, "It's funny, I've never really done this before. But tell me, give me your opinion on the coaching staff."

I was a bit taken aback. We had never had a conversation of any great length, certainly not about the football operation in any meaningful way.

"Mr. Bidwill, this is as fine a staff as I have ever seen," I began. I went around the table pointing to where each guy sat – Ted Cottrell, defensive line coach who went on to be a defensive coordinator with Buffalo and could have been a head coach; Bobby Jackson; Jim ("Don't call me Jimmy") Johnson, who became defensive coordinator with Philly; John Matsko, the offensive line coach; Mike Murphy; Joe Pascale, who went on to become defensive coordinator with San Diego; Ted Plumb; Pete Rodriguez; Fritz Shurmur, defensive coordinator who should have been a head coach too. I went through the staff and explained what each one contributed.

"Joe Bugle has brought in good people. He's a knowledgeable guy. He's got a good eye for talent. There might be an area we could make an adjustment, but I'd prefer to talk about that later."

"Bobby, what would you do if you were in my position?"

"I'd have a good sit down with Joe and I'd talk to him about the strengths and weaknesses of our football team and his staff. Just get a good feel for where his head is at, knowing there's probably a couple of improvements he should make in the staff, and obviously we need another draft and some help on the free-agent side."

We talked for half an hour and when I left I felt really good about the conversation. I thought I actually might have a shot at the general manager's job. I ran into Joe and told him about the meeting. He thought it was an incredibly positive sign.

I was getting ready for a reception later when Joe phoned.

"The old man just called me," he said excitedly. "He wants to see me. I'll see you at the do."

He caught up with me about 90 minutes later. He'd had an hour-long meeting with Bidwill, which was unheard of.

"I feel really good about it, Bobby," Joe said. "Really good. It was the best meeting I ever had with the man. What do you think it all means? I think things are going to be okay."

"I do, too."

I felt as if we were going to get a chance to take a shot at the next step.

On the following Monday, the staff gathered in the boardroom and we began to evaluate the team in preparation for the coming season. We started with the offence – who is our best player? Who is second best? The defence and special teams? Who is the best overall player? Who is our number two? Once everyone was satisfied we asked, where do we have to improve?

We were perhaps 30 minutes into the process, which normally takes between a day and a day and a half. The boardroom had a glass wall and I could see a grim Bidwill stride purposefully towards Joe's office. Sitting beside me, Joe didn't see him. I nudged Joe.

"Mr. Bidwill," I said, nodding towards his office. Bidwill emerged as if on cue. "Mr. B is looking for you."

Joe left.

I watched them walk back into the office. Five minutes later a sombre Joe returned to the boardroom. The discussion stopped. All eyes fixed on him. Joe sat down. His notebook remained lying open where he had left it. He slapped it shut. Thwack!

"That's it, guys," he said. "We're finished."

Shock. Dead silence.

"We're through," he reiterated.

Everyone picked up their material and silently shuffled out of the room. I went to my office and called Kay. No one said a word.

"You won't believe what happened," I told Kay. "I don't know where I sit right now, but I'll go over and see him in a while."

I waited an hour or so and then went to Bidwill's office.

"I'm sorry, Bobby," he said, "and I apologize for not taking your advice but I just felt otherwise."

"Do you want me to start putting together a list of who's available?" I asked.

"That's a good idea."

His confidant on this decision was apparently Tom Gilfoil, an old lawyer from St. Louis. We were in Phoenix – can you imagine? He was a nice guy and probably a very good lawyer, but can you imagine? Halfway across the country, this guy probably attended a few games each year, and he was advising Bidwill on whether to fire the head coach!

"I'll draw up a list of who's out there right now and suggest some guys who might consider the job."

"I'd appreciate it if you'd do that," he said. "Again, Bobby, I apologize for not taking your advice."

I went back to my office and the phone calls began. What happened? What's he going to do? The rumours were flying. It was like a zoo on the telephone. There was a stack of messages – call so-and-so, call so-and-so, urgent – call so-and-so … it's urgent, urgent … an emergency!

Everybody wanted to know what was going on and many wanted

to get their name in for the job. I spent the following two or three days sifting calls and putting my list together.

My first suggestion was offensive coordinator of the Cowboys, Norv Turner. We'd worked together, but Jack Kent Cooke, of the Washington Redskins, also had an interest in Norv. I told Bidwill he was the ideal candidate and we should chase Norv. We talked about the other guys on my list – Dom Capers, who was with Pittsburgh and became head coach of Carolina; Paul Hackett, who had been a pal when I was with Dallas, had moved on to become offensive coordinator for Kansas City; Steve Sidwell, defensive coordinator for New Orleans; Ernie Zampese, offensive coordinator with the Rams; and Gary Stevens, offensive coordinator with Miami.

There were a couple of former head coaches available, such as Joe Gibbs and Mike Ditka. I thought either of them could do a good job for us. Another was Buddy Ryan, defensive coordinator with the Chicago Bears when they won their Super Bowl, and ex-head coach of the Philadelphia Eagles. I wasn't keen on Ryan. Maybe that's because he was so scornful of Jimmy when he was named coach of the Cowboys. Ryan was widely quoted as disparaging Jimmy as "a college coach." "There ain't no East Carolinas on his schedule now," he sniped, suggesting Jimmy's record was padded with wins against schools with no decent football team.

I included a handful of college and university coaches too – Tom Coughlin, at Boston College, who later became head coach in Jacksonville; Dennis Erickson, who became head coach in Seattle; Steve Spurrier, of Florida; and R.C. Slocum, from Texas A & M.

Bidwill's lawyer from Phoenix, Dick Mallory, was going to the Super Bowl and the plan was for him to talk with Norv after the game. Under NFL rules, no team could approach a member of a contender's coaching staff about a new job until after they were eliminated from the playoffs. It was designed to limit and keep such pitches discreet so they didn't draw media attention and become a distraction for the team.

"Here's what's going to happen," I told the lawyer, who didn't know Norv was a good pal of mine. "Jack Kent Cooke says, 'Fuck you.' He's interested in Norv as well, you know. But he doesn't care what the league thinks. He's already let Norv know he's interested. He'll have his private jet on the runway warmed up, and the moment the Super Bowl is over he'll be flying Norv to Washington to sign a contract. He won't let him out of his sight from the moment he walks off the field."

Mallory didn't seem to get it.

"What do you suggest?"

"You've got to get to Norv. Tell Bill, somebody has to get to Norv and tell him not to do anything with Washington at least until he's heard our offer."

He called me from the Super Bowl and told me he managed to say "hello" to Norv at a cocktail party.

"Don't worry, Bobby, I didn't break the rules."

I shook my head. Some guys don't get it.

Norv told me Jack was at the same party and said here's what we'll offer you. No one but Jack and Norv involved. Completely discreet. Jack wasn't going to lose. Norv was on Jack's private jet the moment the Cowboys' team party was over. He called from Washington. "Bobby, you won't believe the deal they gave me. He made me such a hell of an offer I couldn't turn it down."

That's typical of Washington, Dallas, New York. That's how the big dogs do it. Then there's the way the Arizona Cardinals do it. They woke up the next morning and realized, "Yeah, I guess we should have phoned Norv."

—— m ——

A few days later, Bill Bidwill came to see me.

"I'm making the announcement tomorrow of the new head coach."

"What?"

"I'm going to hire Buddy Ryan."

I had trouble not staring at him, mouth agape. I couldn't believe it. No further contact, no discussion. Strange. I didn't even bother to ask why. It didn't matter at that point. He had made his decision and I knew that was the end of it.

On our way to the media conference the next morning, I still harboured thoughts that I might have a shot at being general manager.

As we were going down the stairs, Bidwill turned to Buddy and said, "Oh, by the way, you're the general manager, too."

Buddy seemed shocked. I don't think he wanted it, but he didn't really have a choice. He and I met afterwards but it was little more than a brief introduction. We knew each other by reputation.

"We'll talk more when I get back," Buddy told me. "I'll be back Monday."

He had to move his home and clear up other things before setting up in Phoenix. He was as strange a guy as Bidwill. Neill Armstrong, whom I'd worked with at the Cowboys, used to joke that he was so weird he couldn't believe he hired Buddy on three or four occasions. Like a lot of odd people in football, Buddy was off, but had talent. He had a huge ego, was outspoken to a fault and had a problem being straight with anyone.

Buddy returned and told me he wanted me to be assistant general manager. I agreed, and we shook hands.

Two hours later I got a phone call from Bill Polian, general manager of a new team, the Carolina Panthers, offering me a three-year contract as the assistant GM. They were two years away from taking the field – what an opportunity!

"Oh, Bill, Bill, I can't believe this," I told him. "I just shook hands with Buddy."

"A handshake with Buddy doesn't mean a thing," he said.

"I don't know, Bill, let me think about it."

I went home and talked to Kay about it.

"Oh god, I'm sick about this, Kay. I mean, I'd love to work with Bill. It's a new franchise. We'd start from the ground floor and up. But Buddy and I had a deal and we shook on it. I don't know."

Mike McCormick, president of the Panthers, called me the next morning.

"Bobby, a handshake with Buddy means nothing," he said. "We've got a three-year deal here for you."

"Mike, I know that. I'd love to join you, but my handshake and my word are what I'm about. If I don't back up what I agree to, why would anyone do business with me? I really appreciate it, I'd love to come, but I'm going to stay with Buddy."

What a mistake.

It was the worst year of my life in the NFL. Buddy would sit there, look you in the eye, no, he couldn't look you in the eye, he looked over this way or that – and then he'd be disingenuous. He couldn't be straight. It didn't matter, I'm sure, who it was: player, coach, owner.

If Buddy wanted to cut a player, he didn't do it straight up. He'd sit around the staff room and say, "I don't like that so and so. He doesn't do anything for me." That was the kiss of death. Next you'd hear the coordinator or the position coach saying, "Yeah, you know, I don't know about that guy." Next thing Buddy would tell someone in the media. That's how the kid would find out he was going to be released.

Buddy couldn't bring a guy into his office and say, "We're going in a different direction," or whatever, you know?

It was the same with everybody he dealt with as far as I could see.

Buddy also brought in his twin sons and quite a collection of coaches, two or three of whom were excellent. His sons weren't bad coaches, either, but they reminded me of the old man. I always felt they were keeping something back when they dealt with me.

At the league meetings in Disneyworld, in March 1994, Kay and I took some time to unwind from the internal machinations of the Arizona Cardinals. Sponsors, merchandisers, broadcasters and the teams spared no expense providing a good time. Go on any ride. Free food. Free booze. As Kay and I strolled along an outdoor walkway, we bumped into Jimmy Johnson and Rhonda, Dave Wannstedt, now head coach of the Chicago Bears, and his wife Jan.

In spite of the volatile relationship he had with Jerry Jones, Jimmy had managed to keep his temper in check and lasted two years since I had been fired. With two Super Bowl rings already, he was on top of the world.

"Hey, Kay and Bobby – come join us," Jimmy said.

So we tagged along and were soon ensconced with Norv Turner, now head coach at Washington, and his wife Nancy, Rich Dalrymple, of the Cowboys media relations department, and a handful of others from the Cowboys and Bears organizations. We'd been drinking for more than an hour with Jimmy popping Heineken as if they might go out of style, the entire table in his thrall.

He was boasting of going nose to nose with Jerry Jones in the confrontation before the draft and giving him what for. No one noticed Jerry and his flunky arrive. They were suddenly standing behind me with drinks in their hands, expecting to be invited to join the frivolity.

Jimmy certainly ignored them if he saw them. As I told people later, Jerry didn't understand he had a winner in Jimmy. Jerry, because of his ego, thought he was Al Davis, who is The Raiders. Period. Well, Jerry isn't The Dallas Cowboys. Jimmy and his staff are an incredibly bright group of individuals who are capable of teaching and motivating elite athletes to achieve an extremely difficult goal – win a Super Bowl. You can't buy 40 years of experience. You've got to earn it. This is one business where you can't just walk in and do all the things you think you can do. Jerry thought that if Jimmy were gone tomorrow he could walk onto the field and coach the football team. He couldn't. It doesn't work like a video game.

Jerry soon banged his glass on the table and said he'd like to toast all those who helped him win two Super Bowls. He held his glass aloft and his eyes moved around the table. He saw Kay and then me. "Oh, hi, Kay. Hi, Bob," he said, arm remained raised, his glass awaiting the clink of a friendly toast. I went to raise my own, willing to let bygones be bygones, when Chicago Bears head coach Dave Wannstedt's wife Jan clamped a hand on my wrist. She wouldn't let me raise the glass. Jerry looked around the table. No one raised a glass.

He stared at a sneering, glassy-eyed Jimmy. Jerry slammed his glass on the table. "Fuck you!" he said. "Have your own party." He turned and left.

Jimmy let out a belly laugh. So did a few others. Norv and Dave chuckled nervously. Jerry owned a football team – coaches get fired and they might want him to hire them. Jimmy thought it was the funniest thing on earth. Kay and I excused ourselves, saying we had other commitments.

Back at our hotel, we planned to meet a couple of friends in the bar. We found Jerry at a table holding forth with a gaggle of reporters. We turned and went to bed. This was not going to have a happy ending.

The next morning, I came down for a meeting and the hotel was abuzz. Jerry had told the media he was going to fire Jimmy. Cameramen and videographers staked out the lobby. Everybody knew I had been at the table, so I was targeted for what I knew.

I called Jimmy's room; Kay was there, as she and Rhonda had planned to go shopping. They had heard the news. Jerry's assistant had called to give Jimmy the heads up. Rhonda leaned out the window of the hotel suite. Jimmy and the other head coaches were arrayed on the lawn below for a commemorative publicity photograph.

"Jimmy, Jimmy," she yelled.

Jimmy could see her but couldn't hear a word she was shouting. He phoned the room. Rhonda explained.

"Get packed," he said. "We're out of here."

Whoosh. They were gone.

Jimmy had a place in the Florida Keys, which is where they headed.

Jerry gave a press conference trying to heal the rift, saying it was all a misunderstanding. We'll get it straightened out when we all get back to Dallas, he said. Fat chance, I thought. It never got ironed out.

Jimmy called me later: "You know what that silly son of a bitch did? He gave me $2 million and let me out of my contract."

He guffawed.

—m—

During the off-season, at the height of that year's free-agency action, I got a call from Harold Lewis, an agent in St. Louis. I knew him pretty well. Lewis had helped Buddy Ryan get the job by putting in a good word with Bidwill, and he'd hired another of Buddy's sons, Jim, who was going to law school in St. Louis.

"Bobby," Lewis said, "is Larry Tharpe there?"

Larry Tharpe was an offensive tackle from Detroit who was a restricted free agent. If he got an offer sheet from anybody, the Detroit Lions could match it and sign him.

"Not that I'm aware of," I said.

"I understand Larry Tharpe is on his way there for a workout."

Normally I would know that. "I'll check it out and call you back."

I went down to the locker room and, sure enough, there was Tharpe. I went back up and phoned the agent. "Yeah, Harold, Larry's here."

"Son of a bitch," he says. "I'll tell you what happened. I've hired Buddy's son, and I'm paying him $40,000 a year so he can go to law school. He's taken this kid without my knowledge and sent him for a workout. I'm the agent for this kid!"

I was thinking, geez, is this a Ryan trait? I hung up and phoned a friend in Detroit, Paul Boudreau, the offensive line coach.

"Paul, tell me about Larry Tharpe."

"When I came here he was finishing his rookie year. He's huge, he's athletic, he's smart. But he can't play. I did everything. I bent over backwards to make him into an NFL tackle but I'm convinced he can't play."

"Okay, we've got him here for a workout."

"I understand that – just don't overpay him because he's going to disappoint you," Boudreau said. "He's got a streak in him. He's kind of lazy; he's a good athlete but he's lazy."

With that knowledge, I was sitting in my office when Buddy called.

"Larry Tharpe is going to be our starting left tackle," he said. "Can you draw up the paperwork? Do whatever you have to do when we sign a restricted free agent."

"I've got the forms and everything right here," I said.

"Great. I want to give him a one-year contract for $1 million with $200,000 up front."

That was serious coin. "Boy, Buddy, I think we can get him for a lot less than that."

"No," Buddy replied. "That's what I want to pay him."

"Okay. So who's the agent on this? I need to know that for the form."

"Jim Ryan."

"I'll bring the paperwork down when it's finished."

Ten or 15 minutes later, he phoned back. "Where it says, 'Agent,' just put 'No agent,'" he told me.

Normally I would sign the forms and send them off to the league office and to the Detroit Lions. But I was not going to sign this form.

I walked it to his office and said, "Buddy, you've got to sign this."

In the end, I was glad I did. A few years later, I had to give a deposition. I spent the day in a Miami law office with a lawyer for Harold, a lawyer for Buddy and a lawyer for the Cardinals. The lawyer for Harold went first.

I told my story and authenticated the notes from the Cardinals' personnel files, including those showing I had scratched out the name of the "agent," Jim Ryan.

The lawyer for Buddy went next. As far as I was concerned, he was a seedy little son of a bitch and I wanted to smack him upside the head. He got up and tried to destroy my character, my credibility.

He didn't succeed. Before the trial, Ryan and the Cardinals settled out of court. Harold Lewis told me later he wasn't trying to bankrupt Buddy or do anything to hurt my relationship with the team, but it was wrong what they did. I'm glad he won.

At the January 1995 Super Bowl in Miami, I spoke with Ken Behring, owner of the Seattle Seahawks, and his son, David, also an executive with the team, about moving there to become the general manager. I had truly grown tired of what I considered the organizational dysfunction of the Cardinals. We had a good two-hour lunch. Kay and I thought it would be a great move and take us back into the Pacific Northwest and the orbit of Steve, Scott and the grandkids.

Behring was a car buff from Wisconsin who parlayed his auto dealership, car-wash and real-estate holdings into a fortune. One of his more famous developments was the well-heeled Blackhawk community in the San Francisco Bay area. He had one of the largest collections of Mercedes Benzes in the world. In 1988, Behring and his partner bought the Seahawks.[1]

Ken and I hit it off well. He was looking for someone with lots of experience. But David leaned towards giving a chance to two young men already with the team's personnel department.

The next day, Kay and I were at Leigh Steinberg and Jeff Moorad's party. The super-agents attracted a Who's Who and always had an over-the-top affair. I ran into Stephen Jones, who grabbed my coat

---

1 In 1996, Behring transferred the Seahawks' office operations to Anaheim before selling the franchise the following year to Microsoft co-founder Paul Allen for $200 million.

sleeve, tugging me close as if confiding a state secret.

"I was at a function last night with David Behring," Stephen said, his voice barely a whisper. "He said, 'Tell me about Bob Ackles. Why isn't he still with the Cowboys?'"

Stephen and I always got along.

"What did you tell him?" I asked.

"The truth," Stephen said.

He waited a beat: "Your name isn't Jones."

I laughed.

"I told him you had the job I wanted. You helped me learn it and then it was a case of my name is Jones and yours isn't."

Which was true.

Stephen said he thought I had the job in Seattle.

"We'll have to wait and see," I said.

Moments later I ran into his dad. Jerry did the same.

"Bob, Bob," he said, "good to see you. Come over here a second and let me talk to you."

We stepped away from the crowd.

"I ran into Ken Behring at this function last night," Jerry continued, giving me a distinct case of déjà vu. "I think they are going to hire you."

I was non-committal with him, too. No need to fan the rumour mill. But I started to feel very good about my prospects and thought I might soon have a ticket to Seattle.

—⁊⁊⁊—

Over Easter weekend dinner, Kay and I talked about things with the Cardinals. We both agreed I should leave the team after the draft. I didn't like being associated with somebody I didn't consider a stand-up guy.

I felt I had done good work with the Cardinals, especially orchestrating the 1993 draft when we moved up (by trading troublesome running back Johnny Johnson to the Jets) to grab Garrison Hearst, the tailback who became a key weapon in our offence, linemen Ernest Dye and Ben Coleman. In the fourth round that year, we also drafted running back Ronald Moore, who gained more than 1,000 yards.

In the 1995 draft, Ronald Moore was traded to the New York Jets, along with first- and fourth-round picks, to obtain star wide-receiver Rob Moore.

Since Buddy's arrival, however, my role had greatly shrunk.

Unfortunately, the job in Seattle was not to be. They stuck with the two young guys – one of whom would later become general manager of the Miami Dolphins, the other general manager of the New Orleans Saints.

Still, the day after the draft, on Monday, April 24, 1995, Buddy just happened to phone me before I phoned him. I went down to his office and he couldn't look me in the eye. It was over.

"It's nothing personal," he said.

Right.

Afterwards, I went over to Bidwill's office and said, "Mr. B., I've enjoyed it."

He got upset. He didn't want to see me. He didn't want to be involved in any of that stuff; he hated it.

"I'm just saying if you ever want to sit down over a cup of coffee, I'll be happy to give you an idea of what's going on around here."

"I know everything that's going on around here," he snapped.

"Fine," I said and left.

Before I had packed up my office, Jeffrey Lurie of the Philadelphia Eagles was on the phone to Bidwill asking permission to offer me a job. He didn't know I had been canned – it was serendipity.

Ryan issued a terse news release later that afternoon: "The Cardinals wish Bob Ackles well in his future pursuits and thank him for his contributions to the Cardinals."

He declined comment when reporters called, saying he didn't want to detract from Rob Moore's arrival from the New York Jets.

I wasn't chatty either, saying only, "I enjoyed these years with the Cardinals, and I'm disappointed it ended. I think they have the makings of a good football team."

In Philadelphia, the mood was more upbeat. Jeff Lurie told reporters, "Bob played a big part in helping Jimmy Johnson and Jerry Jones turn the Cowboys into a team that won consecutive Super Bowls. His impact was very broad-based in that he helped build that club by working both as an evaluator of collegiate talent and as director of pro personnel."

He said I would be the third most powerful person in his organization, along with Head Coach Ray Rhodes and him. He couldn't wait for me to get on board. I joined the Eagles as director of football administration.

—⁊⁊—

Kay and I loved living in Philadelphia. We moved right downtown within a block or two of the main restaurant and bar precinct and Veterans Stadium. But Philly is a tough town as far as football goes. They expect to win every game. They don't like to lose.

The city is also full of characters. For instance, hair stylist Toni, who cut my hair, was this fabulous Italian woman who happened to be the favourite of one of the city's most infamous mobsters, Skinny Joey Merlino. He was allegedly an underboss in the dominant Mafia family, a wise-guy heir linked to three murders, two attempted murders, assorted loan sharking and drug trafficking. He and my barber went to school together, and her mum and his mum were really good friends.

She told me he wanted to meet me some time. But I managed to avoid the rendezvous. It was like an episode of the *Sopranos*. It seemed in those days every time you picked up a newspaper another "made" guy was getting bumped off. There was an underworld gang war between the mob in Jersey and the South Philly family. I had visions of being plugged like something out of the *Godfather* every time I went for a trim – an assassin, mistaking me for Skinny Joey, putting two slugs into the back of my head. It didn't happen. Joey was nabbed, convicted and jailed for a long stretch.

—⁊⁊—

Head Coach Ray Rhodes turned out to be a difficult guy. I wasn't sure where he was coming from sometimes. He didn't know me and he didn't really want me, I don't believe. Lurie hired me even though Rhodes was satisfied with demoted vice president John Wooten.

Wooten had spent five years at Dallas and was purged with the arrival of Jerry and Jimmy. I knew him well. He and Rhodes were good friends. Understandably, Rhodes didn't want anyone from the outside, especially someone tied to Jimmy Johnson whom the press said Lurie really wanted to run his team.

I think Rhodes feared I was hired to pave the way for Jimmy's arrival and that Lurie figured he had a better chance of landing Jimmy if I was in place. The kinds of things Jimmy said about me led to more speculation, things like, "Bobby Ackles did more than anybody to rebuild the Cowboys." It was an exaggeration. Jimmy ran a very collaborative operation. The media also presupposed a much tighter relationship than existed.

The rumours had no basis in fact. Jimmy and I spoke once a week or so, no question. But it was usually just to BS. Sometimes, we wouldn't talk for a month or more. There was certainly no Machiavellian plan to engineer a Rhodes ouster and install Jimmy. Rhodes eventually learned I was someone he could work with, that I wasn't someone who meddled. We hit it off after a while. But the beginning was rocky.

I was responsible for negotiating player contracts at a time when the Eagles were up against a $37.1-million salary cap. They had not signed their draft picks and several key financial decisions remained in limbo, including how to re-sign veteran middle-linebacker Byron Evans. I also had to deal with serious problems with our training facilities.

I was actually flabbergasted at the condition of our training camp field. Two months before camp opened, it was a quagmire. The university told me the field was fine: don't worry, be happy. I'd never seen such a mess. "We can't practise on that," I told them. But there wasn't a choice. I got a turf expert in who repaired it a little, but it was just awful. I ensured the Eagles moved the next season.

The field at the stadium and the practice field next door weren't much better. I knew a fellow from Kansas City, George Toma who was the natural turf playing surface expert for the NFL, and he with his son Chip put new fields in for me. I subtracted the cost from the stadium rent.

We had a good year, a solid year – 10-6 – in spite of our quarterback, Randall Cunningham, who was undisciplined. The coaches were always trying to persuade him to follow the playbook. With him, it always was sand-lot football. We could have done better, I thought, if he had bought into the system. As it was, we went with Rodney Peete, our number two, and had a so-so season.

During one game, at Jeff's request, I took Mike Tyson and his entourage up to the team box. He was just out of jail after serving his sexual assault sentence. He wore an expensive suit and a silly grin. The women in the box looked as if Satan himself had arrived. The bartender wanted an autograph; everyone else looked as if they wanted to hide.

The highlight of the season for me was beating Dallas 20–17. We kicked their ass. It was a frigid –7 F with wind chill in Veterans Stadium. The players looked like locomotives huffing and puffing, their breath billowing thunderheads of steam.

Peete was a former backup for the Cowboys so I was happy for him. He managed to engineer a comeback down two touchdowns to win. The defence played phenomenally. We got to Troy Aikman all night, sacking him even on his final play. There were standout plays from the unit throughout the game. Linebacker Kurt Gouveia knocked the ball from Emmitt Smith's grasp on our two-yard line when it appeared he might score. Late in the fourth quarter, the defence stopped Smith again, short of a first down – this time at his own 29-yard line after a fourth-and-one gamble. It secured our shot at the win.

The game was tied at 17 with two minutes left: we managed to push it four yards closer before Gary Anderson kicked a 42-yard field goal with 1:30 to go, giving us our first lead. Dallas was unable to score and we won.

We went on to play the Wild Card game in Detroit. We also played well there, winning 58–37. They were supposed to kick our ass and we beat the crap out of them.

Afterwards, we couldn't practise at home because of the weather, so I arranged for the team to work out at Dodgerville, Florida. It went well, though we still lost in Dallas 30–11 in the conference final. It was a stinging defeat. They drove Peete from the game with a concussion after he was tackled at the Dallas five-yard line with the score still only 3–0.

Deion Sanders, Leon Lett, Darren Woodson, Emmitt and Troy

took it from there and dominated us. Defensive back Sanders set up for a dozen offensive plays as a slot-receiver and even scored a touchdown. He then intercepted Randall Cunningham to set up the final touchdown. Emmitt ran for 99 yards and Troy threw for 253; they pretty well did what they wanted.

Cunningham didn't have a good game, in part because he hadn't prepared much the previous week as he was busy supporting his wife who was delivering their first child. It was sweet revenge for the Cowboys.

Philadelphia remained snowed under and the airport closed after the game so the team jet remained in Dallas. With the season over, many players grabbed commercial flights and headed elsewhere. I told Kay I was going to fly to San Francisco and catch the East–West game; she said she'd skip up to Vancouver and visit the kids.

—⁓—

I had just checked into the hotel in San Francisco when Jimmy phoned.

"I'm going in to see Wayne Huizenga for the Miami job in the morning," he said. "I'll either be 15 minutes or all day. Do you want to come if I take it?"

"Jimmy, I'd love to but I've got two more years on this contract."

"Don't worry about that," he said. "I'll get you out of it."

At the end of the day he called back. "It's all set."

"What's all set?" I said.

"I'm going to the Dolphins and you're coming with me."

"Did you talk to Jeffrey Lurie?"

"Yeah, I found him in the Bahamas."

I couldn't believe it. But Jimmy was chuckling away down the phone line.

"Yeah, that guy Lurie must think I just fell off a turnip truck," he said. "He tried to get a draft choice out of me for you." He giggled.

"I told him we'd give him right of first refusal up to the end of training camp on any player we planned to release prior to us putting them on the waiver wire. And a future consideration."

"You serious?"

"Yep. He thought that was fabulous."

Every Monday morning during camp, I would have to call the Eagles' director of player personnel and tell him who was being cut. They didn't take an interest in anyone. Later in the summer, Jimmy let them have Troy Vincent, a free-agent cornerback as the "future consideration." What that actually meant is he turned down the chance to match the contract Philadelphia had already offered Vincent – $16.5 million over five years.

—⁓—

Jimmy and I met at the Senior Bowl in Mobile a week or so after those initial phone calls and talked about everything under the sun. I would handle the detail stuff in Miami that he didn't have time to deal with. I would deal with the agents, college scouting, the draft, pro scouting and trading – all the behind-the-scenes football business. My title was director of football operations.

I headed back to Philly to pack. Kay and I were in Florida before the end of the following week. As I left old Vet Stadium John Gruden, the offensive coordinator, pleaded, "Bobby, take me with you."

I gave him a wave. In retrospect, given the trouble we had with our offence in Miami, I should have taken him. John was the first really brilliant technocrat I met in pro football – they're everywhere now. He had everything broken down on his hard-drive, every play collated and organized for instant recall and dissection.

The Eagles were eliminated from the playoffs on the 7th of January, 1996, and Kay and I were dining at Don Shula's Steak House on January 23 with Dolphins president Eddie Jones and his wife Marilyn, Jill and Frank Strafaci, and Bryan and Mary Wiedmeier. Eddie Jones would prove to be one of the most knowledgeable and nicest people I've ever met. It was a wonderful evening and we were filled with enthusiasm about the challenges on the road ahead. It was still snowing in Philly.

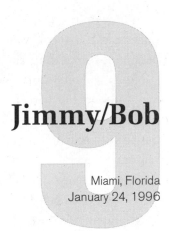

Jimmy/Bob

Miami, Florida
January 24, 1996

JIMMY ARRIVED in Miami and cleaned house. It was different than his arrival in Dallas only insofar as Don Shula had retired. Jimmy wasn't trying to replace by many to be thought a saint ungraciously dumped. He kept a few assistant coaches, but everyone else was gone and Jimmy's crew brought in.

I oversaw the football operation.

Jimmy and I met every morning at 7 o'clock. We'd decide what we were going to do. At 7:30, we'd have a staff meeting and he'd explain his plan. Of course, his guys all knew the drill from being in Dallas or somewhere else with him.

I immediately started working on contracts with Bryan Wiedmeier, VP of administration. We had training camp right out back so that made our job a lot easier in terms of the inevitable forest of paperwork that needs to be done letting players go, continuing negotiations and other preparations for the season. You could go to your office every day, which you normally couldn't do with most teams. We used a hotel that was very close for the players, and I had a room there but I seldom used it.

We faced two major problems – it turned out that fans felt St. Don Shula was forced into retirement and they resented that. Second, Dan Marino was aging. He wasn't throwing as sharply and he was throwing more interceptions. Unfortunately, he was an icon too.

The team had lost a lot of talent as a result of free agency. With the salary cap, it just couldn't pay them what they were worth. They had been first-round draft choices and carried concomitant salaries.

As in Dallas, Jimmy had clear ideas of the players he needed to win. I always felt with Jimmy it was about loyalty. Jimmy expected people he worked with to communicate well, to work hard together but to very much feel as if each and every person's opinion counted. He treated everyone differently, which, paradoxically, really meant he treated them the same. That was evident in the time and effort he put into listening to player evaluations.

Preparing for the draft in early spring, Jimmy spent a half-day with each scout. Later, he would spend time with each of the coaches – one on one. Of course, we also had group meetings where everyone in the room hashed out differences, and assigned a final grade to players overall and at each position.

I created a chart for the scouts and coaches with mock headlines, "Jimmy Johnson's Five Most Important Characteristics for Draft Choices": under "Intelligence" was a photo of me with a hammer, and Jimmy saying, "Bob, hit me over the head next time I want to draft a dumb guy."

Under "Works Hard" was a drawing of a weight lifter. Under "Gym Rat," a rat bouncing a basketball. Under "Character," was the question "Is he a bum?" and a photo of a Bourbon Street bum. Under "Playmaker" was a photo of Zach Thomas beating Buffalo with an interception return.[1]

We had a decent draft but our regular season was only so-so – we finished 8–8, out of the playoffs. Still, not bad for a first year.

I remember David Braley came down for a visit and I took him and his wife to the president's box. It was funny. After the game I had him into the inner sanctum where Jimmy and his staff had sandwiches and beer after the game. He still talks about the encounter.

Jimmy is a peculiar guy, as are most head coaches. Wally Buono is one of the few head coaches I've ever been around who isn't eccentric. I mean, Don Matthews is different. Jimmy has his quirks, too. The

---

1 *Shark Among Dolphins: Inside Jimmy Johnson's Transformation of the Miami Dolphins*, by Steve Hubbard (Ballantine Books, New York: 1997).

truth is a lot of people don't want to be with him when a game is over. If he wins, he can be bubbly. But if he loses, watch out – you don't want to be near him.

As soon as the game was over, wherever we were, Jimmy had to get to a TV set. I've never seen a guy who can watch four different games on four different channels and not miss a beat. He knows the channels the games are on and click, click, click. He's back and forth, back and forth, back and forth. He sits there glued to the set and glugs down his Heineken. He drinks six Heineken on ice – boom, boom, boom.

We won that night, so he was happy when I arrived with David and Nancy. Still, Jimmy was into the highlights of the games and he didn't want to be bothered. Dave, I think, was kind of miffed. Jimmy kept calling to me, "Hey, Bob, did you see this?"

Or calling to a coach, "Did you see such and such?"

David expected Jimmy to be more social. That's not Jimmy.

"He was kind of rude," David said later.

David is worth a gazillion dollars and Jimmy is a football coach. I didn't disagree; Jimmy certainly wasn't warm on that particular occasion – and in spite of his normal personal charm, he could have moments like that occasionally.

After the league meetings in March, Jimmy flew a group of us to Vegas for a weekend of gambling – his girlfriend Rhonda, Kay and I, Norv and Nancy Turner, Dave and Jan Wannstedt, and his lawyer cum agent, Nick Christin. It became a tradition. If the meetings were held in the east we went to the Bahamas; in the west, Vegas. Caesar's Palace comped Jimmy everything – the Ramses Suite and all kinds of perks. He would sign for meal bills of $1,800, $2,500. There were limousines. And Jimmy gave everyone money to gamble with. Jimmy loved to gamble and play blackjack.

In pre-season, we travelled to Mexico City to play Denver in an exhibition game. Jimmy didn't want to go. It was a distraction even though we were there only three days.

We had a big party at the Hard Rock Café in Mexico City and afterwards, at nearly midnight, I sat up with Pat Bowlen, owner of the Broncos, and John Beake, his general manager, at the bar. Their quarterback John Elway appeared.

"Up kind of late tonight," Beake said. "Join us."

Elway sat for a few minutes before lurching into the night. He knew he wasn't going to play more than two series in the next day's game. I finished my drink and said goodnight.

On my way back to the hotel, I passed a cantina that was just rollicking. I looked in and there was Elway. I joined him.

The following morning at the pre-game meal, Jimmy was in a foul mood.

"What's wrong?" I asked.

"Look at those guys," he said, nodding at some of our group.

One of the doctors had gone for a run and arrived for breakfast drenched in sweat. Gary Stevens, an assistant coach, threw up in the entrance to the dining area. Of course, in Mexico it can be what you ate, but Jimmy thought Gary was into the booze.

"Too much laughter," Jimmy growled.

He was pissed. It didn't matter that we won the game, 38–19.

What amazed me were the fans – almost 105,000 people filled the stadium. It was a sea of 7s and 13s, the jersey numbers for Marino and Elway. I thought Mexico was poor, but these were expensive game jerseys and everyone was wearing one. It told me a lot about who was in the seats.

When we got back to Miami, at our first staff meeting, Jimmy unloaded on everyone.

"I don't want to see anyone come into a dining room looking like shit again," he said. "You guys were all out raising hell. You ought to take this seriously."

I talked to him later and confessed my sins.

"I'm not worried about you," Jimmy said. "You might have done some good with Bowlen and Beake. But I don't want my coaches out doing it."

That was Jimmy. Don't let anything distract the team, always reinforce the tone and the message: we're here to win; this is what I expect.

But his mood persisted.

The second season was not to be what we hoped for either. Even when we won our opening game, Jimmy wasn't happy. We beat the Indianapolis Colts 16–10, and he was raging. He was not happy with the offence, the offensive coaches, or the direction of the offence. He threatened major changes at the next staff meeting.

Jimmy came to my office later to get my reaction and I told him I thought he got the coaches' attention.

Offensive coordinator Gary Stevens bore the brunt of Jimmy's anger. Jimmy was furious because he had told Gary to cut down the number of offensive plays in the game plan because the younger players couldn't remember them all. Many only had a chance to practise the plays once.

It's crazy to have such a large play list, Jimmy said. He was really ticked off about it. But Gary didn't take the hint.

That October, we played Chicago on a Monday night and we had a 15-point lead with seven minutes left in regulation time. We lost 36–33 in overtime. Chicago was 0–7 going into the game. We had a three-game winning streak. Can you imagine?

Marino was sacked in the first series of downs, fumbled and turned the ball over to Chicago who scored to go up 7–0. They got through to him all night. The Bears came back from a 33–18 deficit in the fourth quarter to tie the game and take us into overtime. Marino fumbled; they recovered on our 18, which allowed them to kick the game-winning field goal. It was a night of mistakes and an offensive line that failed to protect the quarterback. Porous didn't begin to describe it.

I came down from the press box to the sideline with 9:03 left in the fourth quarter. We had recovered a fumble on Chicago's 32-yard line. One-and-a-half minutes later we scored a touchdown to go ahead by 15 points with 7:26 left to play.

They came back, tied the score with a two-point conversion and then went on to beat us. I was numb. As I ran into the locker room, I passed Wayne Huizenga and his entourage standing in the entrance of the tunnel.

"Bob, piece of shit!" he spat as I jogged by.

I didn't know if he was talking about me or the game. But can you imagine how he felt? The previous night the Marlins, his baseball team, won the World Series.

We made the playoffs with a 9–7 record but finished with three bad losses. The loss to New England in the playoff game was pathetic.

It was Jimmy's first playoff appearance with the Dolphins and we lost in Foxboro 17–3. They manhandled Marino, stole our offensive signals and didn't give us a chance to get on track. Four sacks, nine hurries, six knockdowns, four deflections, two interceptions.

It was the third time we had played them in six weeks and it was a replay of our earlier loss when Dan threw three interceptions and had two run back for touchdowns. On one truly terrible play, Todd Collins grabbed a ball and scampered 40 yards into the end zone early in the third quarter after the defence decoded Marino's signals.

A 38-yard field goal by Olindo Mare at the start of the fourth quarter saved us from being shut out for the first time in Dolphins playoff history, some 31 games at the time. It was a sad, sad day. We recovered an on-side kick after Mare's field goal but fumbled it away on the next play. We managed only 42 yards rushing. Awful.

"When you can't run the football," Jimmy lamented, "you don't have a football team."

He began drinking his chilled Heinekens in the locker room and by the time he got on the plane he was into his fourth or fifth. Jimmy sat in the front row with Rhonda beside him. Eddie Jones, our president, and Bryan Wiedmeier sat across the aisle. I sat behind them on the aisle in the second row, while the offensive coordinator Gary Stevens sat across from me on the aisle seat behind Rhonda.

Jimmy was sucking back his beer and eating taco chips with scorching hot salsa. He loved Mexican food. He had a portable television on which he was watching our in-house video of the game. The more he watched, the angrier he got. He watched the start of the play in which Marino tossed an interception. Jimmy saw the linebacker yelling instructions to the defence, cocking his arm back and forth and Collins moving to the left.

Jimmy realized the linebacker suspected what Marino was going to do. Suspected? He knew. Sure enough, Collins stepped in front of the ball, intercepted it and sprinted in for a touchdown. Jimmy went berserk.

He'd told Gary about this time and time again. Jimmy lifted up the television, which must have weighed between six and eight pounds. He held it up with one hand and flailed at it with the other, yelling

"God damn it! God damn it! How many times have I told you?"

Rhonda grabbed the TV from him and hurled it over her shoulder. It came at my head. Fortunately, I caught it. Everyone gasped. She was apologetic, Jimmy was pissed off and Gary was moaning: "Aw, shit! That wasn't my fault. That wasn't my fault!"

"The hell it wasn't," Jimmy was yelling back.

It was a bad scene.

The next day Jimmy fired Gary. Gary went on to work for the Oakland Raiders as an offensive coordinator. Jimmy said he should have made the move much sooner; Gary just didn't take his hints.

Jimmy went into a funk and didn't speak to any of the coaches for a month. He was very distraught. He was pissed.

In April, before the season started, Wayne Huizenga invited the football staff to his championship 18-hole golf course called the Floridian. It sits on Stuart Island, a private nugget north of Palm Beach, a very exclusive area. It's open for only six months of the year and there are only two permanent members of the club, Wayne and his wife, Marti.

He had 26 full-time pilots at that time for his fleet, which included a 737 that seated 28 people and two executive jet helicopters. Sitting in the back you didn't hear a sound. It was like being in a luxury automobile. We flew up in the two helicopters and a 14-seat seaplane.

Jimmy, Dave Wannstedt, a couple of others and I were in one of the helicopters flying fairly low, hugging the Florida coastline. It was like one of those Vietnam movies. Wayne's birds were forest green and as we came up the coast, another coal-black helicopter headed towards us. The captain opened up the sliding window between the cockpit and the cabin and said, "Jimmy, somebody wants to talk with you."

The pilot handed Jimmy the headset through the small window.

It was the Shark – Greg Norman, the superstar golfer. He was flying down to Fort Lauderdale after playing on Wayne's course.

We landed right at the clubhouse and the floatplane coasted to the dock next to Chi Chi Rodriguez's boat. Just amazing.

About 100 people annually receive as gifts year-long memberships to the club. Wayne has a pro on site and he's built a large, stunning oak clubhouse. Water on two sides, a wrought iron and stone fence around the course. It rivals any celebrated course I've ever seen.

There were 60 boat slips, two guest residences and Wayne's mansion just 10 minutes away. In his garage, he had a Ferrari with only 5,000 miles on it as well as a Viper. I told him if he ever wanted to sell the Viper to let me know. He had all kinds of toys.

Wayne ran putting contests and distributed about $3,000 in hundred dollar bills as prizes. He'd just peel off the hundreds, depending on who won what.

But no matter how many good times like that there were, the football team continued to founder. The problem was also becoming more and more obvious. Dan Marino was the elephant in the room when we talked about what needed to be fixed.

We lost to Buffalo in a Monday night game to go 2–1. It was disastrous. Dan and the offence played pitifully. He didn't have it. He had just turned 38 and looked 38. He was throwing badly and not moving well. Jimmy desperately wanted to make a change but that was political suicide. Dan was the most popular person in South Florida.

The media smelled blood in the water and were all over Jimmy at the news conference after the game. They were still at him the next day. The headlines were nasty. "JJ scolds Marino, offence," the *Herald* trumpeted.

Jimmy called a staff meeting on the Wednesday morning and ripped into the offensive staff. He was very emotional, slamming his fist on the table three or four times – knocking over his Diet Coke, spilling it on my shoe. He got to a point where he couldn't talk anymore and said, "That's all."

With that, he left the room.

He then met with Dan and the quarterback coach.

At 9:15, he met with the team and was very emotional again. He talked about how good the Dolphins could be as a team if they didn't screw it up. He didn't want any finger pointing. Let's fix the problem, not lay blame.

"We are all accountable," he said.

As much as the offence could be taken to task, he said the defence had to pick up too.

I was talking to Jimmy in his office with Dave Wannstedt not long afterwards when Stu Weinstein, our security chief, and Kevin O'Neill, our trainer, arrived.

"This looks like trouble," Jimmy quipped.

Stu said: "The worst."

That changed the mood fast. Just what we needed, a non-football distraction. Cecil Collins, our running back, had been arrested at 4:30 a.m. My first thought was, nothing good happens at four in the morning.

Collins had broken into a woman's apartment by smashing and climbing through the window. Her husband woke up and called the police as Collins fled. The police arrived, learned it was Collins and went to talk with him. But they couldn't get Collins to come out of his apartment. They called Stu, who went over and tried to persuade Collins to come out.

"We finally got him to come out," Stu said, "and the husband was yelling at him, 'You didn't know she was back with her husband. Did you? You dumb f---.'"

"You'd better call his agent," Jimmy said to me. "We'd better get a statement together for the media as well."

I left and called Collins' agent, Jimmy Sexton. I got his answering machine: "Hello, we have a problem, Houston."

We were lucky it was an embarrassment and nothing more.

I thought things looked promising in 1998. We went 10–6 and Dan looked like he might be able to carry us through one more playoff run. We went into Buffalo and defeated the Bills 24–17.

Nothing went right for Bills quarterback Doug Flutie that day. On the first play from scrimmage, he threw a great ball down field only to watch his receiver catch it and cough it up. Our Brock Marion brought it back to our 29-yard line. With 17 seconds left in the game, down by a converted touchdown, and inside our five-yard line, Flutie dropped back to pass. Defensive end Trace Armstrong blind-sided him like a freight train, sending the ball spinning to the ground. Shane Burton fell on it for us at the three. We won!

The Bills had been the Dolphins' nemesis for years and this victory tasted like nectar. It was a rollicking good game that saw us recover four fumbles and make one interception. Our line picked up the blitz, gave Dan lots of time to set up, and our running game was good enough to support his aerial attack. Dan threw only one interception and for the most part controlled the tempo.

The next week Denver crushed us 38–3 en route to the Super Bowl. John Elway killed us through the air and on the ground with Terrell Davis chewing up 199 yards rushing. We had no running game, our receivers dropped the ball and our defensive backs failed to come up with a big play.

Our playoff aspirations were dashed.

Jimmy invited the entire staff down to his place in the Keys that spring. Some of us drove and others came in two Greyhound buses. It was five acres on the ocean.

There was a screen of trees along the road so you couldn't see into the property. Jimmy had an electronically controlled gate and behind that, a tennis court, 2,000-square-foot guest house and a one-bedroom house of about 4,000 square feet.

His home was spread over two levels and featured a large kitchen, workshop, bar and gym. He had a big garage, a pool with a bar you swam up to and a sprawling patio. Jimmy also had a salt water pond stocked with assorted tropical fish. He loved fish and had an aquarium in each of his offices. He found them calming.

The property faced the ocean and also swept around a sheltered cove where Jimmy moored his 53- and 37-foot boats and parked his smaller toys.

Shortly after we got there, Jimmy came out of the house.

Dave Wannstedt and I were in the pool bellied up to the bar.

"Dave, I need you," he said.

He called in Rhonda's girlfriend, Maria, and summoned Stu Weinstein, our security guy. I knew the marriage was about to take place; Kay had let me in on the surprise on the drive down. Stu had a notary public's license and was permitted to conduct a civil marriage in Florida.

Father Leo Armbrust, priest to the stars, was a fixture with the club, and was at the party, but I think Jimmy chose not to have him do the marriage because he wanted no fuss. Jimmy didn't want a big production. Aside from the ecclesiastical issues around Roman Catholics and divorce, Father Leo was also pretty presumptuous. He might have made the mistake of trying to tell Jimmy how to do it.

Jimmy and Rhonda went inside the house, got married and stepped back out onto the patio to make the announcement in their bathing suits and bare feet. The party really started.

Later that afternoon, John Gamble, our strength and conditioning coach, and Mike Westhoff, our special teams' coach, decided to get in an hour or two of fishing before dark. John was number one in the world as a 275-pound class lifter from 1981 to 1983 and a member of the U.S. Weight-lifting Hall of Fame. He and his wife Sharon were good friends of Kay and I. Sharon was also the sister of Oprah's best friend Gayle. We first knew something was wrong when Sharon came to Kay, crying.

"John and Mike aren't back yet," she said, "and it's starting to get dark. I'm worried."

She was really upset.

Kay took Sharon to Jimmy and they told him.

"Don't worry," he said. "The sea is calm. It's flat out there tonight and it's not very deep. John can get out of the boat at any time and only be up to his waist in water. There's nothing to worry about."

He called in to report the missing boaters.

It was an anxious hour or so, but eventually John called. They'd miscalculated the drift of the current and ended up further down the coast than they realized. At twilight, the flickering lights along the coast all looked identical. They pulled in a few miles further along.

The following season on the football field, 1999, Jimmy and I both knew we were headed for a train wreck. The team was improving and the quarterback was declining. What could we do? If he didn't want to go, we certainly couldn't push him. Marino was the most famous, most well-loved person in South Florida.

That's the problem with icons. Marino was making millions. He didn't need the money. He was already a wealthy guy. It was a combination of ego and not being ready to call it quits. He was considered one of the greatest quarterbacks to play the game, but his skills and his ability were letting him down. He had not won a Super Bowl and that haunted him.

Dan had been named Rookie of the Year in 1983 and the following year, in 1984, he had a great chance to win a Super Bowl. He threw for more than 5,000 yards, 48 touchdowns and set records in every category – completions, yards gained, touchdowns. That year the Dolphins went 14–2 but fell to the 49ers, 38–16. After that, Dan struggled with a mediocre team that spent four years wandering in the wilderness without a playoff game. His glory days were sadly a long time ago.

Jimmy's football teams were aggressive and hard running. We needed a trigger man. A Troy Aikman. A Dan Marino in his prime. Dan couldn't do that anymore. He was 38 and his skills deteriorated daily.

We had a mediocre 9–7 season, in part because Dan suffered a pinched nerve in his neck. His arm strength and release didn't come back. We lost six of our last eight games yet we managed to make it into the Wild Card game that year in Seattle. We were the last event in the Kingdome.

Dan was a worry. He wasn't capable of making the spectacular plays we needed if we were to win. We discussed playing backup Damon Huard if Dan struggled too much. It didn't come to that.

Marino passed for only 28 yards in the first half. But he had a great second half, orchestrating three scoring drives to erase the Seahawks' 17–10 lead. Tony Martin made three circus-like catches in a game that was full of cardiac moments.

We were unable to run out the clock and Seattle quarterback Jon Kitna led a last-minute rally, taking the ball down to our 29-yard line with 35 seconds left. On first down, he threw – incomplete. Second down, he stepped back – Joey Galloway made a short curl near the sideline. Kitna wired one to him. Cornerback Terrell Buckley stepped in front of Galloway and grabbed the ball. We won 20–17.

We were ecstatic. Miami had not won a road playoff game since the 1972 AFC Championship game against Pittsburgh. Jimmy told the press, "One win can do a lot of things, especially a win in the playoffs. One win in the playoffs, since the Dolphins haven't done it in 28 years, goes a long way."

Dan's performance put him past Terry Bradshaw and into second place for the most touchdowns thrown behind, only Joe Montana. I picked up a piece of the decrepit Kingdome building as memorabilia – demolition started the next day – as we headed to Jacksonville for the AFC divisional playoff game.

We actually felt like we had a chance. We should have quit while we were ahead. We were humiliated by Jacksonville 62–7. It was the second biggest rout in NFL playoff history. Not since the 1940 Chicago Bears were stomped by the Washington Redskins 73–0 for the NFL title had a team been so brutally outclassed. It was the most points the Dolphins ever allowed in a game.

None of us had ever been so shamed.

"I've never had a game like this in my life," a downcast Dan Marino said afterwards. "Even as a kid, I've never had a game like this."

He threw for less than 100 yards before Jimmy pulled him early in the third quarter. Seven turnovers. We were down 55–7 when the field sprinkler system came on and soaked our huddle. It only added insult to the pain of the loss. Jimmy stood, arms folded, staring blankly at the field. He couldn't believe it. I was incredulous too. Who would have predicted it?

"I guess this thing is full circle," he told the press. "I was on the other side of one of these where we got about seven takeaways from an opponent in the Super Bowl. It was a runaway, but I've never been on this side before."

The game marked the end not just of Dan's career, but also Jimmy's. You can start off bad or you can start off good in a game and usually something changes either for the worse or for the better. We started out bad and got worse and worse. It went downhill like an avalanche.

I've never left a game. During this one, I left the press box at the end of the first quarter and went to sit on the bench dejected. I couldn't listen to it in the press box. It was just awful. It was awful. Everything we did turned to dross. Dan was dreadful. The players looked as if they were sleepwalking.

After the game, sitting on the bus, Jimmy drained iced Heinekens as we waited for a few stragglers. Jimmy always sat in the front row by the window and Rhonda sat beside him. There was a noisy crowd behind police barricades hurling abuse at us in spite of their victory. They were shouting all kinds of vulgar epithets. Jimmy was their favourite target, probably because they could see him sitting there. It was just brutal. Some of the comments were unbelievable – filthy, vile stuff. He just ignored them.

Finally, Rhonda had had enough. She got up. Jimmy tried to stop her. "Ignore them," he said.

But she got off the bus and started yelling back, heading towards this one loudmouth. Fortunately, our security man, Stu, grabbed her before she could breach the line of cops holding back the fans.

"Rhonda, Rhonda," Stu said over and over again as he struggled to get her back to the bus. "Rhonda, Rhonda. Let it go."

The police holding up the barricades looked back. You could see the question on their faces: "What's next?"

I was sure we were going to have a riot. I went to help Stu.

"Come on, Rhonda," I said, "forget them. Let's get back on the bus and get out of here."

Boy, it was tough going home on that charter. It was a tough way to end it, a really tough way to end.

Jimmy announced his retirement the next day. Dan retired March 13, 2000.

Dan didn't deserve to go out like that – the first quarterback to pass for more than 60,000 yards – 4,967 completions, 420 touchdowns. He threw for at least 3,000 yards in 13 of his 17 seasons. His 147 regular season wins was second only to John Elway's 148. Dan retired holding 24 NFL regular season records.

Dave Wannstedt became the new head coach. We'd worked together for three years at Dallas before he went to Chicago. He'd been fired in Chicago and hired by Jimmy the previous year, and so we had another year together under our belts at Miami. I knew it was not going to work. I was Jimmy's guy. Dave had been Jimmy's guy, too, but now it was his team.

Dave and I worked well together but he needed his guy. I could see that. I could never be Dave's guy – and, even if I thought I could be, I knew in Dave's eyes I would always be Jimmy's guy. It would not have worked out.

As well, some guys are not meant to be head coaches. They are great coordinators, they're great position coaches, but they're not meant to be head coaches. Take Buddy Ryan, for instance, who liked to sign #46 after his name because he took credit for creating the old 46 defence. I look at him and Wannstedt and say: those guys were great defensive coordinators. They had a system that worked and they had players who could play within that system.

After working with Jimmy, who was very bright and had a great eye for talent, I knew it was going to be very difficult working for Dave as head coach in spite of our personal relationship. Dave and I were close friends; his wife Jan and Kay were really close friends. We lived near each other and drove back and forth to work together quite often. But I couldn't see it working between us. After the draft, I asked him where he wanted me to fit in and what he wanted me to do.

"I want you to do the same thing you've been doing," he said.

"I don't think that's going to work," I replied.

"Let's give it a try," he insisted.

I appreciated his effort, but I knew it wasn't going to work, and I knew who had to leave. When the XFL offer came, I didn't hesitate.

10

Vince McMahon,
Wrestling and Football

Las Vegas, Nevada
August 7, 2000

I ARRIVED in Las Vegas and hit the ground running. Vince McMahon and his associates had been working on the new football league – the XFL – since the beginning of the year. They had a president, a couple of vice presidents, a handful of general managers, of which I was one, and Dick Butkus, one of the meanest, nastiest linebackers ever to play for the Chicago Bears. Dick was a kind of commissioner called "director of competition."

Bill Baker, a friend, asked me a couple of times if I was interested in coming on board. I had usually sloughed him off. But Jimmy retired, and after, I realized Dave Wannstedt and I weren't going to tango. I talked to Bill again. Our son Scott initiated it. He was with the B.C. Lions at the time and I was still in Miami. He called to see if I could do him a favour.

"I'd really like to get involved in this new league," he said. "Is there any way you could help?"

"Let me make a few phone calls."

I called Bill and he said talk to Billy Hicks, another Dallas crony who was the XFL's vice president of administration. He was the man. Hicks and I had roomed together at training camp, too, and still laughed when we talked about Gil Brandt's liquor tab.

"Never mind Scott for a moment," he said. "How about you?"

"I've talked to Bill Baker a couple of times," I said. "Yeah, I might have an interest. We can talk about it. But what about my son Scott

– you remember him from Dallas, don't you? He's done more training, got a lot more experience in Vancouver, a hard worker."

"There's no question about any of that, Bobby. Tell him to go on-line. We're using a firm called TeamWork Consulting out of Shaker Heights, Ohio. Buffy Filippell is the president. I'll get you the website. That's his first step."

The league got more than 56,000 applications for 112 positions over the three-month recruiting process. Bill called back in late July when we were in training camp for the Dolphins.

"Okay, Billy, I'm ready to talk seriously," I said. "What would you have for me if I wanted to come aboard?"

"You could have your pick, Bobby," he replied. "At the moment, we could use you in Memphis, San Jose or Las Vegas. But why don't you talk to Basil first – fly up and meet everyone?"

Basil DeVito, Jr., had worked with Vince McMahon off and on over the years in various capacities. We talked on the phone and I agreed to fly up. I talked to Kay and, of the three franchises, Las Vegas appealed to us.

We had already discussed the possibility of retiring in Las Vegas. We loved Florida but it was a 12-hour trip, door to door, to see the kids in Vancouver. We didn't want to travel all the time and we knew we would be back and forth. We thought Las Vegas would be a great place to live. We didn't know at the time how good it would turn out to be. With no state income tax, the cost of living there was a lot less than in South Florida and the weather was just the way I like it.

After shaking hands, Basil and Billy wanted to know what franchise interested me. It didn't take us long to agree that I'd go to Vegas as vice president and general manager of the Outlaws. They told me there was a 10-game regular schedule and the inaugural game of the new league was set for Las Vegas on February 3, 2001.

"What?"

I was flabbergasted: "Do we have a team?"

"No."

"A stadium?"

"No. You're going to put all that together."

I was staggered by the prospect.

"I want to bring Scott down as director of operations," I told them.

It wasn't nepotism. Scott could do the job and I could trust him. He would be a key to our success – dealing with logistical concerns, arranging travel and organizing day-of-game operations.

"No problem," Basil said.

They agreed to pay $10,000 to defray the cost of Scott's documentation to work in the U.S. He trained all the other teams' day-of-game staff. Part way through the season, NBC even wanted to hire him.

This was going to be nuts, but it would be exciting.

"How about a coach?" I asked.

They had a handful to choose from. I knew Jim Criner, who was from the West Coast but living in Montana coaching major college ball. He was a Dick Vermeil assistant with UCLA when I first met him years earlier signing quarterback John Sciarra for the Lions. I said he'd be great.

For other positions within the organization, the headhunters set up 27 interviews, whittled down from a list of several thousand. People who applied from California, Utah, Nevada and Arizona got preference. I landed at 10 o'clock in the morning. The XFL had rented Kay and me a two-bedroom condo. I dropped my bags, ordered a van and headed to a nearby hotel to begin interviewing potential employees.

Scott Cobb, from TeamWork, and I started the cattle call at 1 p.m. and conducted interviews pretty well non-stop until 7 p.m. the next evening. Most applicants we spoke to face to face; some we talked to on the telephone. I hired two people immediately – one to handle the financials, one to be director of marketing and ticket sales – John Sandler, vice president of business, and Karen Prescia, director of finance. I had a heck of time finding a media relations manager until I discovered Trey Fitz-Gerald, who was working for the professional soccer league.

We initially worked out of an office at the University of Nevada Las Vegas campus, a small boardroom in the sports administration building. We also rented their field, Sam Boyd Stadium – just over 30,000 seats – perfect for the XFL.

Vince bought the aging Debbie Reynolds Hotel on Convention Drive, just off the strip and half a block from Circus Circus. So we got offices there. Later, he learned he couldn't renovate and expand to create a World Wrestling Entertainment destination resort, which was his plan. So he sold it.

I had to admit, that tendency of Vince's – to passionately adopt an idea and then drop it like a hot potato if it wasn't working – worried me. Vince had created the XFL for the same reason David Dixon, the art dealer, founded the U.S. Football League in 1983 – the NFL was a lucrative monopoly. Vince had an edge on Dixon in that he understood sports and spectacle. He also understood television and the TV marketplace, which was perhaps the over-riding reason he thought there was room for the XFL. He understood that the NFL was not a gate-driven business anymore, it was an industry fueled by television revenue.

—⚉—

Television was the driving force behind professional football as the 21st century dawned. Football is no longer only "a sport," it was and is a very valuable marketable commodity. Consider, the broadcast rights to NFL games for the period 1998 to 2005 were divvied up and sold – CBS paid $500 million per season, Fox $550 million, ABC Monday Night $550 million, ESPN Sunday night $600 million. The total package for the eight years was $17.6 billion – averaging $78 million per team for each year, whether they won or lost or sold a ticket.

Vince's highly successful cocktail of glitzy, spectacle-style wrestling as a lucrative television commodity made him believe he could do the same with football. His idea was to turn the entire stadium into a television studio. Most of the two-dozen-or-so cameras were situated on one side; we sold seats on the other side first so viewers always saw what looked like a full stadium. Ticket prices were scaled to first fill areas most often in view. You had to pay through the nose to sit on the side with the cameras. Eight players on each team were miked so fans could also hear what was happening on the field.

We had a camera on wires – the one everyone uses now. Vince was the first to use that – bring viewers right in over the huddle and the subsequent play. We also had two cameramen wearing pads and white helmets on the field with hand-held cameras. Talk about getting up-close to the action.

Vince's vision was attractive. He really did understand television; he and his partners had deep enough pockets to absorb initial losses; and it seemed they were willing to listen to professional football men when it came to the on-field product. I thought it might work and the prospect of being in on the ground-floor helping to build not just a team, but an entire league – what a challenge. That excited me. That's why I got on board. But it nagged at me that I might have got into bed with a group of guys who had watched football on television and said, "We could do that."

And Vince made mistakes.

For one, he put the play-by-play announcer and colour commentators among the fans. That's what they do in wrestling, and Vince thought it would work in football. That's also why he hired celebrity pundits – most of whom didn't know anything about football – to be outrageous and add to the circus-like atmosphere. Those decisions hurt us because we had an uphill battle getting people to take our football "product" seriously.

The most important element, though, was NBC. Vince originally had a deal with his wrestling broadcast partners – UPN and TNN. But Dick Ebersol said the Peacock network must have the rights. He thought the games would be a perfect lead in for *Saturday Night Live*. NBC had lost the NFL rights a few years earlier, and he was sure a partnership would be ideal. He talked the NBC board into becoming 50/50 partners with Vince in the XFL – they didn't just buy the rights; they bought half the league.

Vince was very much larger than life. He and his wife Linda and their two kids, Shane and Stephanie, were committed and very involved in the XFL. I got to know him a little better than most because he and I have two mutual friends.

Angelo Mosca, the great Hamilton Tiger-Cat player, called me when he heard I was in Vegas and said he was coming for the opening game. "I used to wrestle for Vince's father," he said. "When Vince was a kid he'd wear these suits with huge shoulder pads. I used to grab him by the pads and shake him. So you tell McMahon next time you see him that King Kong is coming to Las Vegas for the opening game and I'm going to kick his ass."

I saw Vince at training camp and I told him, "Vince, I met you at the league meetings in Chicago and a mutual friend of ours called me. King Kong said he is coming here for the opening game and he's going to kick your ass!"

He almost fell on the ground laughing. Basil, who was with us, didn't know what to make of it.

Our other mutual friend was Curtis Iaukea, a big Hawaiian tackle who played for the B.C. Lions back in 1958–59. He also wrestled for Vince's dad. Curtis performed under many names, including King Curtis Iaukea, Prince Curtis Iaukea, the Wizard, the Bull and the Master. He was enormously popular in Australia and also played the part of a sumo wrestler in the 1963 movie *The Three Stooges Go Around the World in a Daze.*

His father was the chief of police in Honolulu, but Curtis was a wilder kind of person. He dropped out of the University of California Berkeley, which is why he ended up playing for the Lions. He and I roomed together at the Admiral Hotel in his rookie year. I was still in high school and working as the assistant equipment manager. Curtis captivated me with his stories. B.C. traded him to Montreal and he played a year there before he got into professional wrestling.

After he started wrestling, I saw Curtis only occasionally. But I always looked for him whenever we visited Hawaii. I found him one time wrestling Sweet Daddy Siki. It was packed and a lot of fun. I went back stage and we had a brief reunion.

Later, Curtis said the effects of steroids and the physical toll of football and wrestling ended his career. His forehead was thick with scar tissue and he must have weighed 400 pounds the last time I saw him. He had a boogie-board stand on Waikiki Beach and I sat for hours listening to his stories. He claimed to be descended from the greatest indigenous chiefs and took Kay and me to a luau out by Diamond Head that featured three roast pigs cooked in a pit buried with hot rocks, Hawaii's most famous star Don Ho and all kinds of entertainers from the mainland and the islands. We had a marvellous time.

Curtis still followed football closely and called to wish us well the moment he heard about the XFL.

—ᴍ—

With the business side coming together, I needed a team.

The league decided the four western teams would train in Las Vegas so they could scrimmage against each other and accelerate preparation for the season. The four eastern teams trained in Orlando. But first, there was a draft in Chicago at which we all got to choose our players. Again, Vince had a good concept.

Instead of individual teams signing players, the league signed players. If you wanted to play, you applied to the league and got on the list. Bill Baker and a couple of others would scrutinize the bona fides and if it all checked out, the player was in the draft. Teams could nominate players onto the draft list but they had to make information available to every other team.

Players were paid through the league office and everyone earned the same base salary, roughly $45,000, though quarterbacks got a little more, $50,000, and kickers a little less, $40,000. After every game, players from the winning team split $100,000, about $2,500 each. If you were on the roster and played in the game, that was an incentive. The bonus pool for "The Big Game at the End," as it was called, was $1 million. Players in the championship could expect to receive about $25,000 each.

We took over a couple of banquet rooms in the hotel to get ready for the draft. We looked at a lot of tape. In the end, I thought we ended up with a pretty fair selection.

Chicago was wild. There were more than 500 people – Vince, Basil, directors of World Wrestling Entertainment, Dick Ebersol and all the NBC crew. Vince started to address the crowd and somebody's cell phone went off at the back of the room. You could see his jaw clench. He looked down; he looked up. Finally, he said, "You better turn that cell phone off or I'm going to shove it where the sun don't shine."

Vince gave his speech, introduced everyone and kicked off the draft. It was televised and ran pretty well. They really did try to be professional.

The first game was like a Super Bowl in spite of all the nay-sayers. Several people I respected told me, "You'll be lucky to sell 2,000 season tickets."

We used every trick in the book. We unveiled our jerseys and uniforms – black and gold with a cool logo – on the strip at the Harley Davidson Café with our sponsors and loads of media. Everything we did we turned into an event. We picked these fabulous cheerleaders, the cream of the crop of local gorgeous showgirls.

Vince hired Jay Howarth, from Los Angeles, to travel around the league and select, groom and train the cheerleading squads. We set up in the MGM Grand Theatre and put 125 women through their paces – from high-school cheerleaders to strippers. There was even a woman who was an undercover Las Vegas police officer. She ended up managing the team. Another beautiful woman had to be cut because we found out she was a $1,000-a-night hooker. None of the high-schoolers made the cut. It was really something. We sold season tickets based on photographs of those girls. Their outfits and routines were amazing. I'm sure guys bought tickets solely to watch the cheerleaders. No wonder by the time we kicked off we had 10,000 season tickets sold.

A couple of days before the game, we released some cheap seats pretty well on top of the bleachers. We created five rows of temporary seating and on the ticketing computers you could see them getting snapped up. They disappeared one at a time – pop-pop-pop – around the stadium. They sold out within the day.

People flew in from all over the country because, regardless of the on-field product, we ensured this was an event. Everyone was impressed.

Five o'clock the night before the first game, our staff went around and pasted Sorry-Sold-Out signs on every ticket wicket. It was unbelievable. All the hotels that turned down ticket packages thinking they could pick them up on game day were frantic.

"This is Caesar's! We need 20 VIP tickets."

"Geez, I'm sorry, we don't have a seat left."

There was some screaming because the high rollers now had trouble getting tickets. We had held back a few seats around the broadcasters, and we helped out those we could. New York, New York and a couple of the smaller casinos really stepped up to the bar for us. We really appreciated their support. We did a great promotion with New York, New York because we played the New York-New Jersey Hitmen on opening night.

Scott got a New York Taxi, one of those almost-trademark canary-coloured hacks. At the team-and-NBC-sponsored tailgate party before the game, we let people take a sledgehammer to it to raise money for charity. We ran all kinds of crazy promotions. The players even had nicknames stitched onto their jerseys. I loved running back Rod Smart's moniker: "He Hate Me."

First possession was determined by Las Vegas safety Jamel Williams and the New York-New Jersey Hitmen's safety, Donnie Caldwell, facing off in a grab for the ball at midfield. Williams won.

On our first possession we went down the field but stalled on the 33. Paul McCallum kicked a field goal. McCallum became the first player to score in the history of the XFL. He had been released by the Saskatchewan Roughriders after seven seasons to play with us.

We dominated the game and our quarterback Ryan Clement threw for two touchdowns to lead us to the 19–0 win.

The ratings of that first telecast were gargantuan. But the critics were not impressed. We got hit by a tidal wave of negative press.

Shame on NBC. Shame on the network of the Olympics, Sarnoff and Garroway, Huntley and Brinkley, Gowdy and Costas for selling out to the dark side of gratuitous violence, tawdry titillation and lousy football, otherwise known as the XFL.

Leonard Shapiro, *The Washington Post*

The premise of the XFL is to appeal to male viewers aged 12–24 – the same audience with which the WWF thrives – and it's clear there will be nothing highbrow or low-key about the shows. From the preponderance of shots of barely clad cheerleaders to cameos by snarling WWF wrestlers to the fascination with nonsensical nicknames stitched on players' jerseys to downright silly 'interviews' with fans, there was little question the XFL is more about spectacle than sport.

Howard Fendrich, *The Associated Press*

For however much longer the XFL lasts, there's really only one score-card worth keeping. It's the one that notes all the sellouts who lent their names, careers, reputations and consciences to this predictably unmitigated garbage.

Phil Mushnick, *New York Post*

Like a blight that has crept from the low-rent fringes of cable to network prime time, the XFL mingles violence, voyeurism and even politics into one trashy Saturday night show that suggests how the lowest television culture is gaining mainstream respectability.

Caryn James, *The New York Times*

Where was the hemorrhaging? Where were the gurneys? Where was the crack of spine against helmet? We wanted mayhem, dog. The XFL gave us football. What were they thinking?

Paul Daugherty, *The Cincinnati Enquirer*

It didn't take long for the novelty factor to fade and the widespread criticism to have its effect. Ratings were cut in half for the second game.

NBC finished last among the four major networks in prime time that Saturday, just a week after beating ABC, CBS and Fox. The preliminary overnight rating was reported as 5.1, meaning an average of 5.1 per cent of television homes in the country's largest 49 markets tuned in at any given time. That was down from 10.3 the previous week, even though it was an exciting game – the Los Angeles Xtreme pulled out a 39–32 victory over the Chicago Enforcers in double overtime.

The same audience fall-off had crippled the USFL – the writing was on the wall.

"We remain a work in progress, and our numbers last night are exactly where we said they would be the last six months," Ebersol said.

The main play-by-play voice changed, as wrestling announcer Jim Ross took the microphone from Milwaukee Brewers broadcaster Matt Vasgersian. Ross became the in-booth partner of Minnesota Governor Jesse Ventura. The change didn't help. We fell off the map.

I think we oversold the game – and the league. We had less than six months to prepare. We didn't have the time to put together the kind of on-field product that was needed. We were generating Super Bowl-style hoopla but the football was wanting. Even worse, we were doing it every week.

Our quarterback Chuck Clements was injured in training camp. So we started with number two, Ryan Clement. He got hurt after a couple of games. Our number two was maybe good enough to lead a .500 team. With number 3, Mike Cawley, we were out of luck.

We were running from six in the morning till midnight to generate interest and enthusiasm. Our staff worked exceptionally hard. We finished the season 4–6. We simply weren't good enough. If we had been a winner, we were to host the championship game. That was Vince's goal: "The Big Game at the End" in Vegas. It wasn't to be.

There were, nevertheless, successes. In terms of market penetration, we were the best of all XFL teams with a 17.9 per cent reach. Vegas had about 560,000 people at the time and we sold 100,030 tickets. New York had 7 million and they only sold 130,513, a 1.9 per cent market penetration. They played in the Giants stadium, which is tough – 70,000 seats. They were rattling around in there. Memphis did well too; in a market of about 640,000, they sold 86,303 tickets for a 13.5 per cent market penetration. The market penetration of other teams fell off sharply after that.

Our target was 100,000 in total ticket sales for the five home games of the season. We made it, but it wasn't easy. The stadium seated 37,000 but after we installed the huge television screen, set up fireworks platforms and erected enormous signs bearing XFL logos, we lost several sections, which reduced it to 32,000.

Aside from the ticket targets, there were also sales goals for merchandising and sponsorship. Vince and the league spent a fortune. But attendance tailed off everywhere but San Francisco, where they were fairly successful at selling the franchise and were drawing, on average, 31,000 a game. There wasn't enough success, though.

In the end the league lost $75 million. Yowzah!

We talked a lot afterwards internally about what we could have done differently. A lot of teams had structural problems. I warned them when I first came on board that the lines of authority and reporting in the management structure would not work. They didn't listen. At the major forensic session we held on April 24 at the league head offices in Stamford, Connecticut, the organizational structure was among the biggest suggested changes on the agenda.

In a nutshell, the difference between the NFL and the XFL could be easily understood – one league was an exclusive men's club (with the exception of a single woman owner) and the other was a single man's mansion. In the NFL, each team was individually owned and operated and each owner had a vote in decisions. Vince made all the calls in the XFL. If you wanted to change a rule or operating procedures in the NFL, you needed to persuade people it was a good idea. Vince could just make the decision.

—⚬—

All the vice presidents and general managers attended the year-end business autopsy meetings. The coaches were scheduled to arrive later for a similar kind of dissection of the year on the field. Over the following two days, we worked intensively. Vince was very positive.

"In all fairness to you guys, if I was to do it again, I'd give you at least a year to prepare," he said.

Vince reassured everyone that in spite of the staggering loss, there were good signs. It was important to remember, he said, that the NBC contract covered half the losses, continued for another year and ensured the league enjoyed television exposure.

"I'm in it for the long haul," Vince said. "The next 20 years, or longer."

He envisioned the league growing from eight teams to 10 in two years, expanding again to 12 teams in four years. The football would be improving, he said. It really was amazing the XFL did as well as it did and sold as many tickets, given it was thrown together in roughly six months. He was right.

Vince also had thoughts about the on-air product. He had come around and realized we didn't need the crazy celebrity hoopla. We didn't need broadcasters sitting with the fans. We needed people who knew football, not entertainers. I thought Vince's vision was a good one. Pretty smart thinking, really.

The following morning, Basil and Billy Hicks called me aside.

"Bobby," Basil said, "what I'd like to announce at this meeting today is that you are going to head up a group and you'll deal with the general managers in terms of finding out what the business problems are and make a recommendation on how the teams should be restructured."

I returned to Las Vegas and met with our supervisory staff to brief them on the meetings in Stamford. I told them everything was optimistic. Kay and I had a Mexican vacation planned, and I wanted to send Basil the report beforehand, so I threw myself into its production. It turned into my blueprint for a football franchise.

The biggest issue was making the football decision makers accountable to the general managers, who had to worry about the team's budget. Football decisions were being made by coaches and the league's head-office staff. The GMs who were responsible for the finances, only found out later in many cities.

I sent my report to Basil on May 3. It more or less fleshed out what the general managers had said during the meetings in Stamford. There were concerns about the lines of authority and the problems with budgeting that lack of accountability created. The general managers felt they were often the last to hear about decisions that had a major effect on their team's bottom line – trades and injuries, for instance. I made several recommendations and said we needed to talk about other things.

Basil, these issues, concerns and recommendations are growing pains due to our "work in progress." We have now progressed to a point where we must go forward. Each team still requires a lot of support from the League, however, the General Manager in each XFL City should be head of his household.

If you have any questions, please call me Monday – May 7th, as I will be out of town Tuesday – May 8th through Monday – May 14th and back in my office May 15th.

Regards,
Bob

Just as Kay and I were packing to fly to Mexico, Basil called me and was very enthusiastic about the recommendations. "I'm going to take it to Vince," he said. "It's great!"

He couldn't have been happier. I was very pleased.

—⁂—

Four days later, on May 11, Kay and I were at a bar in Puerto Vallarta when Scott called with the news. We returned to our hotel room to learn Vince had pulled the plug – the XFL would close its doors July 27, 2001.

NBC apparently told Vince it wasn't prepared to televise the second season. Vince went to UPN and TNN, who were carrying Sunday games. Their noses were still out of joint from being jilted by Vince originally when he partnered with NBC. They remained ticked off and they played hardball with Vince over money.

Vince told his board of directors about the predicament and their answer was succinct. "Vince, this is not our baby. Football is not our deal."

My immediate thought was, oh god, we've got to cut our vacation short.

We headed to the airport to grab a standby flight. I had a month to close the operation. It was a sad experience because I felt we had built a heck of an organization – the young staff had done an incredible job in less than a year. We had to sell off the property and return the office jerseys, helmets and cheerleaders' uniforms to the league. Vince didn't want those on e-Bay. Anything else we could sell or give away.

I got the league to extend Scott's contract for a month so he could remain in the U.S. under his work permit. I had a two-year contract as did all the general managers and head coaches. The assistant coaches and others had one-year contracts.

Vince sent all of us a note September 4th. "It is with a great deal of respect and appreciation that I write you this letter today. I greatly appreciate the risks and sacrifices that all of you made in joining the XFL. I also appreciate the unbridled enthusiasm you brought." On the note to me, he'd added: "P.S. Well, Bob what can I say? It just didn't work despite your extraordinary effort. But nothing ventured, nothing gained. We have been rolling with the punches all of our lives. Let's keep rolling, best of luck."

The one thing I would add, I have yet to receive a call from someone saying Vince stiffed them and they didn't get paid.

—◊◊◊—

Once the office closed, Kay and I decided we'd stay in Vegas. We always thought we might retire there. I enrolled at the University of Nevada Las Vegas in the fine arts program. There were calls from NFL teams, but most wanted me to go back to scouting. I didn't want to go back on the road again. Scouting is a tough row to hoe.

A nice NFL pension started flowing my way at 62, about the time my XFL contract ran out. I was in good shape financially and in no hurry to find work. I was happy to retire and go back to school. It had been a great career – 35 seasons in the CFL, 16 years in the NFL and an unbelievable year running the XFL team in Vegas. My wife and best friend Kay and I decided that unless I found something extremely challenging, we would winter in Las Vegas and summer at Schooner Cove on Vancouver Island where we had a condo on the water.

We had numerous things we wanted to do before we headed to the big football field in the sky – important things like spending more time with our sons, Steve and Scott, their wives Sherri and Theresa, and our five grandchildren. We had not travelled much outside of North America because of the demands of my job. Travel was high on our list. I was also a closet oil painter and wanted to do more of that. We were looking forward to retirement – campus life, painting, drawing, writing and learning about black and white photography ... that is, until David Braley called on March 14, 2002.

Big Losses and Psychology

B.C. Place Stadium, Vancouver
September, 2004

FROM THE moment I abandoned retirement, it took until the start of the 2004 season to fully believe that the B.C. Lions were going to sip from the Grey Cup. I stood on the practice field and watched Wally Buono supervise the workout. I called over our media relations director, Diana Schultz, and asked her to snap a photograph.

"Get a picture of them," I said, pointing across the field. "Those five young men could be the best group of quarterbacks ever on a CFL practice field at any one time – Dave Dickenson, Giovanni Carmazzi, Casey Printers, Jarious Jackson and Spergon Wynn. I don't think you'll see five guys on a practice field who are that capable, that good."

I thought it was a great omen and a huge indication of where we were as a team. Wally and I both thought we would bury the semifinal loss to Toronto and be a contender for the Grey Cup. But the Argos beat us handily 28-7 and we both knew it would take a few wins to truly assuage the pang of that defeat. Three of those quarterbacks had played in the league. Carmazzi was better in practice and unproven, but he had taken a few live snaps, and Wynn was the same. Carmazzi was with the 49ers briefly as a backup and I liked him better than maybe the coaches did.

Printers was the real find. Rick Gosselin, from the *Dallas Morning News*, one of the most knowledgeable football writers in the country, turned me onto him. I think an NFL team could use Gosselin as a resource in their draft preparation. He's that good. He studies the game, he has very good rapport with a lot of head coaches and he understands.

Gosselin, Tony Wise, offensive line coach of the Chicago Bears, Harvey Greene, media director of the Miami Dolphins, and I used to go on hockey trips together. Gosselin is from Detroit and a huge hockey fan. We went to see one of the last games at the Montreal Forum and had a great weekend. The next year we went to a game at Maple Leaf Gardens and a junior game in Guelph. We did it for about five years.

When I came back to Vancouver I called Gosselin and said, "How's the draft coming? Who's coming up?" We talked about players. He said he saw this quarterback who wasn't going to be drafted but who looked like a CFL player – Casey Printers.

I wrote his name down on my pad and called Wally. I asked him if Printers was on anyone's negotiation list. The list was kept at the league office and if a player was on it no other CFL team could negotiate with him. He's that team's property. That doesn't mean you can leave him on there forever, let him die on the vine and not offer him a contract. The list protects you while you work out the athlete, look at tape or do whatever you want to do and offer him a contract.

"No, he's not on a list," Wally said.

"If you have a spot," I said, "put him on ours. I hear he's a pretty good CFL-style quarterback, a pretty good athlete."

We put him on our negotiation list and ordered tape.

Printers didn't get drafted and no one offered him a contract. We made a move in 2003 and signed him in May just before going to training camp.

We found Buck Pierce at a free agent camp in Portland. His story was a duplicate of the movie *Invincible*[1] – an ordinary blue-collar guy overlooked by the pros who gets a chance and grabs the brass ring thanks to his hustle, heart and talent. Buck saw our advertisement on the Internet for an open tryout and drove up from his home in

---

1 The movie is about Vince Papale, a 30-year-old part-time bartender/schoolteacher, signed in 1976 by newly appointed head coach Dick Vermeil in Philadelphia after a publicity stunt, open tryout. He played for three years for the Eagles on special teams and as a receiver.

California to Oregon. He hadn't got a sniff from the NFL. Wally signed him right on the spot.

Most of the quarterbacks who play in the CFL are not going to be able to cope in the NFL. They have different athletic skills. Most. There are a few who can and do succeed in both leagues. Warren Moon was simply a superstar. Joe Theismann, too. Doug Flutie made the transition eventually, but he initially came out of the USFL, got a shot with the Chicago Bears and died.

By Flutie's second time around, the mentality of the game in the NFL had changed. They had come to see there was value in quarterbacks who could scramble. Quarterbacks always had been rated on their ability to drop back and pass. If you wanted movement, you wanted the pivot moving around in the pocket. You didn't want him running around out there where he could get hurt. You wanted him in that protected space – drop back, look around, step up and throw the ball. Today, athletes have changed so there are big, strong, fast quarterbacks who can drop back and throw the ball or scramble and scamper for a first down.

Still, most quarterbacks who are successful in the CFL are suited to the Canadian game with the longer, wider field. More space on our turf demands more all-round athleticism from our pivots as opposed to the American field, which restricts the quarterback's movements and is better suited to those with stature who can see down field, have a good arm and the size to take punishment. Dave Dickenson, who is only five-foot-11 inches and 180 pounds, got spot play for about 18 months in the NFL. He excels in Canada.

Returning from my Mexican vacation earlier in the year, I felt good about the Lions' prospects and pretty well threw off the gloom of the loss in Toronto. I thought we put together a good draft and we were an improved team. It roared out of the gate chalking up win after win.

Then Dickenson got a concussion.

I thought we might be in trouble, but Printers stepped into the breach and he was brilliant. With Printers at the helm, we had the best regular season record in club history going 13–5 – and the most consecutive wins at 9. We finished on top of the Western Division.

Casey set a CFL record for highest single game completion average of 90.9 per cent, 20 out of 22 against Hamilton. He was voted the league's most outstanding player. We had eight Western Division all-stars. The team performed as I thought it should.

In the playoffs, we got a scare from Saskatchewan and squeaked past with an overtime win 27–25. It gave us the much-desired re-match with Toronto in the 2004 Grey Cup.

Dickenson was healthy again, so Wally went with him as the starter in the Grey Cup. We lost 27–19.

Played at Frank Clair Stadium in Ottawa, it was the first Grey Cup game in the nation's capital since 1988. We looked good with Dave taking the team down field after the opening kickoff for a score. He was good on several short, precision passes and then bang – he wired one to Jason Clermont, 7–0. The Argos missed on a field goal attempt and Dave started deep in his own end. But again, he found Geroy Simon, Ryan Thelwell and Antonio Warren added nine on the ground to get us out of trouble. By the end of the quarter, Dave had held the ball for 11 minutes. Fantastic.

In the second quarter, we were plagued by kicking problems and a penalty in the red zone that allowed Damon Allen to dive across from the one for a touchdown. It put the Argos ahead. We managed to tie it, but before the half ended, Allen found Robert Baker to put Toronto back in the lead, 17–10.

In the second half, Dickenson and the offence played well, but Allen and the Argos managed to put more points up. On our final pos-session, Dickenson came within inches of hitting Geroy with a bomb. Those inches were the difference between a win and a loss.

Jason Clermont was named the Most Valuable Player and "most valuable Canadian" but that was scant consolation. The Argos, our arch rivals – our nemesis – had defeated us again. I had been certain this was our year. We were a good team.

Of course, the armchair critics were all over us: why didn't we play Printers? There were many, many fans who believed we made a mistake going with Dave Dickenson since he had been out for so much of the season. Printers was especially steamed.

I got back to Vancouver and my old high school coach, Lorne Cullen, phoned.

"I thought you might like to hear my opinion," he said. "You did the right thing going with Dickenson. He's the guy who's going to win for you."

I didn't worry anymore. Lorne was one of the most astute football guys I ever met. I think he missed his calling. Next to Jimmy Johnson and maybe Jackie Parker, Lorne understood the game better than anyone. He followed it closely and, to his mind, Wally did the right thing not replacing Dickenson with Printers. Funny to say, but that made me feel better.

A.J. Smith, general manager of the San Diego Chargers, sent me a note:

Hey, Bobby, I know you just lost the Grey Cup but what you have done since you went back to B.C. has been remarkable. They were down and out with poor attendance before you went back to take over. I know and remember from scouting at the B.C. games. Keep it going. You will be back.

I hate to lose, and to lose like that to the Argonauts, again, was too much. I couldn't wait to start the new season given that frustration. Couldn't wait. If 2004 was not to be our year, I said, it was written in the stars – the Lions will win in 2005 because the Grey Cup will be played in their building. That almost became a mantra with me. We will win; it is pre-ordained.

We tuned up the team in the off-season. I was brimming with optimism. This was the year. This was the year. I was sure of it. I was sure I would deliver to David a Grey Cup.

I had a bit of a shudder in training camp watching Printers. It was obvious he hadn't done a lot of work in the off-season. He complained regularly about his shoulder. In his first year he exhibited a strange throwing motion, but he seemed to correct that as he went along. Now he was back doing it again and showboating every time he threw a bad ball, which was often. He'd look over at the coach and grimace. "I don't know what's wrong, coach."

When we went 8–0, I shuddered again. I began to worry. Oh, oh. This was too good.

That was when the media started to talk about an undefeated season and everyone started to speculate. That kills you. I'm not a superstitious person, but I felt nauseous. The players start to get an unrealistic goal into their heads and they lose focus. I could see it happening. We already had a growing problem with the mounting tension between the quarterbacks.

The Dickenson–Printers contretemps was cleaving the team. We were in trouble. I knew it. Wally got to a point where he wouldn't announce who his quarterback was going to be until almost game time. All that did was trigger debate that the quarterbacks weren't being treated fairly.

Printers had a Cinderella season, no question. He got a lot of attention as a result. Yet Dave came in for the playoff game because we thought he was our best chance to win. Printers couldn't accept that.

I say, look at the game tape. The offence played pretty well except for a couple of plays. Our defence let us down and our kicking game was just awful. The kid, Duncan O'Mahony, stunk. He did a good job all year kicking away from the return man; we got into the Grey Cup and he did the opposite. Plus, he could have kicked it further. Our field position was awful.

In the off-season, the media had fuelled the quarterback controversy and in training camp you could see it simmering. Printers didn't help it. He had the spotlight and he liked it. He thought he was the greatest thing since sliced bread. It was always a controversy, game in, game out.

Dickenson handled the whole situation as best he could, but Printers was immature and wouldn't let it die. He wanted to be the centre of attention. Distractions kill you and the Printers conflict was a fatal disease. Every week the rancour grew worse. Every week the focus was on the quarterbacks, Printers or Dickenson, Dickenson or Printers. Printers couldn't handle it if he wasn't played. He pouted and sulked.

Dickenson, by contrast, was a pro. Even in San Diego, by his second year, Dave exuded the confidence of a veteran. He is our player rep, voted by the players, not only as a leader in the locker room, but also a leader in the union. You don't see a lot of quarterbacks in that position; it's usually an offensive lineman. Dave has a good personality for the job. Everyone has confidence in him because they've seen how he handles himself. He's won. Players believe that even if he throws an interception, he's still going to get it settled down and find a way to turn it around and win.

Football is such a mental game. That's why you always see these athletes jawing at each other. Say a player drops a ball in the last game, misses an interception or gives up a touchdown, they'll be on him. Some of them are worse than others. But they do it because at this level the smallest edge is all it takes.

That's where Jimmy Johnson revealed a lot of his brilliance. He studied industrial psychology and was really into mental sharpness – the psychology of the players and the team were his domain. In Dallas and Miami, for instance, he used a billboard in the dressing room. In Dallas, Bruce Mays, one of his assistants, started putting items on the billboard Monday or Tuesday in preparation for the Sunday game. In Miami, it was Dave O'Conner who would paste up, say, a quote from the opposing team, a comment someone made about the Dolphins or one of our players. He'd fill the board with snipes and jibes just to incense our players and underscore the theme: these guys don't think you are very good. Jimmy used a lot of motivational tools. He had studied psychology and knew how to apply it – a very brilliant guy.

With B.C. in the 2005–06 seasons, I saw firsthand the effect of mental distraction on an otherwise solid team. I don't think Printers handled the situation very well at all. I guess because he was young, he didn't figure out how to deal with the situation. People were telling him he was better than he was, based on the previous year's perfor-mance. He'd had an unbelievable year and then he was benched in the Grey Cup. Many people told him he should have been the quar-terback. He believed we would have won had Wally let him play. He thought he should be the starter.

I agreed with Wally, and I worried the dissension would under-mine the gains we had made. Sure enough, in spite of our fine start, the team began a swan dive. It turned into one of the most disappoint-ing years I've ever had with a football team – going to the Grey Cup the previous season and losing to Toronto, going into this season with a better football team, going 11–0 – then failure.

Geroy Simon, Jason Clermont and Ryan Thelwell each had phenomenal seasons, Brent Johnson was a monster on defence with 17 sacks, Barron Miles snagged six interceptions and Aaron Locket, our kick-returner, burned up the league. We won first place in the West, chalking up the best record in the league (12-6) while we were in a death spiral mentally.

We had a late game comeback in the Western Final, but the Eskimos deserved to beat us 28–23. They went on to win the 2005 Cup 38–35 in our building. To host the Grey Cup and not to play in it. That hurt.

Vancouver did a wonderful job hosting the cup. Scott Ackles was the general manager for the entire affair and Water Boys founders – Moray Keith, Tom Malone, Jamie Pitblado and Dennis Skulsky, chairman of the 2005 Grey Cup – proved invaluable. Pamela Anderson, who had long ago gained stardom after being caught on camera at a Lions game, was parade marshal. We had done so much and come so far. We were doing terrific at the box office; our business couldn't have been better. We had boosted our marketing budget from $1.1 million in 2002 to $1.75 million. We had made an amazing turnaround and were an integral part of the community again. Yet at a time when we should have been showcased, we were in the stands. I watched sourly.

I felt as bad as when we lost to Ralph Sazio's Argonaut team in newly opened B.C. Place back in 1983. Ralph had been an assistant coach with the Eastern All-Stars in 1956 when I was the equipment manager, the year of the horrible plane crash. I really wanted us to beat him, especially in our brand new stadium.

This year felt worse. We were still struggling with our offensive line; it wasn't where we wanted it to be. We were still putting the pieces together I realized. It was a year when rather than taking the next step, we didn't take the next step, and we didn't get any better. The team in 1963 lost a Grey Cup but had gone through the fire and come out the other side tempered and matured. They came back and won. In 2005, we made the same harrowing journey, but it didn't appear we had made any progress. It all seemed to come down to the quarterback injuries and the controversy. This loss was more depressing. I knew we had brought it on ourselves. The quarterback controversy had distracted us as a team. We had allowed off-field issues to defeat us on the field. We had paid dearly for our lack of focus.

In the off-season, Printers went for a tryout in the NFL. We offered him an extension that would put him beyond the NFL's $230,000 US rookie minimum. It wasn't enough. He asked for a salary far in excess of what we thought he was worth. He wanted to be the highest paid player in the CFL, up there in the $400,000 range with Dickenson. We thought he needed to prove himself. He wanted to see what the NFL would offer him.

Canadian contracts contain a window that allows players in their option year to try out for the NFL. Each year the league loses as many as a dozen players who survive an NFL training camp but are released at some point during the cut down. Printers was an exception. Normally, CFL players who go down already have been through one NFL camp, sometimes two, before they come north. Printers was fresh blood. No one had really seen him. He was one who had slipped through the cracks in the draft.

That happens – athletes who aren't going to be taken in the first few rounds sometimes elect to come to Canada first. They play a year or two in the CFL, mature, go into an NFL training camp and blow the coaches away: where did this guy come from? Now the player understands what it takes to make it. He's better equipped than he would have been as a rookie fresh from the draft.

Wally and I held our breath. Printers' return could herald another disaster. If he came back, we would likely have to trade one of our quarterbacks – but which one? The fan base was split right down the middle between Printers and Dickenson. And that always has to be a factor when you are rebuilding your fan base. It would be a difficult decision.

We both sighed with relief when Printers signed with Kansas City. That might be the last little touch we need, I thought – harmony in the locker room.

Winning

B.C. Place Stadium, Vancouver
November 12, 2006

SASKATCHEWAN is an ideal opponent for us in the Western Final. We are guaranteed a massive crowd because the Green Tide rises for a Rider game. Rider Pride. The Green Machine. People can live somewhere for 25 years, but if they spend 25 minutes in Saskatchewan, they'll cheer for the Riders forever. Go figure. I love it – because it spurs ticket sales. You always get a good box office when Saskatchewan comes to town. Already, I know they have convinced themselves they're winning the Grey Cup. And they call every time to ask if they can bring their locomotive – that infernal machine they like to ride around the field after scoring.

"No," I tell them. "Not in our house."

Can you believe that? They want to turn our home-field advantage into their home-field advantage! Not here. Saskatchewan is the only team you get that from. They did that in Calgary to win the semifinal. But it's our house; we invite – and we understand those tricks.

The Riders were looking for revenge for their playoff loss two years before. Their kicker, Paul McCallum, who had played for me in Las Vegas and scored the first ever points in XFL history, shanked an 18-yarder for Saskatchewan in overtime and we defeated them here 27–25. He was on our team now. So kicking our ass would be even sweeter for them. They could kick his, too.

The stadium was almost full – 50,084! I was pleased with that. The sound was LOUD. I was more pleased with that. That was our home-field advantage. We didn't need a locomotive. We had had a great season.

We won the coin toss and Ian Smart took the kickoff 32 yards, slashing downfield into Saskatchewan territory. Dickenson went to work quickly. He threw to Jason Clermont for 16 yards, then another short toss, bang, to Joe Smith for four yards. A third went to Geroy Simon for 13. That's what I wanted to see. We were already threatening. First down on their 18-yard line.

Another completion to Geroy for four yards, then a try for the touchdown to Geroy across the middle under the safety, but it was knocked away – incomplete. We settled for a McCallum field goal – three points, which was better than zip. We were on the board, I thought.

The Saskatchewan offence under quarterback Kerry Joseph went two and out. We got the ball back on our own 35.

Dave began with a short pass to Ryan Thelwell for four yards. On second, Dickenson went to Kendrick Jones bolting down the sideline. He went 21 yards and we were back at centre field. Dave was picking and choosing his targets.

Smith went up the middle for seven yards. Paris Jackson gave us another first down. They came with the blitz. The line stood up the rush, and Dave threw it deep. Downfield, Geroy was open against James Johnson, dashing ahead of him by easily four or five yards and nothing between him and the end zone. Geroy was at full gallop but Dave overthrew him.

After our punt, Saskatchewan took over, pinned near their goal line. They made a one-yard gain from Keith, and then Joseph took his first time-count violation because of crowd noise. A good indicator, I thought. That pushed them back – half-way to the end zone – to the three-yard line. Under enormous pressure on the next play, Joseph scrambled about the end zone and dodged behind the goal post before he managed to find Jason Armstead sprinting across the field. He made the catch at their 37-yard line and the Riders were out of trouble.

On the next play, our defensive back, Lavar Glover, bit on a fake and grabbed Armstead – a pass interference call. The penalty took them to our 44. Joseph tried a forward shovel pass but it went awry. His next try was incomplete, too, and Luca Congi had to punt.

I didn't like everything I was seeing.

We were pinned in our own end – we were at the 13 when Joe Smith lost the ball. Damn. Their big lineman, Scott Schultz, punched the ball free as Smith hit the line. Rider Omar Morgan recovered it in the resulting melee on our 18-yard line.

In the next offensive series, our 13th man – the crowd – our home-field advantage came into play magnificently. Joseph managed to get his first play off but the pass was incomplete. Then he couldn't get the ball hiked on time because no one could hear the snap count. Time-count violation. Yes! Saskatchewan 0–Fans 2!

Second down repeated but it was now 15 yards. The play clock went to zero again. What do you know – he didn't get it off. Another time-count violation. Saskatchewan 0–Fans 3!!

Second and 20, and they were back at our 26.

Finally getting a play off, Joseph backpedalled under pressure. He escaped the initial clutches and grabs, slipped forward and Carl Kidd nabbed him. Yes! End of the major score threat. Congi would hit the field goal from about 40 yards but that was better than giving up a touch-down. Our defence and fans had kept Saskatchewan out of rhythm.

Down on the field, I could see Saskatchewan coach Danny Barrett complaining about the crowd being incited through the PA system and Jumbotron screen. Ha, ha! I wished I could hear what they were saying. "It's our house, Danny! It's our house!" I thought.

We bobbled the short, high kickoff and Dave went to work. He handed it to Joe Smith who cantered through the line for seven yards. Dave hit Clermont across the middle for the first down. The pocket collapsed and Dave went down, just past the line of scrimmage trying to escape the rush. Under pressure again – come on, Dave – yes, he stepped up, there was no one in the middle, and Dave took off. He slid head-first. That's tough. That was a quarterback who wanted it. A 26-yard gain took us to the Saskatchewan 35-yard line.

It was the last play of the quarter and he was under pressure again. They were chasing him and he bolted. Go, Dave, Go. He slid feet-first this time after eight yards. Thanks.

Buck Pierce went in for the short yardage snap. Buck handed it to Smith who smashed into a stone wall. He didn't make it.

Wally sent in Jarious for the gamble – third and one. He was stopped initially. Shit, he was losing the ball. Shit, okay, he got it back under control and he went through the pile for the yardage.

The next play was a big gain of eight yards for Smith.

Second down, Pierce in again for the short yardage play, handed off to Smith. He got it. First down.

Dave returned and was flushed from the shotgun. He threw it away. It was a good call but too bad he didn't see Clermont wide open in the flat.

On second down from the 14, Dave saw Paris Jackson in the end zone, running away from James Johnson, leaving him in his dust. Dave fired a torpedo. The racing Jackson leapt – he went almost horizontal – stretching, stretching … before bringing it in and tumbling out the back of the end zone. Touchdown! Yes! 9–3.

Saskatchewan continued to have trouble with the noise; it caused mass confusion for them. Two more procedural penalties. Congi gave up a safety touch – 12–3.

Dave went to work again – completed a pass to Thelwell, who was wide open for 10 yards. Dave was picking on James Johnson, the Roughriders' outside defensive back. He was giving our receivers too much of a cushion and Dave was killing him. He completed the pass to Paris Jackson – good block, and a gain of nine.

Buck Pierce, back in, handed off to Joe Smith; he was tackled in the backfield. We were eating up the clock and really controlling the football. Jarious Jackson, six-foot-one and 230 pounds, was in on the third down gamble again. Into the line, rolling over, spinning left, he was tough to stop. Stacked up at the 27 – first down!

Dickenson came back in – with a completion to Paris Jackson for a gain of two, a completion to Clermont for seven (a great diving catch) and back to Clermont again for a 22-yard catch off a nice little post route. Clermont was born in Regina but I doubt that made the Saskatchewan fans feel any better. From the five-yard line, Dickenson threw wide to Joe Smith – touchdown!

That's what we wanted. Dickenson was masterful.

What a change from the previous year to see three quarterbacks working together! It made me think of the previous year's dissension.

Casey Printers had been in the stadium. He wanted to be on the sidelines and wandered onto the field during warm-up. Wally spotted him. We found one of our box owners and asked if they'd play host for Casey and his agent. They said sure. Wally, the players and I all felt his presence on the field was a distraction. Wally told Casey that and offered him the box seats. He chose to leave and watch the game on television.

The offence went two and out the next series. But the Saskatchewan return man, Dominique Dorsey, fumbled McCallum's 60-yard punt, and our linebacker Tyson Craiggs recovered it. Dickenson wasn't able to put it away during the next series, but we picked up another field goal.

Saskatchewan came up empty again.

Dickenson came back on the field and burned James Johnson again. Johnson was even getting help on the play from David Bush. It didn't matter. Dickenson connected with Paris Jackson, who made a spectacular 35-yard catch, fighting off both defenders, for a touchdown. We were up 29–4 at the half.

During the break I went down to the president's suite, shook a few hands and talked with Pamela Anderson. She was going through her latest marital spat with Kid Rock. I couldn't even begin to imagine the life she led, but I had to admit she was always fabulous with the Lions. Anytime we asked her to get involved in a promotion, she always said yes.

I was feeling very good but not ready to think about Winnipeg and the Grey Cup game.

People say a game is "out of reach." It's never out of reach. Anything can happen. The game is so damn goofy anything can happen. Few would believe it, but Saskatchewan could still beat us. People who understand this game know how quickly you can undergo a reversal. One moment, you are coasting to a win; next, you're wearing goat horns.

I remember playing Montreal in the 60s and in the last quarter we were tied – we even might have been a touchdown ahead. George Dixon scored three touchdowns in minutes. From the same damn place on the field. We lost.

It scares the hell out of me that you can be that stupid, that anyone can be that stupid as to be beaten three times! Gee, after two, don't you think they might get him out of there and do something else? So is it a breakdown of coaching? Is it a breakdown of a player? Could the guy not do the job, and the opposing team uncovered that he couldn't do the job?

There were a few moments in the Saskatchewan game when I had shudders of such disasters recurring. It's mind-boggling to me sometimes, sitting up there and not able to do anything. And yet when you sit down with the coach the next day and look at the tape it's obvious to everyone. Amid the fog of the game, players and coaches can get distracted and make the wrong decision …

It felt like earlier this year when we were playing well enough to win our second game with Saskatchewan, and didn't. I remember the play. Dickenson dropped back to pass – he had one receiver coming across underneath who was double covered, three going deep down one side, two on the other sideline. There's a chance of a completion on the sideline. The read is pretty easy and a smart quarterback like Dickenson should throw it to the sideline anyway. If it's late in the game, all the receiver has to do is catch the ball and step out of bounds. Dickenson threw it into double coverage, it was intercepted – end of game. We lost.

Here is a very smart quarterback, yet you look at that and ask, why did he throw it there? Why did he do that? Why did he throw the ball the one place it was going to be intercepted? He just misread the defence or he decided, "I can make this throw," because he does make those throws in between three defenders sometimes. He's an experienced quarterback. He knew. So why didn't he make it? Who knows? That's why coaches pull their hair out. They say Dickenson maybe had 12 bad reads all season. That's incredible. Yet the chain of decision-making continues to frustrate. Why didn't he see the obvious? Even though he had played and seen similar situations over and over, he didn't read the situation. It boggles the mind.

With two minutes left in the third quarter, I had a shudder of concern. Saskatchewan's Kenton Keith slid out of the backfield, stepped in front of our middle linebacker, Javier Glatt, grabbed a short pass and sprinted downfield for a 38-yard touchdown. Glatt didn't have a chance to catch him – that was a mismatch. One is built like and runs like a gazelle, the other is more of a slow-moving freight train. Damn.

On our very next offensive play, Rider Davin Bush stuck his head onto the ball and forced Geroy Simon to fumble. Rider linebacker Jackie Mitchell jumped on it.

Now, Saskatchewan had it on our 33-yard line. They ran for seven, and passed to Dominguez on the eight-yard line. If I were a religious man, this is when I would pray. They were in the shadow of our goal post, you could feel the momentum moving their way. It silenced the crowd. I thought darkly, oh no, here we go.

Joseph threw it to the corner, Dominguez drew an interference flag, and the refs marched the ball half the distance to the goal line. It was a gimme. This was serious, serious trouble.

From the four-yard line, Keith took a pitchout on a fake reverse and ran it into the end zone. I began to grow worried; after the convert it was 32–18 with a full quarter to go.

The collapse didn't happen. McCallum got revenge for his playoff shank – ironically, against his old team. He kicked another two field goals and Joe Smith added his second touchdown.

Rob Murphy, who played seven years in the NFL, and the other members of our front line, Angus Reid, Kelly Bates, Sherko Haji-Rasouli, Jason Jiminez, were pillars. Dickenson and the offence displayed a killer instinct. They did not take their foot off the Riders' throat. It ended 45–18. A crusher.

I thought we were going to win the cup from the moment Wally and I breathed that sigh of relief when Casey Printers signed with the Kansas City Chiefs. Coming out of camp, I knew we were a good football team. All I worried about was staying healthy, particularly Dickenson. But I saw Buck Pierce's ability and Jarious Jackson's – either one could step in and I stopped feeling uncomfortable at the thought of those guys being in there. That's why it was wonderful to see them take turns in the Western Final.

Dave generates comfort with his athletic abilities, his intelligence and his knowledge. He's been around a long time and he understands the game. Buck and Jarious are more limited in their knowledge of the game; they haven't played as much as Dave. As a coach, you're a bit more limited with those guys. But I like their athletic ability and by putting them in and giving them experience, you nurture and develop them.

You never get completely comfortable during a season. But I thought the team could win any time it stepped on the field. I definitely felt that way by mid-season – this team could beat anybody on any day as long as we went out and played like we can play. Most of the games we did.

We played pretty good football all year and I liked our defence. Every day at practice when I was with him in Dallas and Miami, Jimmy Johnson had the entire defence do a drill in which they all chased the ball. It wasn't a long drill. But they did it every day until it became rote. The defence would line up across the field; a runner with the ball would set off down the sideline and the defence en masse would give chase. Each member of the defence, depending on where he had lined up, would take a different angle in the pursuit. The drill teaches players about choosing a pursuit angle and staying in their lane. It's a great conditioning exercise and accentuates what a defence must do: move like a school of fish, a single unit. It's also good from an aerobic point of view; it keeps the defence fit.

Dickenson did go down during the season, which raised some concern. He had a high ankle sprain, and those are bad because they take longer to heal. If you start running on one too soon, you can re-injure it. Dave's really a tough guy and, like most players, his instinct is to play through the pain. But I didn't want him doing that in this case because he would be out for a lot longer.

That's why trainers are so important. They can help an athlete recuperate a lot faster than the average non-athlete. An injury suffered by an amateur athlete might take three months to heal; a professional athlete might be better in three weeks because they're getting treatment three times a day.

The big concern for Dave, though, was the problem with the concussion. Head injuries always make an athlete think about continuing – or not continuing. That's why Troy Aikman retired. He could have had a longer career if the possibility of serious damage hadn't arisen.

He'd had a number of concussions and doctors had advised him that he was gambling with his quality of life later on. When you have a wife and young kids you think about those things. Dave has a young wife and a young child; he had to think about the future.

We were fortunate, too, in that Dave was invaluable on the sidelines. He worked well with the young quarterbacks. He sees what's happening. It takes a long time before a lot of guys actually get the picture. Until you are shown or until you learn it, you are looking at an abstract swirl – 24 men in motion. Once the light goes on, well, it's a Zen moment.

Dave has played enough football, seen enough football and looked at enough tape that he sees what's happening and he knows what's happening. His situational awareness is amazing. When he throws an interception, he knows he shouldn't have let the ball go. He knows he shouldn't have thrown it there. And he knows that the moment the ball is out of his hand. A lot of quarterbacks don't know that. They throw the ball out there and then say, "Oh, I didn't know that guy was going to be there."

Dave knows the defence; he knows there's every possibility of that linebacker being there. It takes a lot of work, a lot of time, a lot of study. Some guys don't ever master it. But the good quarterbacks have paid their dues.

The best young quarterback I ever saw was Payton Manning as a rookie. Just watching his dedication in drills was something else. I was sitting in Indianapolis on the bench while he warmed up with his receiver, Marvin Harrison. They'd start on about the 30-yard line and Harrison would sprint to the goal line and cut sharply to the corner. Manning would hit him right over his shoulder on the outside, so only he could catch it or it went out of bounds. They did this 30 or 40 times – and this was only 90 minutes before a game! That's why he is the winner he is. He and his receivers did that every day, except maybe one day a week. Their success is not an accident; it's by design. They know what it's all about.

There was little time to savour the Western Final victory. That was one of the frustrations of the playoff schedule. The coaching staff immediately had to begin work on the game plan for the Grey Cup. And with not much time. Normally, they would have a day and a half to prepare for the next week's game. This week, they would be on a plane Tuesday morning. They had less than a day. They also would have no access to the computer server once they got to Winnipeg. They had to do a lot the old-fashioned way. Still, it meant at Wednesday's practice, instead of running through the game plan, the players had only a piecemeal plan.

It's a lot more work for everyone preparing for Grey Cup and there are a lot more distractions. The coaches must zero in. They don't get much sleep that week. They're working and meeting together and individually with players, gathering as a team, trying to put everything together. They really have a tough week and at the same time they are expected to attend league functions and entertain 150 to 200 members of the media at practice.

The office staff, too, must organize a circus. There were 140 people to transport from Vancouver to Winnipeg. The league had done some preparation – they reserved hotel rooms for both teams, players' wives and some support staff. It also blocked off seats for the team on a flight Tuesday morning out of Vancouver.

Scott and Andrea Savard, office administrator, organized a staff meeting after the team reception that followed the Western Final win. Two dozen others were travelling too. Today, players like to take their kids, and it doesn't matter how old they are. The Felions cheerleaders' travel was arranged because they had been slated to attend a competition in Winnipeg anyway. There were all sorts of arrangements to be made.

Wally, Scott and I met first thing Monday and tied down the loose ends. Wally's wife, Sandi, Kay and the other wives got involved. I began to worry from the moment I went through the newspapers. We were such heavy favourites, I worried the team would be overconfident, especially after our dominating performance against Saskatchewan. Wally had worked hard on that issue over the last few weeks, emphasizing what had happened the previous year. I fretted more when they announced the All-Star team and the CFL Player Awards nominees. We cleaned up.

We started winning the night before the awards, even, when Brent Johnson won the Walby Warriors Award. He got a $60,000 pickup truck. The following night, Thursday, he won two awards and Geroy won two as a fan favourite and Most Valuable Player. There was only one award all week we didn't win (the Special Teams award) and we didn't have a nominee.

For us, it was a clean sweep and sometimes when you do that, god, I thought, not again, not this close … I had the jitters. We had not faced any real adversity during the season. Not really. I also thought the media were playing up too much the disparity in talent. We were seven-point favourites.

Wally brought in our sports psychologist, Frank Ledato. He also talked to the team early in the week. "They're all going to be telling you how good you are, how great you are, how you are the favourite. You're the favourite now, and you'll probably be more of a favourite by game time. Everybody's going to say, 'Oh it's done, why do you even have to play the game?' But you do have to play the game."

The team was pretty loose all week: serious but not uptight. They enjoyed being there. I hoped it was an indication they were confident enough to know that if they played well they would win, but loose enough to still have fun. That's difficult when you are the odds-on favourite. There were few people picking Montreal to win. That's a detriment.

I think the team had matured. Looking around the locker room, you could feel the players thinking back to two years earlier, thinking back to the previous year's collapse, knowing that they could have, should have. They were thinking back to all the distractions of the previous year with the quarterbacks: Casey Printers–Dave Dickenson, day after day. Casey Printers–Dave Dickenson, every day, pound, pound, pound … But this year I sensed a focus. The players kept their heads. They were mature. They were confident but relaxed and, most of all, focused.

We had a Lions Den celebration – a huge gala fan get-together – on the Saturday before the Grey Cup from one to six o'clock. We took over a ballroom in the hotel. There were bands and cheerleaders from all the teams. It was a humongous event, very well organized, really well choreographed. Our staff – Scott, George, Lui, Jen, Terri, Phil, Justen and more – did a great job. David Braley got up and said a few words.

The players came back from morning practice and were led up through the back of the hotel and the kitchen, onto the stage in the ballroom. It was a cavernous room and packed. People went wild. We introduced the coaches and the players. We all sang "Roar, You Lions, Roar!"

Then the players mingled with the fans and signed autographs. It was marvellous. Scott had been to Winnipeg twice previously to ensure everything went smoothly. Not all coaches go along with these kind of events, but Wally was cooperative.

The players didn't do much afterwards except prepare for the next day's game. Saturday night was the only night Wally imposed a curfew. Kay and I hit every function we could but still called it a night about 11. I remembered there was a time when it was three in the morning every night of Grey Cup week. Not anymore.

I stood all through the game. David Braley and the B.C. Lions had a box with room for about five people – David and his wife Nancy, Kay and I and Bob O'Billovich. I stood at the back. I didn't want to sit. I went outside half the time. My stomach was queasy. Sometimes I stood on top of the steps beside the press box to watch. I was just too damn nervous.

Montreal won the toss and elected to receive.

Anthony Calvillo, in his fifth Grey Cup, started with pretty good field position on the 35. He went downfield for O'Neill Wilson, incomplete. Second and 10 – he threw it away. Otis Floyd pressured him.

The punt by David Duvall went out of bounds and Dave Dickenson took over on the 25-yard line. His first toss was to Joe Smith up the sidelines for a first down. Then he hit Geroy for another first down.

Dickenson won as a backup in 1998, lost in the 1999 Grey Cup with the Stamps and lost again two years ago with us. He wanted to win this one.

Paris Jackson pulled down the next throw for a gain of five yards. Three plays, three completions, three different receivers. That was the way, Dave.

Jackson snared the next one as Montreal threw a blitz at the B.C. line. First down – another 14 yards. Four for four.

Next down, Dave ran for another first down. He had injured his ankle against Montreal in September, and then suffered the head injury.

Buck Pierce came in on first down and handed off to Joe Smith. He bulldozed his way for a handful of turf. Second and four, with Dickenson back in, they brought the blitz, and Chip Cox nearly intercepted the pass to Clermont.

McCallum kicked the field goal – 3–0. Better than nothing, I reminded myself.

Montreal took over at the 40-yard line after a 16-yard return on the kickoff. Calvillo handed off to Robert Edwards and he was eaten up by our line. Second and six, Calvillo threw a quick release pass to Byron Anderson, first down. But they threw a pick and the penalty erased the gain and made it second and 16.

Six receiver set, Calvillo threw another quick release ball, but the Als came up shy by about two yards and punted.

This time, Dickenson had to start from our 18-yard line.

Joe Smith, the rookie running back, romped through a gaping hole in the line for a 17-yard gain. Dave gave it to him again.

Montreal came with the blitz on the next play. I watched wide-receiver Geroy Simon stay in and actually make a block. That's a thing of beauty – a receiver throwing a block. Thelwell was open and made the grab. That gave us third and inches from our 44, Wally gambled and sent in Jarious Jackson. He tucked in between the left guard and made it easily. It was a great surge.

Across the middle again, Dave hit Thelwell for another first down. A handoff to Smith, then downfield to Paris Jackson (this time Jason Clermont came over to help block the blitz).

Buck Pierce came in, dropped back and was sacked. Loss of 9.

Dickenson came back, another blitz, but this time it was picked up by the line and Dave completed his throw to Thelwell. But short of a first down.

We settled for another field goal – 6–0. Better than nothing, as I said.

Calvillo took over, dropped back, his line collapsed, he was in our grasp: he dropped it. Fumble! Yes. Middle linebacker Javier Glatt picked it up. The offence was back on the field.

Dave gave it to Joe Smith, then tried to pick up the first down himself when the defence stiffened on second down. We were forced to kick another field goal – 9–0.

Better than nothing, but come on!

We were kicking their ass on both sides of the ball, yet we kept coming up with three points instead of seven. That can come back to bite you in the butt. That was my concern. We were better than this team but we were not putting it in the end zone.

I stood outside.

Calvillo again had a dreadful set of downs ending up on his butt on the final play of the first quarter. No first downs in the quarter. I took scant solace.

Dickenson started the second quarter just across the 50-yard line. Smith, who scored 116 yards rushing against Saskatchewan, stormed ahead for six. Second down, incomplete pass. The Als finally got some pressure on Dickenson and we had to give it back. McCallum hammered a 51-yard punt that angled out of bounds at the two-yard line. No return. A textbook kick for this situation. Well done, Paul.

The struggling Montreal offence continued to sputter. The team had had a difficult year – coach Don Matthews fell ill and left his job four weeks before the end of the season, although he was still an advisor. That kind of emotional loss matters more than many people think. We got the ball back with fabulous field position.

Dickenson took it down inside Montreal territory and threw a rocket that Paris Jackson jumped halfway to Mars to grab. He's six-foot-three, and he was fully extended and well off the ground to pull it down. Montreal's Chip Cox, who's only five-foot-nine, didn't have a chance.

Buck Pierce came in for the next snap and pitched to rookie Ian Smart, who sprinted like a bat out of hell 25 yards into the end zone. He was cut the first week by the Alouettes. Sweet revenge. 16–0. That was better.

Calvillo came up empty again. The defensive line just shut him down and the secondary suffocated the receivers. Three and out again.

Dickenson took over on our 20-yard line. The play-action pass went incomplete. He hit Geroy shy of the first down. We kicked it away.

From his own 45, Calvillo handed off to Robert Edwards who bounced outside, lowered his shoulder and plowed his way forward for close to a first down. The former New England Patriots' property, he went 137 yards against the Argos in the Eastern Final, and was coming off his second consecutive 1,000-yard season in the CFL.

Just when the Als looked as if they had something going, though, Korey Banks came from the backside and hammered Calvillo. Second sack. Next play we flushed him again. The Als missed the field-goal attempt. Still 16–0 with less than five minutes until the half.

Dickenson on the next series hit Lyle Green, who slipped out of the backfield and grabbed the toss for close to a first down. Jarious Jackson came in for the short-yardage plunge.

The defence batted down the next pass attempt. And the next.

The Als got one more crack before the half.

Ben Cahoon made a great catch and turned it up-field for a good pickup. In the hurry-up offence, the Als' Robert Edwards slipped after taking a handoff. Next down, our Korey Banks, a super pickup from the Ottawa Renegades in the dispersal draft, knocked another pass down, sending Calvillo back to the sidelines. But the Als got on the board with a field goal – 16–3.

They were getting a bit of momentum and all I could think was, no, no, no – we're better than this, we're better than this! They could turn this around. If they go into the locker room, down less than two touchdowns … All it takes is a fumble or an interception. It should not be this close.

Fortunately, we got the ball back.

Starting on the Montreal 50 with 33 seconds left, Dickenson threw an incompletion. Away from the play, Kendrick Jones took a penalty, and that moved the ball to the 39-yard line. Dave came back and found Paris Jackson on the sideline. He ran a beautiful out pattern and Dave wired him the ball. They blitzed on the next play and sacked Dickenson. Next down, they caught Dave again.

McCallum hit another 30-yard field goal, his fourth, to end the half – 19–3.

The Alouettes started on the ground in the second half with Robert Edwards but didn't get anywhere. They stayed with Edwards again and came up two yards short.

We started from our 33-yard line.

Dickenson, who used five receivers in the first half, started on the ground as well with Smith off right tackle for a gain of four. The blitz knocked down the next attempted pass and we were forced to give the ball back.

Calvillo threw away his first attempt. Brent Johnson, who led the league in sacks, buried him on second down. Third sack of the day for our defence.

Smart gave us a good return and Dickenson again started with tremendous field position. He hit Thelwell for a gain of six.

A few moments later, they flushed Dickenson and chased him. He was tripped and as he fell, the ball came loose. It was clearly a fumble. Cox picked it up and jogged towards the end zone as the officials indicated they had blown the play dead.

The replay showed the ball was clearly loose before the whistle went and I cringed.

The Als would have a first down; they should have had a touchdown. We dodged a bullet. But we were still in the crosshairs.

Calvillo struck for a first down immediately. He came back and completed a short hook pattern. The Als went without a huddle and the pass went awry. They were forced to punt – a beauty, it turned out, that pinned us on our own one-yard line.

Smith took it up the middle, churning ahead for seven. Dave gave it to him again, but the Als' defence stopped him this time and we were looking at punting from our own end zone. We surrendered a safety – 19–5. They were within two touchdowns. Not a good sign. If they had been allowed to run in the fumble for a touchdown, they'd be within one.

Calvillo hit Cahoon, who skipped ahead for a six-yard gain, and handed off to Edwards who ran off left tackle for the first down. He picked up another first down in the air to Thyron Anderson, on our 20. I was beginning to fear the Als had something going. He hit Cahoon again. Robert Edwards took them down to the four-yard line.

Chris Wilson jumped the gun and it took them to the two – that gave them an extra down as well. It was first and goal. Robert Edwards took the handoff and went airborne before the defence slammed him back. But he broke the plane of the goal line.

The Als were back in the game, trailing only by a converted touch-down. A team that should have been out of it in the first half was back in the game. Those points we squandered were back to haunt us.

We nearly gave it away on the kickoff return, but managed to re-cover the fumble on our own 35. On the next play, Dave nearly threw an interception. I thought we might be snake-bit. He called a draw play next and ran for a first down. Well done. That said everything to me. Relax. That was an incredibly gutsy call given our position. Dickenson wanted this game. He ran for another first down to end the third quarter.

We banged away with the run, pushing them back, picking up an-other first down and eating up the clock. A quick pass from Dickenson to Simon on the 25. Buck Pierce went in for an end-around but the defence shut it down.

McCallum kicked his fifth field goal. I hoped we wouldn't need the points, and then I saw the flags on the field. Too many men against Montreal. What a mistake! We had a first down and another chance.

Under pressure, Dickenson rolled out on first down and threw it away. On second and 10 from the 13, the Montreal defence again blitzed, and Dickenson threw incomplete. McCallum came in and kicked his fifth field goal – again – 22–12.

We had given Montreal hope, and that is always dangerous.

Calvillo came back on the field, but our defence shut him down.

Dave returned and gave it to Smith, who churned ahead for a gain of about eight. Pierce came in and gave it to Smith, who came up short. McCallum kicked his sixth field goal to tie a Grey Cup record held by three other kickers – 25–12.

The Als refused to die. With about eight minutes left, I went down to the field to watch the rest of the game, afraid to stop worrying.

Edwards came back and fought for 17 yards. Calvillo hit Cahoon again. Then he, too, called a quarterback draw, put his shoulder down and charged ahead. He nearly got the first down; they got the remain-ing yard on the next play.

He hit Robert Edwards on the sideline for another 10. Calvillo nailed Cahoon running a post. First and 10 from the 17.

They missed on the first try. Incomplete. Cahoon whined loudly about interference. Second down, Dave Stala made a great catch over the middle for the first down. He also got a face-mask flag that took the ball to the two-yard line. This was gut-check time.

Edwards got the call, but our defence stood him up. Yes! On second down, they gave it to Edwards again and the defence not only stood him up, they swarmed all over him before he even reached the line of scrimmage – linebackers Carl Kidd and Javier Glatt flew over the top to make contact. Edwards fumbled. Otis Floyd fell on it.

The Montreal coaches didn't challenge the referee's call even though on the replay screens it looked as if the ball came out after Edwards' knees were down. All I thought was, whew! Another bullet just whizzed past.

They score and it is a whole new ball game. I thought, now we should be able to bury them.

Dickenson led the team away from the end zone as time ticked away. It was ball control at this point and Dave managed to run the clock down to less than two minutes. McCallum gave up a safety to deny the Als field position and the possibility of a quick touchdown.

The Als started from their own 35, trailing 25–14. Hail Mary time. Dave Stala in the end zone made a diving try. Incomplete. A short completion to Cahoon. One last stab to Terrence Edwards, tipped, incomplete. It was over. We had won! Wally Buono had his fourth Grey Cup, Dave Dickenson his second, his first as a starter, the Lions their fifth, and I my third.

It was organized chaos on the field after the game because everyone, rightly so, wanted to be involved – the families, the players and the coaches. There was also a crush of media trying to get shots and conduct interviews. The locker room was similar madness. Champagne sprayed everywhere.

It was terrific to see David Braley in the middle of the celebration, beaming as they presented him with the Grey Cup. He had given a lot to the league and the Lions. He represented what it was all about. He was ecstatic.

In the locker room, David was one of the boys. He was much closer to the players than I am. He can be that way. He's in Hamilton.

He doesn't have those guys all the time saying, "Hey, Bobby, you know, I'm worth more money." I have to stay at arm's length.

Regardless, at that point, we were a team and we had won. Everyone was ecstatic. Of course, the cup got broken.

We had a big party in the hotel – the players, their wives and kids, friends, some of The Water Boys. We had a buffet, beer, wine and sodas. It was a fantastic feeling. Around the room, I saw perhaps the best Lions team ever. It had lots of character; it also had lots of characters. A good group of people.

I was as excited as hell to be there; I was excited as hell to win. I tried to compare the elation – this was thrilling, similar to 1985 in that I felt very responsible for the outcome. It was completely different with the 1964 win – I was just happy to be along with the guys back then. They were right there and I was right there with them – it was a very physical, in-the-moment experience. I was just blown away at being there, just blown away by that win. In 1985, it was as if I were being rewarded for 10 years of hard work – it was an incredible monkey off my back to win that first cup as a general manager, as the person who had planned and worked for years to bring that team to the field. The 2006 cup was different again, but it too felt like a reward for a lot of hard work. We had so many great young people who had worked extremely hard to make this happen.

Winning a Grey Cup can't help but be a wonderful feeling, a fantastic sense of accomplishment. But I saw the 2006 win in perspective more than I saw the others. I'm older. I understand more. It represents something different to me now – not just victory on the field, but success at many levels achieved by the organization. I no longer see it as an end: it's a process.

As the party rolled along, Wally and Neil McEvoy had to finish the season's work. Rosters closed at midnight the day of the Grey Cup game – the official end of the season. That year, 2006, was special because it was the last year without a salary cap. If you extended a player's contract before the end of the season, the cost was applied to that year's budget – not the next year's when the salary cap would come into place. This meant you could legally spend money over and above the cap and not be fined. With that in mind, Wally and Neil put the finishing touches on the last of the contract extensions. We extended seven players of the 10 we had identified and hoped to extend. That gave us a very good nucleus for the following year, with a great age spread and mix of veterans and young players.

What a year 2006 had been! Ernie Stautner had died. Jim Trimble had died. Annis Stukus had died. Denny Boyd had died. Jackie Parker had died. We had won the Grey Cup, but the larger flow of life went on.

My job now was to pump up revenues to where they should be. They're not there yet, although we've done well. When I arrived in 2002, we weren't spending the money we needed to spend in the community to promote the club. You've got to spend enough money to drive revenues.

The team does most of it. If you have a quality, winning football team you usually have a good gate. But, as I think the Lions' experience before I arrived showed, you also must have an overall business plan, follow it up with solid community promotion, the right advertising and marketing strategies, and aggressive ticket sales – all of those things must drive what you're doing. With the Grey Cup, we had an enormous opportunity.

We put together a system to ensure the cup appeared at as many events in the course of the year as possible – personal, player events and big media extravaganzas. We took it over to Victoria and the B.C. Legislature so the provincial government could be part of the celebration.

Then we started the draft process again, the free-agency cycle, the U.S. college players, NFL Europe. We started talking about where we could improve. A team can never stay the same. If it stays the same, it will lose. You've always got to try and improve your roster even when, like us, you're in pretty good shape. The journey had to begin again and new obstacles had to be overcome.

Wally gave me a report on the team. Our top three players were Canadian. That was important. If you have quality Canadians, you can find American players for the other positions. There is just such a huge pool of football talent south of the border for us to choose from we can usually find those other guys in America. Finding talented Canadians who can play at a professional level was more difficult.

Wally's report told me where we were – Geroy Simon had an

arrow going up, which means he's a top player. An arrow going sideways and then up is a solid player with an upside. An arrow going sideways and down means a solid player but with concerns. That was Dave Dickenson because of his age and injuries. Clermont had a horizontal arrow and an asterisk – I interpreted that to mean he was not going to get any better physically than he was then. Carl Kidd is just a great team guy but he was at the end of his career. You hate for it to happen, and he hated for it to happen. I was going to talk to Wally, but I knew I shouldn't because, sure enough, if I did he'd end up on our injured list all year. You can't fall in love with players. You just can't.

The head coaches who are successful don't fall in love with their players. I think that's why Wally has had success. He loves the players, he really enjoys them, but he's very disciplined when he grades them. He does not let his feelings cloud his evaluation of what they can do for the football team. I try to do the same on the business side.

We have hosted three Western Finals, and we hosted the Grey Cup once. We went to the Grey Cup twice, and we won one. We're ahead of our business targets in many ways. I'm relatively pleased with ticket sales. The first "sold out" sign went up on the final game of the 2003 CFL season. We could always do better, but I'm relatively pleased with the progress we've made in five years. With the 2006 cup, we had a chance to up the bar.

You have to make sure you keep building on your base. I've never put a number on my goal. There was a 30,000 season-ticket base when I left the Lions in 1986. In my mind, I won't be successful until we hit 30,000 again. I'm not sure that's possible. I won't know until I get there. But I've never had so much fun. I enjoy the challenge and there is a lot more to do. I would like to see the stadium regularly filled. I'm not sure we can do that either – but those are my goals. I have them on my list.

I'll work as long as I feel good and I'm healthy – as long as I feel we're making some progress and as long as David wants me to work. I have a contract, but my contract with David is more of a handshake. During Grey Cup, David said to me there was an employee at the league office who was fired this year shortly after he had a pacemaker installed. He confided, "I'd never fire someone with a pacemaker."

As we were walking off the field the other day after practice I mentioned, in a serious tone, "I got that pacemaker put in."

He stared at me.

I laughed.

Recognition spread across his face and he guffawed.

Epilogue

I STARTED in professional football as the B.C. Lions' water boy in 1953, and the job cost me streetcar fare. In 1954, the players each paid me $1.00 and tips for cleaning their shoes or other chores. I got $500 a year from the club as the assistant equipment manager, and that was the year Kay and I were married. I didn't start drawing a regular pay cheque until 1960 when I became equipment manager. I used to tell reporters I'd been assessing talent since I was equipment manager – if a rookie looked as if he was going to make the club, he got new cleats, otherwise it was retreads.

I have vivid memories. For instance, I remember By Bailey scoring the first-ever B.C. touchdown in 1954. We were heading north and it was a short yardage running play, from inside the five-yard line. I remember the photograph of By alone in the end zone. He didn't power over with guys hanging off him. He didn't end up on his back. He was out in the open. He feigned into the line and skipped around the right side and in untouched. The stadium erupted like Krakatoa!

I remember Sonny Homer as if he were here today, too. He arrived from junior college in 1958 with speed. Blazing speed. You didn't have many Canadian kids with that kind of speed. He played as defensive back, but they moved him over to receiver, and he excelled. He and Joe Kapp worked a lot together. His hands weren't the greatest. They never were really soft hands. Some receivers have hands you don't hear the ball hit – like Mervyn Fernandez or Geroy. They catch the ball effortlessly, like a dancer who hardly touches the floor. Sonny's hands were stiffer but working with Joe improved them.

Sonny had good height but only one kidney and had to wear a pad around his abdomen, which was cumbersome. It was courageous for him to do that – the wrong hit and he was dead. But Homer loved the game; he loved to be in the locker room. The guys were always giving him what for, and he loved the guys. That camaraderie is so important I think. The feeling in a good locker-room is familial. On championship teams, I have found the bond is as close as blood. That's why so many players hang on to their careers until the very end – it's tough to give up that feeling of belonging, of being needed, of being part of something greater than yourself.

Strangely, I always think about a play in the 1964 Grey Cup that Willie Fleming made, a running play in which he turned inside out probably the best defensive back in the country for years, Garney Henley. He was as good on defence as Fleming was on offence. But Henley got turned around and couldn't make the play. Willie just blew past him and on into the end zone.

I remember, too, Neal Beaumont in 1963 returning an interception from our end zone, 120 yards for a touchdown, with Big Emery Barnes running down the field with him, throwing a block to ensure the score. That was a game breaker. We beat Saskatchewan that day 26–6! Those are moments I cherish; they're worn smooth from recall. They're also rare.

I remember people more than plays.

I've thought about which was the best Lions team I knew up close. The 1964 team had a strong leader and quarterback in Joe Kapp, an outstanding running back-receiver in Willie Fleming. We had a very strong offensive line. Tom Hinton, who played guard, was perhaps the best offensive lineman that I have ever seen personally in terms of technique. Hinton was as quick as Fleming in three steps, which is as fast as greased lightning, and he was as powerful as Tom Brown, our great middle linebacker. Hinton was extremely smart and he was passionate about the game. We had an outstanding defence – the best defence I had seen up to that time. We also had very good special teams, a good punter and a good place-kicker. Solid coaching.

That team had all the components.

In 1985, we had a strong quarterback in Roy Dewalt, while Fernandez was the Fleming of his day. I think Mervyn may have been the best receiver who ever pulled on a Lions jersey. We'll have to see how Geroy Simon does. Anyway, the 1985 team had a good quarterback, a great receiver, a solid offensive line, an excellent running back in John Henry White and a great defence. Of course, we had Lui Passaglia, as well, great special teams and Don Matthews as coach. Again, all the components.

The 2006 version of the Lions had strong leadership, solid coaching, a super leader in Dave Dickenson, a great receiver in Geroy, and a very, very good running back in Joe Smith. With those two American tackles, a great offensive line, and an outstanding defence, even our return game was pretty good. But is it the best yet? Hmmm. I believe they very well might be. But let's see if they can repeat.

Is Dickenson a better quarterback than Kapp or Dewalt? Maybe at this time he is. In this generation in the CFL, he is the best. But he's a different athlete than his predecessors. The nature of the game has changed and the size of the players has changed. If you look at the 1954 team, our biggest offensive lineman was probably Laurie Niemi, who played at 260 pounds or so. The best lineman on this team is 310 pounds. And many linemen are playing the position at 360 pounds. In every position, they're bigger, faster and more skilled.

The athletes have changed. Kids today are coached constantly and, as they get to higher and higher levels, especially in the U.S., they receive specialized attention. In college and university, they have 10 to 12 assistant coaches instead of three or four. If an athlete makes it to pro football, there are as many as 20 assistant coaches in the NFL, six to eight in the CFL. They are virtually assured a personal trainer south of the border – certainly they're going to get more personal attention than they've received since mum held them for the first time. But even here, professional football players are well looked after and well schooled in the game and their position.

Coaches spend hours looking at tape and tracking players with evaluation programs. Every play is broken down and analyzed. A player is evaluated on every play from scrimmage, from every angle.

There is no place to hide. Similarly, when they game plan, coaches can pull up the opposing team's complete play-by-play record – here's what they do on third and a long two yards, here's what they do if it's third and six. They can see every down. All the clips are right there on the computer hard drive. By contrast, for the first 25 years or so, all we had was a head coach and two assistants. Can you imagine the difference?

Those are the reasons athletes are better today. They get individual attention and they work harder in the off-season. It's a full-time job. The average player might take a month off after the season and then start focusing on training camp. Professional athletes train year round. In the past, players went home at the end of the season – most of them to full-time jobs – and didn't think about working out until the coach's letter arrived announcing training camp.

Still, Fleming, Fernandez and Simon were all in that upper echelon as athletes. They were all in that elite class of professional, world-class talent. Each of them had that royal jelly. They were all character players.

We probably had more characters in 1964, but things have changed a little bit. Pro athletes in those days were more into, "Let's go to the bar and have a few." That's long gone. The 1985 and the 2006 teams collectively said prayers. That would have started a fight among the 1964 squad. Who's to say which approach is right? Today you can join in or not; there's no pressure one way or another. Every year is different, every journey each team makes is unique – they only happen to end up at the same place if they become champions. That's one of the lessons football teaches – that it is about the process. Every step matters. You must focus on every play to win a game, to build a winning season, to emerge a champion.

The Canadian Football League is a small business and the players who play in this league play because they love the game. They really love the game. I'm not saying they don't in the NFL. But some of our players are earning $40,000 a year. That's not huge money.

A Dave Dickenson is making over $400,000 and we have a few that are in the $100,000 to $200,000 range, but most earn under $100,000. It's not the gravy train.

I'd hate to see the CFL die.

Talk about the NFL coming to Canada scares me as a CFL fan. It would be the death knell for our league if the NFL set up in Toronto. I'm all in favour of exhibition games or even a league game or two being played here, but we don't need a franchise. It would suck the life-blood out of our league. It would be a loss not just for sporting fans, but for the country, I think. The Grey Cup is a unique and storied part of Canadian culture and our history. We would be poorer as a nation if it were to disappear. I felt so strongly when I heard the latest rumours that the league was interested in starting or moving a franchise to Toronto, I called NFL commissioner Roger Goodell's office in New York and spoke with him. He told me there was nothing to worry about and that there were no active plans to expand into Canada. Just to be sure, I also spoke with Greg Aiello, his right-hand man. We had worked together in Dallas and I knew he'd give me the straight goods.

"Geez, Bobby, I think those were off-hand remarks the media picked up – pure speculation, I'm sure," Aiello said. "That would be so far down the road."

"I'm just telling you it will kill the CFL," I told him. "You know how those people start. The media start with a rumour and then begin feeding off it. Before you know it, it's happening and happening soon. If people have a lot of money they can do what they want, but it will kill us."

"I don't think it's a problem."

"It might not happen in my lifetime," I said. "I don't think it will, but it really will destroy the Canadian Football League."

"That's so far away," he replied.

"I know there was a group who talked to New Orleans when their building was damaged about bringing the franchise to Toronto and selling it," I told him. "I understand they offered $1 billion to move it to Toronto."

"All just speculation, Bob."

"It seems to me it would be a shame if the league had to fold because of three or four greedy people in Toronto. And that's the way I look at it."

I rang off.

I've now talked to a number of people – senators, politicians, wealthy people, ordinary people, the media – and I'm going to continue to talk about it because I sure don't want to see the Grey Cup game disappear, especially just because a few people in Toronto need an NFL franchise to feel good – to feel they're "major league."

That's really what it is, isn't it? Ego.

It's not that Toronto can't support a franchise. Of course they can. It's a big place with lots of money. But to have 70,000 people enjoy an NFL game in Toronto, you will murder eight CFL franchises. You will eliminate the economic benefits, the players, the support staff, the money that the Grey Cup brings into each host city. The economic impact of the Grey Cup in Vancouver was between $46 and $48 million.

You can watch the NFL on television – we get every game here. Other than for a few people and one city, what is the advantage of a franchise – except, as I say, for a few greedy people to turn $1 billion into $6 billion, while screwing the rest of the country.

—⁂—

The NFL is a different kettle of fish – because it is huge. It's a different game. The athletes are different: in general, they're about 20 per cent bigger, faster and more powerful. Still, the same values hold sway in each league.

The football business, like other businesses, runs on relationships. As I made my way in professional sports, it was emphasized over and over again that winning depended on the relationships I forged – the friendships and business associations I made were the difference between success and failure.

I sit surrounded by memorabilia – hundreds of sports books, a couple of feet of shelving with mentions of me, signed game balls, a Schenley Award ... Down the hall there's another room, across town there's a storage locker, a thousand framed pictures, an equal amount awaiting framing, shots of me with cups, with mountains of equipment, with this great player or that team.

They filmed *Any Given Sunday* while I was with the Dolphins. There I am with Nick Nolte, who was supposed to be the head coach before Al Pacino got the role. I met Cameron Diaz, who was a really nice, down-to-earth person. She came to one of our games and took photographs from the sideline.

I still remember what she told me about marketing a film: "Word of mouth, Bob," she said. "Word of mouth is the best marketing you can get. Advertising can help get you a start, but if the word of mouth is bad – the film is dead."

It's the same in football. If the fans don't like the product and you don't have good word of mouth on the street, your franchise is dead. To a large extent that's why the Lions got into trouble in the 1990s.

I feel like a packrat. And who would have guessed it more than 50 years ago when, as a 15-year-old, I wandered onto that field in East Vancouver and told Annis Stukus I wanted to be the water boy. Who would have guessed it would lead to this?

Not that there haven't been personal as well as professional challenges along with the milestones. My oldest son, Steve, went through a few hard years in his teens. I think because of football. My youngest, Scott, has always had an interest in football. For Steve, football probably detracted from his life. Although he probably would say he enjoyed the association, he wasn't associated. He wasn't close to it. I was gone because of football. I was gone a lot.

I remember Steve during high school; he was in a place they called The Pit, where students went to smoke. The vice principal arrived, and shouted the first name that came to him: "Bobby Ackles!"

Steve snapped. "I'm not Bobby Ackles, I'm Steve Ackles."

It bothered him, that association. "I'm me. I'm not…"

I think we had a good relationship, but he preferred to spend time with his friends.

There's roughly four years' difference between them – Steve was born September 6, 1961, and Scott was born on May 29, 1965 – and it made a difference.

With Scott, he followed football. He knew about it, he wanted to be part of it. Steve was always arm's length away from it – and, indirectly, me.

—ɷ—

Steve's first love was always the outdoors. He met Sherri, got married, had three kids. Sherri works at Overwaitea on the Island, and their life together has been very good.

Steve put up stoically with our lives being run by football. I know he would have sooner been hunting and fishing than watching someone run back a punt. He's a conservation officer in Nanaimo and his kids now are fine young adults – Robert is 25; Ashley and Kyle, 22.

Scott used to work with me at training camp. He had just turned 21 when they announced I was going to Dallas. He had graduated from the broadcast journalism program at BCIT and was working locally in radio but didn't really like it. So he came to Dallas with us.

In Dallas, Scott worked with the Cowboys video department as a volunteer. He also worked at one of the local cable companies as a camera operator. Paul Hackett's son was playing football, and on Friday nights we generally all went to watch him play. That was the ritual in Texas. Friday night is high school football night, Saturday is college football and Sunday is pro football.

Scott would take a camera and videotape the game for Paul. The contacts and the experience were invaluable. Scott worked the Cowboys' training camps and game days. He saw this was a good business and said, "I like this business."

When he got an opportunity, Scott worked for the B.C. Lions in day-of-game operations during Glen Ringdal's time as president. Scott was the first person I hired in the XFL. He's always done a great job. In 2003, we decided to host the Grey Cup game and the league awarded us the 2005 game. David thought it might be too soon, but I put Scott in charge of it and he assembled a team of young people who I believe put on one of the finest festivals in Grey Cup history. That's one reason shortly after the Lions won the Grey Cup last year, he was courted and then named senior vice president of the Calgary Stampeders. He and Theresa have two great kids, Kasey and Robyn.

I couldn't be more proud of our family and I realize how fortunate I've been.

I worked all the time in the early years and that only changed while I was retired. I always worked like I do now, putting in pretty long hours. This past weekend I spent all Saturday in the office, Sunday, two hours in the morning, and then I spent four hours at radio station CKNW judging a promotion contest. I enjoyed it, but it's a Sunday and you don't have many Sundays.

I sound sometimes like I'm ready for retirement again, but I keep taking on new projects.

—ᴍ—

I went to bed at 11 last night because I had to finish paperwork. I am raising money for a YMCA early childcare project, Nanook House. Doing something for those who can do nothing for you in return can be very satisfying. There's my work with other community organizations, too. There are all kinds of little projects that I'm involved with that consume time, aside from the Lions.

My life changed when I retired and went to school. Then I had nothing to do. I had my classes, but I was off the treadmill. It wasn't like this. Today, I have a timetable and timelines – certain things have to be completed by certain dates. But I like it – and it has kept Kay and me always engaged.

We got involved in every community in which we lived. We went here, we went there, and we went to see everything. In Dallas, or whatever city we were in, every weekend we would drive out and see a different part of town or an outlying burgh. We did the oddest things sometimes that enriched our lives.

I remember one Sunday in Dallas after reading about a rattlesnake roundup. We drove out to what looked like a deserted town two hours beyond the city limits.

You could hear the snakes as you approached this ramshackle house with a sign promising rattlesnake milking and more. We paid $2 to enter. Inside, the rattling noise was deafening. There had to be 250 or more writhing rattlers in a metre-high, Plexiglas enclosure in the centre of the main room. You could walk around the outside. There were three young men standing in this big box amid the snakes. At one point, the rookie, they said, got into a sleeping bag, lay down and let the others put a bunch of serpents on him. We watched him wriggle out of the bag without getting bit. His concern wasn't the rattlers on the bag; it was the snakes behind him, rampant, tails shaking franti-cally. It was April, so they were said to be docile, apparently; if it had been hot, they would have struck.

We did things like that all the time.

—⁜—

Every place we lived, we got out into the community. We met the community. We enjoyed ourselves wherever we were. We also had a ton of people come visit us, all kinds of people – family, friends, col-leagues, and other Canadians passing through who knew of my work with the Lions.

Yet, I admit it was also an insular life. I gauge that by my taste in music. They don't even ask me anymore for my suggestions on what to play in the stadium. My favourites – "Come Fly with Me," by Frank Sinatra, "Live at the Sands" with Count Basie and his Orchestra, or how about, "MacArthur Park," by Richard Harris, the seven-and-a-half minute version (I have it by every artist who's ever done it)?

In many ways my life has been lived in a cocoon of football and 50s camaraderie. The Vietnam war, the civil rights movement, disco, Ronald Reagan … few of the issues that rocked society during the last half of the 20th century rocked the locker room. In the late 60s and early 70s, the attitude quotient went up. But that would be about it.

Societal concerns were peripheral. It's not that all those issues weren't important. It wasn't that they didn't matter. They most cer-tainly did. But we came together to play football – to win a champi-onship. That was always our focus, no matter what league, no matter what team. It was about football.

—⁜—

But over the years my appreciation of football has changed. Working in the locker room, I came to realize, I was inside a very small box for the first 10 years of my career. Every year those of us in that box had our pictures taken by the team photographer. That was it. That was the football team. Those guys were right there in front of me and I lived it with them. My view of the football team was inside that picture frame, that small box on the wall.

The day I became a full-time employee with the Lions, my world changed and my perspective began to change. It started to enlarge. I could no longer have a beer with the boys and it took me some time to adjust. It hurt me to be working in the equipment room without the friendships. That began to open my eyes and forced me to appreciate the business side of a football team – the part that was outside of the framed picture on the wall, but oh so necessary to it. The next year I was completely removed from the locker room and became part of management. That first season, though, was tough – I became part of the administration, I was different. I had moved outside the box.

As a general manager, it became evident to me that there were a lot of people outside of that box – people who never appeared in a team photograph, people who were neither player, coach or trainer, people who made decisions and whose effort was also key to building a championship team and winning. The job enlarged my frame of reference and opened my eyes to the complexity, the veritable jigsaw puzzle that needed to be assembled to make everything work, to win. And I liked putting it together more than I liked being in the belly of it. I preferred the boardroom to the locker room. I really liked putting it together. I still do.

I always had running with the bulls in Pamplona on my list of personal to-dos. These days my list says: taking pictures of the running of the bulls. Setting goals is important. It's also important to keep those goals in perspective and to be realistic. It's difficult to be a good manager and to build a winning team.

Finding the right people is hard. It's not about what somebody tells you. It's about sitting down and talking to them face to face and getting a feeling about them. Do they have the passion for what you want them to do? Or what they want to do? They might have a diploma or a degree, they might even have some experience. But is this something they want to do every day – and do well every day?

I've never had to get up and go to work in the morning, and I don't like to hire people who look at work as a chore. I have a passion for what I do and I expect it from those I hire. Football isn't a job to me, it is a vocation. Having worked with the likes of Tom Landry, Jimmy Johnson, Jackie Parker, Eagle Keys, Don Matthews and Wally Buono,

I have come to expect excellence. Why aspire to mediocrity?

What have I learned?

I do have a message about leadership, success and building a winner that I deliver when asked to address convocations or after-dinner groups. I refined it over the years as I stole ideas from people. It isn't brilliant or fancy. I don't say that it's the best or most perfect expression of what works and what doesn't. I'm not even saying you should follow it, but it's what I think worked for me.

It boils down to two basic tenets – hire good people and let them do their job. Otherwise, I think, being a leader and being successful demand primarily a lot of common sense. You must be loyal, disciplined, dedicated, well prepared and get the most from your talent. There is no magic formula, no easy road, no wand or potion to do the hard work for you. You must hold to your values and be engaged with your community. That's how you become a leader, that's how you succeed, that's how you build a winner. Unfortunately, and people generally hate to hear this, you've also got to have luck – a healthy sprinkling of the proverbial pixie dust.

That's what I had in spades.

I look back on my life and career and feel like the luckiest man in the world. Few people get to spend their days doing something they love with those they love. I shake my head at what seems now a sepia-toned memory – me chasing Annis Stukus across Heather Park on a sunny afternoon in 1953, tugging at his sleeve – "Coach, coach, can I have a minute? I applied to be the water boy."

And the words that set my life on its path: "Tiger – put him to work."

The water boy. What an incredible journey – Grey Cups. Super Bowls, the Dallas Cowboys, Jerry Jones, Jimmy Johnson, Oliver Stone, Vince McMahon, those decades with the B.C. Lions, children, grandchildren … what a path. Who would have guessed the journey would still be going on? Who would have guessed I'd be eagerly awaiting the kickoff of the 2007 CFL season as part of a team hoping to win the Grey Cup? Who would have guessed that future half a century ago, watching that fresh-faced, teenaged water boy? Not me.

Select Bibliography

Dent, Jim. *King of the Cowboys: The Life and Times of Jerry Jones*. Adams Publishing, Holbrook, MA: 1995.

Hubbard, Steve. *Shark Among Dolphins: Inside Jimmy Johnson's Transformation of the Miami Dolphins*. Ballantine Books, New York: 1997.

Kramer, Jerry with Dick Schapp. *Distant Replay*. G.P. Putnam's Sons, New York: 1985.

Parcells, Bill with Jeff Coplon. *Finding A Way to Win: The Principles of Leadership, Teamwork and Motivation*. Doubleday, New York: 1995.

Skrien, Dave with Dick Beddoes. *Countdown to Grey Cup: The Story of the B.C. Lions*. McClelland & Stewart, Toronto: 1965.

Smith, Emmitt with Steve Delsohn. *The Emmitt Zone*. Random House: New York, 1993.

St. John, Bob. *Tex: The Man Who Built the Dallas Cowboys*. Prentice Hall—A Division of Simon & Schuster, New Jersey: 1988.

Stamborski, Jim (editor). *J.J. Straight Talking—Jimmy Johnson's insights, outbursts, kudos, and comebacks*. Lifetime Books Inc., Hollywood, FL: 1998.

Index